The Afterlife of Toyotomi Hideyoshi

HARVARD EAST ASIAN MONOGRAPHS 447

The Afterlife of Toyotomi Hideyoshi

Historical Fiction and Popular Culture in Japan

Susan Westhafer Furukawa

Published by the Harvard University Asia Center
Distributed by Harvard University Press
Cambridge (Massachusetts) and London 2022

The Harvard University Asia Center publishes a monograph series and, in coordination with the Fairbank Center for Chinese Studies, the Korea Institute, the Reischauer Institute of Japanese Studies, and other facilities and institutes, administers research projects designed to further scholarly understanding of China, Japan, Korea, Vietnam, and other Asian countries. The Center also sponsors projects addressing multidisciplinary, transnational, and regional issues in Asia.

Cataloging-in-Publication Data is on file at the Library of Congress.

ISBN 9780674267916 (cloth) | ISBN 9780674267923 (paperback)

Index by Lori Morimoto

♾ Printed on acid-free paper

Last figure below indicates year of this printing
32   31   30   29   28   27   26   25   24   23   22

For my family

Contents

Illustrations

Acknowledgments

I first encountered *Taikōki* in a graduate seminar I took with Tom Keirstead at Indiana University. The early conversations I had with Tom and Sumie Jones about the numerous possibilities and nuances surrounding Hideyoshi narratives were invaluable in setting me on the path to this book. I am thankful to Sumie for the many opportunities she gave me to read and translate Edo period texts. My advisor, Richard Rubinger, read and discussed many early drafts of this work with me. I am grateful for his meticulous eye and for all that he taught me about how to use primary source materials. I was also mentored by Michael Dylan Foster, Michael Robinson, and Michiko Suzuki. All of these people contributed to my thinking on this book. My cohort was small, but the friendships have been lasting. Much appreciation goes to Sandrine Catris, Lori Morimoto, and Vance Schafer.

In many ways this project really began at DePauw University on a Tuesday morning twenty or so years ago. My undergraduate advisor, Paul Watt, met with me weekly to talk about my burgeoning interest in Japanese literature and answered my seemingly endless stream of questions. Those conversations with Paul convinced me not only that I wanted to be a Japanese literature scholar, but also that I wanted to be one at a small liberal arts college. At DePauw, Yasuko Ito instilled in me an appreciation for the intricacies and idiosyncrasies of the Japanese language, and Tom Chiarella nurtured my love of writing. I will be forever indebted to all three of them.

When I pursued my MA degree in East Asian Studies at Stanford University, I benefited greatly from the guidance of my advisors, Jim Reichert and Miyako Inoue, whose encouragement and insight still inform the way I approach my work. At Stanford, I also had the good fortune to study and converse with a great group of fellow graduate students: Claire Cuccio, Karen Fraser, Mark Gibeau, Hank Glassman, David Gundry, Shu Kuge, Elizabeth Oyler, Anna Schonberg, Christopher Scott, Ethan Segal, Roberta Strippoli, and Robert Tierney.

My initial research in Japan was funded by a Fulbright U.S. Student Grant for Dissertation Research. In Japan, Watanabe Kenji at Rikkyo University was a fierce supporter and patient guide as I worked my way through the numerous and varied *Taikōki*-related source materials. Kojima Naoko helped make it possible for me to return to Rikkyo to work in the summers of 2010 and 2016. Abe Kazuhiko generously served as a guide and mentor on all things Hideyoshi and provided me with materials from his personal collection when I could not find them anywhere else. My thanks also go to the docents at Kōdaiji Temple and the curatorial staff (Hisano Tetsuya, in particular) at Saga Nagoya Castle Museum for meeting with me and answering my questions.

While I was in Japan, I enjoyed the camaraderie of a remarkable group of fellow researchers and am happy to be working with many of them today: Tove Bjoerk, Kendall Heitzman, Gergana Ivanova, Nick Kapur, Lisa Onaga, Erin Schoneveld, May-yi Shaw, Kari Shepherdson-Scott, Lily Anne Welty Tamai, Sarah Thal, Benjamin Uchiyama, Molly Vallor, Chingshin Wu, and Kirsten Ziomek. Erin has continued to be a great support (and a discerning reader) in the years since. Tove and I spent hours discussing our research in the carrels at the old Rikkyo University library. I am thankful for those conversations as well as for all of the times she has tracked down materials in Japan for me when I have not been able to get there to do it myself. And Sarah was a lifesaver when the pandemic shut down my access to research collections.

In the United States, I am grateful for the many conversations about this project with colleagues and friends. As I worked on my dissertation, Aletha Stahl helped me with the earliest drafts of these chapters. Several days at the Popular Culture and Social Change dissertation workshop of the Association for Asian Studies in Philadelphia in 2010 came at a crucial time in the development of this project and were tremendously helpful.

I have benefited most from my ongoing friendship with Jeni Prough, who I met at the workshop and who has been a constant and insightful sounding board. Akiko Takenaka and David Spafford provided a much-needed critical reading of my dissertation that helped me discover ways to make it into a much better book. Thank you to Alisa Freedman and two anonymous readers for their incisive comments on an earlier version of chapter 4.

At Beloit College, I am surrounded by incredible colleagues in the Department of Modern Languages and Literatures as well as in the larger campus community. Akiko Ogino in the Japanese program has been a dedicated colleague and friend. Joy Beckman, Britt Scharringhausen, and Daniel Youd read drafts of some parts of this book, and I benefited significantly from their perceptive comments. Many others—too many to name—have been encouraging along the way. Everyone should be lucky enough to teach at a place like Beloit! Funding I received from the Mouat family and the Beloit College Book Grant were integral in helping me finish this project. The Mouat Junior Professor of International Studies endowed chair made it possible for me to return to Japan for several summers and pull together many loose ends, and the book grant gave me a semester away from teaching when I needed it most, greatly facilitating the completion of the first draft of this book.

Besides the funding I received from Beloit, my research has been directly supported by a Fulbright U.S. Student Grant for Dissertation Research, U.S. Department of Education Foreign Language and Area Studies grants, a Philanthropic Education Organization National Scholar Award, and a McNutt Fellowship from Indiana University. Grants from ASIANetwork (the Student Faculty Fellow grant) and from the Luce Foundation (the Luce Initiatives on Asian Studies and the Environment grant) made it possible for me to pursue research related to heritage and historical tourism in Japan.

Many thanks to the editors and other staff members at the Harvard University Asia Center. Bob Graham has guided this project to completion with unwavering efficiency and care, even as we faced the myriad challenges wrought by the pandemic. I also thank Karen Thornber and the two anonymous readers who provided such detailed and astute feedback and Kristen Bettcher and Jeanne Ferris at Westchester Publishing Services for such meticulous editing. Their comments helped improve this book tremendously.

The Westhafers and the Furukawas have supported me in various ways over the years. I am particularly grateful to my parents, Joe and Anne, who always encouraged me to pursue my passions—even if they took me an ocean away from home. Their unwavering support has meant the world to me.

Writing a book while teaching full-time and raising a family is no easy task, and I am forever grateful to everyone who has helped us. My three youngest children, Luke, Clare, and Nico, have never known life without this book, and like them, it has grown out of the things I have learned along the way. I am thankful for all the times they waited patiently and lovingly for me while I worked on this project on the other side of the door or the other side of the world. Their humor, their persistence, and most of all their ability to always help me keep things in perspective have made me a better person. My oldest daughter, Yukie, has been there from the beginning, and I am deeply grateful for her patience and encouragement, especially during the lean years. And finally, Naoyuki: this book has been a test of endurance, and Nao has shown that absolutely nothing can stop him or us. Without his steadfast support, this book would not exist.

In the end, this is all for Nao.

A Note to the Reader

In this book, Japanese words are written using the Hepburn romanization system. In cases where the words do not appear in the English dictionary, they are italicized. Long vowel sounds are marked with macrons except in cases where the word is commonly used in English.

Japanese names are traditionally listed with surname first. This is the convention I have followed throughout the book. On second mention, individuals are identified by their surname except in cases where they are typically referred to by their given name in Japan. For example, Toyotomi Hideyoshi is referred to as Hideyoshi in Japan, so I will use that name here.

The period starting with the end of Toyotomi rule has been called both the Edo period and the Tokugawa period. Throughout the book, I use the term "Edo period" to refer to these years and place its start date in 1600, the year Toyotomi troops were defeated by Tokugawa supporters in the Battle of Sekigahara.

Finally, unless otherwise specified, all translations are my own. I take full responsibility for any mistakes.

Abbreviations

INO	*Izumo no Okuni*
NHK	*Nippon hōsō kyōkai*
NMRSZ	*Nagai Michiko rekishi shōsetsu zenshū*
SRZ	*Shiba Ryōtarō zenshū*
YEZ	*Yoshikawa Eiji zenshū*

Introduction

> Whether a nation is settled in peace or disrupted by conflict de-
> pends on if its rulers discern the righteous way. This will deter-
> mine whether good politics or bad politics reach every corner of
> the nation.
>
> —*Taikōki*, Oze Hoan

So begins *Taikōki* (The records of the Taikō), a twenty-two-volume
biography that maps the rise and fall of Toyotomi Hideyoshi (1537–
98), the samurai leader who unified Japan at the end of the sixteenth
century. Oze Hoan's (1564–1640) *Taikōki* was first published in 1626, and
versions and spin-offs of it amazingly still resonate with readers four centuries later. Oze's *Taikōki* was one of the earliest examples of historical
writing about Hideyoshi. This text has influenced and inspired a seemingly endless number of Hideyoshi-*densetsu*, or Hideyoshi-*den*. From
oral tales to kabuki plays, from manga to popular historical fiction novels, and from critical films to television dramas, the past four hundred
years have seen a near-constant stream of stories about Hideyoshi based,
at least in part, on Oze's text.[1]

This book investigates *Taikōki*-influenced Hideyoshi-*den* and explores
the question of how history, popular culture, and the present intersect.
In the process, it analyzes the relationship between sociocultural contexts,
entertainment value, and the construction of popular historical narratives.
What is it about the story of Hideyoshi that makes it so resilient and relevant, and how has his story continued to shape and be shaped by the
people who reproduce and consume it? How and why has the narrative
of Hideyoshi's life not only persisted but also thrived in the centuries since
his death, and what are the implications of a sixteenth-century samurai's
story being used so freely in the twentieth and twenty-first centuries in
Japan? To talk about the confluence of writing and media about Hideyoshi,

I have chosen to use the term Hideyoshi-*den*.[2] The word *densetsu* is usually translated as legend, folklore, or tradition. The use of the term here not only signals that there are many well-known tales about Hideyoshi, but also that these tales have become an important part of Japanese tradition. The study of Hideyoshi-*den* highlights the rise and fall of a complicated hero who has been employed as a national symbol throughout the centuries since his death and whose story, like those of other complicated heroes, demonstrates how views of history and the past are fluid and often influenced by what is happening in the present. By exploring the various ways Hideyoshi has been interpreted in the years since his death, this investigation of *Taikōki*-influenced Hideyoshi-*den* addresses the question of how history, popular culture, and the present intersect and begins to untangle the intertwined relationship between sociocultural contexts, entertainment value, and the construction of popular historical narratives.

Popular representations of the past are everywhere in Japan, from cell phone charms to manga, television dramas, video games, and young women dressed as their favorite historical figures hanging out in the hip Harajuku district of Tokyo. But how does this mass consumption of the past impact the way consumers think about history and what it means to be Japanese? The multiple fictionalized histories of Hideyoshi published as serial novels and novellas before, during, and after World War II demonstrate how imaginative re-presentations of Japan's past have been used by various actors throughout the modern era. Hideyoshi, Japan's earliest aggressor in East Asia (his troops invaded the Korean peninsula—then known as the Choson peninsula—in 1592 and 1597), has become a metonym for the complicated relationship between Japan and other East Asian nations. This analysis of portrayals of Hideyoshi in the twentieth century examines how and why discourses on Hideyoshi, as seen in popular historical fiction, shifted during World War II and in the immediate postwar era. The reinterpretation of history in popular culture reflects various contemporaneous discourses, and these emerging discourses on Hideyoshi redefine the way individuals understand the history that is being depicted. Hideyoshi's efforts at self-legitimation and the resulting cult of personality combined with the inconsistent behavior that marked his leadership have contributed to multiple interpretations of him in both history and popular fiction.

Of the so-called three unifiers of Japan, Oda Nobunaga (1534–82), Toyotomi Hideyoshi, and Tokugawa Ieyasu (1543–1616), it is Hideyoshi who has made the strongest impression on subsequent generations. Most Japanese people seem to have two or three favorite anecdotes about Hideyoshi: he warmed Nobunaga's sandals in the breast of his kimono; he built a castle in a day; he outsmarted and outcharmed his enemies. These and other tales about Hideyoshi have been told repeatedly and have taken on a life of their own. By attaching himself to an up-and-coming star in the form of Nobunaga, Hideyoshi ultimately outlived and outperformed him, thanks to what many touted as his impressive combination of charisma, negotiating skill, and ability to read other people. By the end of his career, Hideyoshi had accomplished something practically unheard of at the time: he had risen from complete obscurity to become arguably the most powerful ruler Japan had ever seen.

His rags-to-riches story—of an uneducated farm boy from the humblest of beginnings and with very little in the way of social or financial capital who rises to the top—is one that continues to draw an audience. Yet this man who showed great ingenuity and perseverance on his way to becoming the ruler of the realm is also remembered for the ruthless violence he perpetrated against both friend and foe at the end of his career. The way these very different aspects of Hideyoshi's life have been handled in posthumous writings about him illustrates the broad range of possible interpretations and makes him a fascinating figure for the study of literary afterlives.[3]

Research about the reinvention of famous historical figures is not new, especially in Japanese studies. Much work has been done on Sakamoto Ryōma, the forty-seven loyal retainers (also known as the forty-seven *rōnin*) [masterless samurai]) and the Akō vendetta, Saigō Takamori, and others.[4] What makes Hideyoshi an outlier is the way he sought to manipulate his image and reinvent himself well before others started doing it for him. He was acutely aware of what he hoped his legacy would be and played an active role in creating it. He was what Stephen Greenblatt calls a renaissance self-fashioner,[5] and his tales about himself set off a fiction boom that continues to this day. The case of Hideyoshi is interesting not only because there is an abundance of popular historical fiction about him, but also because Hideyoshi's ability to control his own narrative while he was alive impacted the vibrancy of stories about him once he was gone.

When we consider the shifting historical narratives of Hideyoshi, Narita Ryūichi's notion of the three axes of historical fiction offers us a useful framework. The three axes are the time in which the story is set, the time during which it was written, and the time during which it is being read.[6] Not only can these three axes not be divorced from one another, but any analysis of them that attempts such a separation misses the potential richness in the text being studied. When Nagai Michiko's narrator in *Ōja no tsuma: Hideyoshi no tsuma Onene* (The monarch's wife: Hideyoshi's wife Onene) reminds readers to consider the context of what women experienced in the sixteenth century, for example, she is relying on the layering of these axes to help her story resonate in ways it might not otherwise.

As a historian using the writing of the well-known historical fiction writer Shiba Ryōtarō as a lens to better contextualize his analysis of the scholarly debates about historical fiction in the 1960s and 1970s, Narita concludes that "for both authors and historians, there is no good answer to the question, 'What is fact?'"[7] His close readings of several of Shiba's novels as well as of the history of the debates between writers and scholars about the nature of historical fact leads him to conclude that any argument positing that history is based on "fact" while fiction is based on "fabrication" is too simple and misses the point. Discussions of "historical fact" and "fictional fabrication" aside, historical fiction is often based on historical sources without being bound by them in the same way that historians and other writers of the historical record often are. Given this flexibility, historical fiction writers are able to attribute meaning to the characters of the past they describe and give them human emotion and personal depth that might be missing from the historical record. This ability to create characters and stories about human suffering and triumph from historical sources appeals to a general readership in a way that historical manuscripts often cannot. And historical figures like Hideyoshi who lend themselves to being variably interpreted over long periods of time make for the best historical fiction characters.

Narita argues that historical fiction in general, and the widely read works of Shiba, in particular, have provided readers with what Pierre Nora calls a "realm of memory" (*lieu de memoire*). Shiba's fiction has made its way into most households in Japan, but it has also heavily influenced how readers think about history. Nora describes a realm of memory as "any significant entity, whether material or nonmaterial in nature, which by dint of human will or the work of time has become a symbolic element of the memorial heritage of any community." Nora is interested in what he refers to as a "new approach" to history that focuses on reinterpreting it from varied perspectives and in "symbolic terms." He refers to this as "history of the second degree."[8] In various *Taikōki* and *Taikōki*-inspired tales, Hideyoshi has come to symbolize much more than himself, and this analysis of *Taikōki*-influenced Hideyoshi-*den* is very much an analysis of history of the second degree as it highlights the role historical fiction plays in the construction of memory and identity.

As Alexander Bukh explains, historical narrative is essential to the construction of national memory because it plays a central role in ensuring that the collective memory is shared by wide swaths of the national community. Bukh writes: "In order for these events to become genuinely national, i.e., shared by a large part of the national community and related to the present, these events are recreated and reinterpreted through museums, monuments, works of art, but also through historical narratives, which are present in texts such as school textbooks, historical novels, and memoirs. Collective memory of the national past is an integral part of the national present, or of the present national identity."[9]

This analysis of representations of Hideyoshi in the twentieth and twenty-first centuries examines how and why historical narratives about Hideyoshi, as represented in popular historical fiction, shifted during World War II and in the immediate postwar era. The reinterpretation of history in popular culture reflects various contemporaneous discourses, and these emerging discourses on Hideyoshi redefine the way individuals understand the history that is being represented. Hideyoshi's efforts at self-legitimation and the resulting cult of personality combined with the inconsistent behavior that marked his leadership have contributed to multiple interpretations of him in both history and popular fiction.

Analyzing varying versions of Hideyoshi's story over time, starting with Yoshikawa Eiji's 1930s newspaper serialization of *Shinsho Taikōki* (The new Taikōki) and ending with a close look at two Hideyoshi-centric tourist sites popular in the twenty-first century, this book reveals the ways stories about him encourage readers to remember a past that often did not exist. Although I engage here with discourses of historical memory and use historical analysis as one entry point into the topic, my methodology relies on close reading of various texts to uncover the power (the vibrant afterlife, if you will) of iterative narratives about Hideyoshi.

Hideyoshi and Taikōki

Chapter 1 provides much more detail about Hideyoshi and the origins of *Taikōki*, but to orient readers, here are the basic contours of his story. After early years spent in poverty, hardship, and obscurity, Hideyoshi entered the service of Oda Nobunaga in 1558. As Hideyoshi rose through the ranks, eventually reaching the position of *taikō*, or retired imperial regent, he put into practice many innovative policies that would become the framework for the Tokugawa government (1600–1868) and have a long-lasting impact on Japan. He disarmed the peasants and required samurai to take up residence in castle towns. He ordered comprehensive land surveys and population censuses that required all peasants to be registered on tax rolls and to live in their fiefs unless given permission to go elsewhere. And in 1590, he succeeded in unifying the domains in Japan under his rule.

At the same time, however, toward the end of his life and political career, Hideyoshi made a series of decisions that have tarnished his legacy. He ordered the suicide of the tea master Sen no Rikyū, his trusted advisor, in 1591 and ruthlessly murdered the entire extended family of his nephew and heir, Hidetsugu, in 1595. In an effort to take over Korea and eventually China, Hideyoshi launched two unsuccessful invasions of the Korean peninsula, in 1592 and 1597. In attempts to expand his power well beyond Japan's shores, Hideyoshi sent messengers to the Chinese, Koreans, Spanish, Portuguese, and others declaring his intention to create a Japanese empire. This "pretension to empire," as Mary Berry calls it, led to the two failed invasions of the Korean peninsula, which Hideyoshi had expected to conquer easily on his path to invading China.[10] Letters written by Hideyoshi late in his life show him to be a man with delusions of success and grandeur on the Asian continent. The same letters also reveal a seemingly jealous yet indulgent father who is obsessed with issues such as who can and who cannot kiss his young son's lips and whether his mother and wife are taking proper care of their teeth. Even as Hideyoshi's behavior as a ruler became more erratic and despotic, his focus remained very much on his family.[11] Hideyoshi died in 1598, having failed to conquer Korea or establish a government stable enough to ensure his young son's rise to power. Regardless of what the last few years of his life did to Hideyoshi's legacy, however, he died fully in control of a Japan that was more unified than the country had been at any previous point in history. The contradictions between the prudent leadership and effective administration of his early career and the cruelty of his later years have sent many historians and writers of fiction on a quest to make sense of his seemingly inconsistent behavior.

The shaping of Hideyoshi's literary afterlife, the Hideyoshi-*den*, began in earnest when Oze's biography was published, less than thirty years after Hideyoshi's death. A Confucian scholar and former vassal of Hideyoshi's nephew, Oze was both intimately familiar with Hideyoshi's life and also constantly seeking to interpret the events he recorded as lessons for his readers. Oze's writing about Hideyoshi becomes a morality tale that is part fiction and part biography.

In twentieth-century rewrites of *Taikōki* one can see what Yael Tamir calls "deliberate forgetfulness and misrepresentation"—interpretations made easier by the fact there are plenty of "blanks" in Hideyoshi's early history that have been and continue to be filled in by various authors in various ways.[12] Hideyoshi, as a humane warrior who invaded Korea, was a perfect representation for Japan's shifting national identity in the 1930s and 1940s. And when postwar Japan became focused on economic development, Hideyoshi's so-called ingenuity and superior interpersonal skills were heralded as excellent examples for a Japan that sought to reidentify itself as an economic leader. In short, World War II–era and postwar Hideyoshi rewrites highlight parts of Hideyoshi's life and career that depict a wide range of often unexpected Hideyoshis.

Historical Fiction and Sakuhingun (*Media Conglomerates*)

Oze's *Taikōki* and later reinterpretations of it in popular fiction of the twentieth and twenty-first centuries are part of a long tradition in Japan of consuming the past in various ways. Whereas historical fiction as a genre is often closely tied to the development of stories of national identity or national character, its use extends beyond questions of nationalism and well into the realm of popular entertainment. So although on some level historical fiction in Japan has helped connect great memories of the past with national character and a "reawakening of national history," as Georg Lukács argues, there is much more happening with Hideyoshi's memory.[13] More recently, Jerome de Groot articulates a broader definition of the role historical fiction can and does play in society. This definition is more closely aligned with the role Japanese historical fiction has played in the twentieth and twenty-first centuries in Japan. De Groot writes: "A historical novel might consider the articulation of nationhood via the past, highlight the subjectivism of narratives of History, underline the importance of the realist mode of writing to notions of authenticity, question writing itself, and attack historiographical conventions. The form manages to hold within itself conservatism, dissidence, complication, and simplicity; it attracts multiple, complex, dynamic audiences; it is a particular and complex genre hiding in plain sight on the shelves of a bookshop."[14] This "complex genre hiding in plain sight" has a long history in Japan.

One of the earliest forms of historical tales in Japan is the *gunki-mono* (warrior tales), a prominent genre of medieval literature. Traditionally these tales were encountered as written text (*yomimono*) or recited material (*katarimono*). They were sometimes chanted by itinerant *biwa hoshi* (lute priests) who traveled with battling troops and recited well-known tales of brave and heroic warriors. The earliest of the *gunki-mono* dates to the tenth century, but some of the most famous, such as the *Tales of the Heike*, date to the thirteenth and fourteenth centuries.[15] From chanted accounts of twelfth-century battles by *biwa hoshi* and entertaining *kōdan* (dramatic oral storytelling of well-known narratives) of the Tokugawa or Edo period (1600–1868) to the recent *rekijo* (history girls) fad, engagement with the past has been a popular pastime in Japan. Even today, history is consumed widely in popular culture—in the form of manga, anime, video games, novels, and films (to list a few).[16] The seeming omnipresence of stories about the past in Japanese culture today highlights the power that the stories and the images they evoke have over the popular imagination.

During the Edo period a vibrant popular literature scene developed to meet the needs of an emerging *chōnin* (urban commoner) class, and the popularity of historical tales surged in the form of Kabuki, *jōruri* puppet plays, and *kōdan*.[17] Thanks to these performances, which often took historical events as their topic; the introduction of mass (woodblock) printing; and increasing rates of literacy and literary consumption, historical tales flourished.[18] Popular historical fiction has provided a critical voice since its inception,[19] and during the Edo period, well-known playwrights such as Chikamatsu Monzaemon (1653–1725) drew on the Japanese literary practice of adapting stories from the past to comment on current events and indirectly criticize the strict social structure enforced by the Tokugawa regime.[20]

Historical fiction experienced another surge in readership in the 1910s and 1920s with the growing popularity of *taishū bungaku* (mass or popular literature) and an ever-expanding magazine audience.[21] Others have written at length about the definitions of and distinctions between *jun bungaku* (pure literature), or literary fiction, and *taishū bungaku*.[22] The fiction discussed in this book falls into the latter category. It has traditionally been considered low-brow and of lower literary quality than pure literature, but it has also often sold more widely due to its accessibility to a general audience. Relevant to this discussion, popular historical fiction is just that: popular. It is widely available, highly readable, and undeniably entertaining.

In his essay "History as It Is and History Ignored" ("Rekishi sono mama to rekishibanare"), first published in 1915, the well-known Meiji fiction writer Mori Ōgai (1862–1922) notes the challenges inherent in trying to distinguish between history and fiction: "The kind of work I am now writing does differ from the fiction of other writers. I have not in my recent historical works indulged in the free adaptation and rejection of historical fact common to this type of composition. . . . In studying historical records, I came to revere the reality that was evidenced in them. Any wanton change seemed distasteful to me."[23] Ōgai's engagement with the genre highlights the difficulty he seemed to have in reconciling his role as a fiction writer and his strong conviction that he should be faithful to the information he uncovered during the course of his research. Eventually, it became difficult for him to include anything in his writing that he didn't find in the historical sources he was referencing. He explains, "Just as I disliked changing the reality in history, I became bound by history in spite of myself."[24] His view of "wanton change" to the historical record as "distasteful" led him to write accounts that were increasingly closely bound to that record. Toward the end of his career, Ōgai wrote mostly *shiden* (biographical literature), which he serialized in various newspapers. As Marvin Marcus writes, with these *shiden*, "Ōgai persisted in administering daily doses of documentary minutiae to the nation's readers, thus challenging their values by trying their patience."[25] Ōgai's insistence on sticking ever closer to the original source materials made his works increasingly distasteful to many of his readers.

Ōgai's attempt to articulate the relationship between fact and fabrication and to address issues of historical accuracy was the beginning of an ever-evolving discourse between historians and writers of historical fiction in Japan. The question of the role played by writers of historical fiction in the interpretation of historical facts is one that writers have grappled with throughout the twentieth century. The writers of historical fiction that you will encounter in this book have faced similar challenges—some welcome and some not—in working with their source materials.

The goal here is not to resolve these ongoing discussions about how historians and writers of historical fiction should go about their work or to distinguish what the two groups do. Nor is it to judge the differences in value between the two types of writing. Instead, the focus is on how the historical record, or lack thereof, opens the way for particular types of interpretations and how and why those interpretations have changed over time.

What has made historical fiction so popular in Japan? First, historical fiction is often quite accessible to readers, using well-known stories and familiar language to draw them into often exciting tales of heroism and loyalty. Second, historical fiction provides readers with a refuge in an often idealized, simplified past. The historical fiction that was popular in the 1920s gave readers a longed-for sense of tradition in the midst of growing uncertainty due to increasing capitalism, urbanization, and eventually militarism. Third, historical fiction has served as an outlet for social and political commentary that might otherwise be banned. By setting stories in a distant past, writers can force (or facilitate) discussions of socially or politically touchy topics. Historical fiction writers are able to comment on their milieu through the guise of narratives set in the past. Tales based on the life of Hideyoshi or the forty-seven loyal retainers are good examples of this use of historical fiction. Fourth, such fiction can serve to validate the modern state and its founders while also providing stories that people living through periods of suffering or change can relate to. Its romanticization of history at moments of change highlights glorious heroes of the past while also providing models for contemporary readers to be encouraged by and emulate. Although historical fiction does not always romanticize the past and produce praiseworthy heroes, when it does, it can be quite effective in motivating readers to support national ideals.[26]

Perhaps the most famous example of how a story of a historical event has taken on a life of its own in Japan is the account of the forty-seven loyal retainers and the Akō vendetta (1701–1703), portrayed most famously in the puppet play *Kanadehon Chūshingura* (1748). The initial incident occurred on the morning of April 21, 1701, when Asano Naganori (1667–1701), lord of the Akō Domain, drew his sword and attacked Kira Yoshinaka (1641–1703), a senior advisor to the shogun.[27] Because this incident occurred within the walls of the shogun's castle at a time when he was hosting envoys from the imperial court in Kyoto, it was a particularly brazen act that could not be ignored by the *bakufu* (the Tokugawa government). Asano was ordered to commit ritual suicide the same day, leaving his retainers masterless and without a domain. They spent the better part of two years planning their revenge. In early 1703 they attacked Kira's Edo mansion and took his head, declaring they were fulfilling the wishes of their deceased lord. They then presented the head to the grave of their lord before turning themselves in. This time the government took a little longer (more than a month) to decide the fate of the forty-six retainers held responsible for the assault on Kira's mansion. They were eventually ordered to commit ritual suicide, which they did on March 20, 1703.

The story of the forty-seven loyal retainers immediately captured the popular imagination. Though the details of both the initial incident and the act of revenge that followed twenty-two months later—as well as details of the way the *bakufu* responded to both episodes—were debated by scholars and officials for years to come, the first play about the forty-seven loyal retainers was written immediately after the events and performed within months of their revenge attack. The show was quickly shut down by authorities, most likely for fear it would incite anti-*bakufu* sentiments. Three years later, the famed playwright Chikamatsu Monzaemon wrote the oldest surviving play based on the story. By setting the story in the past and making it part of a series of plays centered on the fourteenth-century figures Ko no Moronao and Enya Hangan from the well-known fourteenth-century epic *Taiheki* (Chronicles of great peace), he avoided censorship. This approach also established a precedent that has been followed by subsequent *Chūshingura* writers. Takeda Izumo, Miyoshi Shōraku, and Namiki Senryū employed this strategy when creating *Kanadehon Chūshingura*, arguably the most influential account of these events.[28] The loose disguise of the *Taiheiki* story served as an easily decipherable shorthand for eighteenth-century audiences, enabling this story of government resistance to be retold under the watchful eyes of *bakufu* censors as a story of loyalty and justice in which the forty-seven are clearly portrayed as heroes.

Satō Tadao has written a thorough analysis of the events, their aftermath, and the various popular works the events inspired. For Satō, *Chūshingura* is an ideal *sakuhingun* with the power to shape-shift and appeal to a wide range of people.[29] Satō defines a *sakuhingun* as a historical event or person whose story can be produced in a number of varied formats such as plays, novels, movies, and television and appeal to a broad audience (figure I.1); it is, in a sense, a media conglomerate centered on a certain historical moment or tale.[30] Some examples include Miyamoto Musashi, Shinsengumi, Sakamoto Ryōma, Mito Kōmon, the Soga brothers, *Taikōki*, and of course *Chūshingura* (the focus of Satō's study).[31] Satō describes a set of characteristics that contributed to making a historical event or person eligible to become a *sakuhingun*. First, the event or person should have to do with a topic that is well established and thought to bring good luck. Second, *sakuhingun* are often (but not always) about people who have experienced premature and often heroic deaths. Third, *sakuhingun* stories often have a broad cast of characters who can be developed or explored. Fourth, *sakuhingun* are stories that often include a journey of some sort. And finally, *sakuhingun* stories are often connected to everyday life and politics in ways audiences find meaningful.[32]

Based on Satō's definition, both *Chūshingura* and *Taikōki* have characteristics of *sakuhingun*. Both have been reproduced in a wide range of media. Both have resonated with readers over several generations, showing incredible longevity, and both seem full of narrative possibilities. Interestingly, though, *Taikōki* has been the subject of far less research,

FIGURE I.I   An image from the manga *Toyotomi Hideyoshi: Ihon Taikōki* (Toyotomi Hideyoshi: A variant Taikōki) that shows a young Hideyoshi (then called Hiyoshi) running away from home and toward his future. Original story by Yamaoka Sōhachi and manga by Yokoyama Mitsuteru (Kodansha, 1995). Image from the author's collection.

despite the fact there have been a great many versions of it. For example, a recent search for the term "*Taikōki*" in the National Diet Library holdings revealed that the library has accumulated more than 250 works with that word in the title, starting with Uroko Gataya's 1710 *Taikōki*. The most recent title in the collection is the 2018 manga *Sengoku otome retsuden: Netorare Taikōki* (A Warring States his and her biography: The stolen *Taikōki*). Some other titles include *Donguri Taikōki* (Acorn Taikōki, 1959), *Kyabaree Taikōki* (Cabaret Taikōki, 1966), and *Onna Taikōki* (A woman's Taikōki, 1980). When the items are organized by date, interesting observations can be made regarding the story's rise and fall in popularity. For example, clusters of *Taikōki*-related texts appear whenever Hideyoshi and *Taikōki* are the subject of one of the annual historical drama series of the popular televised NHK annual *Taiga dorama* history drama series. Although *Taikōki* has been studied much less thoroughly than *Chūshingura* by scholars, most likely due to the breadth of the former's content (numerous events over nearly sixty years of a man's life versus two brief but compelling incidents with a large cast of characters), the latter's longevity and durability are instructive when thinking about *Taikōki*.

Stories such as *Chūshingura* and *Taikōki*, which are particularly adaptable due to their potential for multiple interpretations and wide-ranging implications, manage to stand the test of time because of their narrative flexibility and their ability to speak to themes that resonate with readers. Furthermore, audiences are drawn to stories like *Chūshingura* and *Taikōki* because they are so rich in the retelling. Portrayed in the traditional performing arts of Noh and Bunraku, for example, the stylized representation of a shared tale is particularly rewarding for a historically literate audience. The joy of consumption, then, comes not from the fact that what is being offered on stage or in the pages of the newspaper is historically accurate but because these are retellings of familiar stories. Indeed, the differences reflected in the choices made by the author or playwright are what appeal most to the audience. In its very construction, historical fiction acknowledges the conscious rewriting and criticism of history that has been going on for generations, making it a valuable contribution to the discourse of invented tradition in Japan.[33]

With themes of heroism, sacrifice, and bravery, *Taikōki* and *Chūshingura* both also fit into what Barbara Ruch calls Japan's "national literature." Ruch notes that national literature is national precisely because, by its nature, it is not exportable. Such literature refers to "a combination of themes, heroes and heroines, predicaments, ethical dilemmas, resolutions, and emotional attitudes" that are particular to a given nation.[34] She argues that a national literature is "a certain core of literary works the content of which is well known and held dear by the majority of people across all class and professional lines, a literature that is a reflection of national outlook."[35] According to Ruch's definition, texts like *Taikōki* or *Chūshingura* are national literature because both are made up of well-liked and well-known recurring themes, and both offer comfort to readers as they also reflect national character. Ruch's definition of national literature resonates well with the nature of Hideyoshi-*den*. The stories about Hideyoshi speak to Japanese readers because they meet so many of the criteria Ruch suggests. These stories never "shock or revolutionize" but instead include themes of loyalty, hard work, and commitment that are repeated and that reflect the national character.[36]

Simultaneity and Entertainment Value

Why has historical fiction about Hideyoshi remained relevant to Japanese readers and worked so well as a realm of memory? A significant factor is the critical role that entertainment value plays in making historical fiction relevant. Hideyoshi's image has been present in popular culture over the past four hundred years, not only because his story is malleable, but also because it is quite entertaining. As our social media and meme-saturated world demonstrates, what is entertaining and widely available gets the most views, and what gets the most views has the highest potential to influence national discourse.

Ozaki starts "Taishū bungaku no omoshirosa" (The entertainment value of popular literature) in his *Taishū bungaku* (Popular literature) by stating matter-of-factly, "Many people think popular fiction should not be boring."[37] He notes that unlike pure literature, popular literature is created for general readers and sells based on their response to it.[38] Ozaki continues: "If popular literature is not interesting, it is safe to say it will fail. We cannot, therefore, talk about popular literature without addressing the issue of *omoshirosa* (entertainment value)."[39] Though it may seem self-evident that to sell, literature needs to be entertaining,

Ozaki's argument is significant because he asserts that entertainment value is the defining component of popular literature, and interest level is the determining factor in whether or not a person or event becomes the subject of popular fiction. Ozaki focuses his analysis of Hideyoshi's popularity in fiction on this question of *omoshirosa* and being *omoshiroi* (interesting or entertaining) and notes that just as entertainment value distinguishes popular from pure literature, so too, a high potential for entertainment is what has made the genre of popular historical fiction so successful.

Ozaki's argument can therefore be linked to the common conception in Japanese discourse that Hideyoshi is the most interesting of the three unifiers. Hideyoshi's position as the most interesting of the three affords him greater space within the popular imagination. The Hideyoshi historian Kuwata Tadachika argues that stories about Hideyoshi are far more interesting than those about Tokugawa Ieyasu because Hideyoshi's story had more twists and turns.[40] Similarly, Ozaki points out that even though Tokugawa Ieyasu was the more experienced leader, Hideyoshi, with his seemingly endless narrative possibilities, made for better *kōdan* stories and is therefore the more popular of the two.[41] Although *kōdan* initially gained popularity during the Edo period, it persisted into the modern era. Hideyoshi's ongoing presence in this quintessentially popular genre illustrates his entertainment value as well as his consumer appeal.[42] During the Meiji period (1868–1912), transcriptions of these *kōdan*—called *kaki-kōdan*—eventually became the basis for the popular fiction of the twentieth century. Being a go-to subject for *kōdan* meant being a regular topic in early books. So Kuwata's suggestion that Hideyoshi is far more interesting than his predecessor Nobunaga and his successor Ieyasu, and Ozaki's suggestion that stories about Hideyoshi make for better *kōdan* both confirm that stories about him are naturally suited for widespread consumption.

The popular appeal of these accounts of Hideyoshi's life has been augmented by the fact that stories about him often emerged in formats readily consumed by the masses, such as newspaper serials and television programs. Benedict Anderson writes that newspapers offer a simultaneity—linking disparate events and facts simply because they occurred within the same period of time—that structures the reader's sense of national identity.[43] Because stories about Hideyoshi are often serialized in newspapers and

FIGURE I.2 An installment of Yada Sōun's *Taikōki*, serialized in *Hōchi Shinbun* from 1925 to 1934. This installment was published on October 27, 1925. Image from author's collection.

comic series and on television, they present a similar type of simultaneity. This gives readers a dual sense of simultaneity. First, there is the shared experience of reading a story together that makes them identify it as a national pastime. Second, the fact that the past is repeatedly being consumed simultaneously with various versions of *Taikōki* allows readers to feel a particular connection to Hideyoshi and the past he represents to them.

Kuwata's own story illustrates this point when he articulates the sense of simultaneity that he felt when reading Yada Sōun's *Taikōki* (fig. I.2), which was serialized in *Hōchi shinbun* from 1925 until 1934:[44]

For people like me, who were born during Meiji, the end of the Taishō period coincided exactly with our young adulthood. It was about the time

we were studying hard in college that *Hōchi shinbun* . . . a large newspaper
began serializing a historical novel which took *Taikōki* as its topic. The author, Yada Sōun was already well-known for *Edo kara Tokyo e* (From Edo
to Tokyo). . . . [45] As I graduated from college, began working at the Historiographical Institute at Tokyo University, got married and started my
family, I continued to take the newspaper in order to read this story. Because
Yada Sōun's *Taikōki* was serialized for twelve years in *Hōchi shinbun* from
the end of Taisho through the beginning of Showa,[46] this story impacted
an entire generation that was reading it every day like I was.[47]

Kuwata is not specific about the way in which his generation was impacted. Indeed, it would be hard to speculate exactly how each reader
was influenced by Yada's text. What is clear, however, is that the experience of reading about Hideyoshi's exploits and successes spoke to Kuwata
as he set out on his own career. Furthermore, this was an experience that
Kuwata believed he shared with others of his generation.

Simultaneous consumption is only part of the story, however: the
facts that Hideyoshi's story has been told so often and for so long also
contribute to the tales' likability. They are tales "that Japanese at all levels of society [want] to hear recounted again and again."[48] And stories like
Hideyoshi's that are told repeatedly over time tend not only to be better
liked, but also more influential. Just as Kuwata's generation came of age
with Sōun's *Taikōki*, so subsequent generations followed the numerous
rewritings of Hideyoshi's life, which have become part of an ever-changing
national narrative. David Henry argues that the popularity of the
children's tale *Momotarō* is not only because it has been consumed simultaneously by entire generations, but also because it has been recycled so
often. Henry makes a connection between simultaneity, consumption,
and repeated production that can also be applied to the discussion of
Hideyoshi.[49] In addition to the fact that iterations of *Taikōki* have been
widely distributed, read, and watched throughout the four hundred years
since Hideyoshi's death, multiple iterations have led to more iterations
and consumption has led to more consumption (fig. I.3). In a sense, the
reason for Hideyoshi's popularity in historical narratives is irrelevant.
Are stories about Hideyoshi popular because there are so many of them?
Or are there so many of them because he is such a popular topic for historical fiction? In the end, the cause and effect do not really matter because

FIGURE I.3   A page from Yada Sōun's illustrated *Toyotomi Hideyoshi: Taikō no maki* (Toyotomi Hideyoshi: The Taikō volume), published by Kōdansha in 1938. Image from the author's collection.

the net result—multiple and simultaneously consumed serializations of stories about him—means that Hideyoshi has remained part of the national discourse for the better part of the past four centuries, and our understanding of his presence there enables us to understand his readers and the contexts in which they were reading.

In discussions of enduring works of Japanese literature, Oze's *Taikōki* has often been overlooked despite the fact that it has all the makings of the type of national literature Ruch describes and that it has been the source of many *sakuhingun* materials about Hideyoshi. The following chapters explore how *Taikōki*-related fiction about Hideyoshi serves as a barometer for various social and ideological shifts in Japan, and they also highlight the role that historical fiction and historical narrative can play in influencing those shifts.

Chapter Outline

Starting with Oze's seventeenth-century text to lay the foundation, this book analyzes the depiction of Hideyoshi during Japan's war years and through the years of the country's rapid economic growth. Throughout, the focus will be on how Hideyoshi's self-fashioning, authorial intent, and sociocultural context contribute to the multiple and repeatedly consumed posthumous popular accounts of his life—accounts that have remained part of the popular imagination for centuries.

In chapter 1, "Toyotomi Hideyoshi and *Taikōki*: A Fictional Hero Emerges," the factors that have made the character of Hideyoshi and the various versions of his biography, *Taikōki*, so enduring are the focus of analysis. This chapter shows how Hideyoshi's vibrant literary afterlife results from the blanks in the historical written record about him, his own attempts at self-fashioning, and the dynamic role Oze's *Taikōki* has played in popular culture from the Edo period onward.

Chapter 2, "Hideyoshi's War: Yoshikawa Eiji's *Shinsho Taikōki* (The new Taikōki) and Hideyoshi as World War II Hero," considers the manipulation of Hideyoshi's image during the 1930s and 1940s, focusing specifically on Yoshikawa's *Shinsho Taikōki* (in Yoshikawa's *Yoshikawa Eiji zenshū*, 1950)—the story of Hideyoshi's life from the age of six until he established himself as leader of the realm. Not long after Yoshikawa began serializing his *Shinsho Taikōki* (1939–45) in the *Yomiuri* newspaper, that publication hosted a roundtable discussion that became the basis for a series of articles that it published over the course of several months. With titles like "Hideyoshi, Japan's Collective Hero" and "War and the Problem of Inadequate Provisions," these articles were part history lesson and part blatant propaganda: the link between Hideyoshi and the newspaper's support for the war is unmistakable. This chapter shows how articles printed immediately before and during the serialization of this novel position Yoshikawa's text within Japan's war propaganda machine and how Yoshikawa, like other popular fiction writers at the time, was implicated in this process by the type of Hideyoshi he created.

Chapter 3, "The Salaryman Samurai: Hideyoshi as Business Model," takes up the story of Hideyoshi and *Taikōki* during the early postwar period. After the Occupation government lifted the ban on stories about famous warriors, Hideyoshi-related fiction flourished in the 1950s and 1960s. This fiction was published concurrently with management manuals that used Hideyoshi and other sixteenth-century warlords as models of business success. As demonstrated through these manuals and novels, at a time when Japan was beginning its economic ascension and simultaneously distancing itself from the allied Occupation, Hideyoshi became the businessman's hero. To consider the contradictory discourses about Japan's past that these works expose, this chapter analyzes several business manuals as well as the *Sarariiman shusse Taikōki* (Taikōki of a salaryman rising up in the world) series by the well-known movie writer Kasahara Ryōzō, *Shinshi Taikōki* (The new historical Taikōki) by Shiba Ryōtarō, and *Tsutsui Junkei* (Tsutsui Junkei) and "Yamazaki" (Yamazaki) by the science fiction parody writer Tsutsui Yasutaka.

Chapter 4, "The Women of the Realm: Hideyoshi as Social Criticism," looks at works by Ariyoshi Sawako (1931–1984) and Nagai Michiko (b. 1925), two famous female writers of historical fiction, which reflect a growing resistance in the late 1960s and early 1970s to the apotheosis of premodern Japanese warriors. Ariyoshi's *Izumo no Okuni* (Okuni from Izumo) and Nagai's *Ōja no tsuma: Hideyoshi no tsuma Onene* (in her *Nagai Michiko rekishi shōsetsu zenshū*) question the patriarchal forces at work in the telling of history by portraying the lives and struggles of women in Hideyoshi's immediate circle as well as others in his realm to provide new interpretations of Japan in the late sixteenth century. Focusing on how their female characters respond to constraints placed on them due to their position in the patriarchal social structure, both novels offer clear criticism of Hideyoshi and sixteenth-century Japanese society through the eyes of their female protagonists. Although Ariyoshi and Nagai may not have had feminist agendas when writing about Hideyoshi, an increasingly public discourse on gender roles sparked by the growing women's liberation movement led to these new, insightful readings—which run counter to views of Hideyoshi as a great hero and leader.

Chapter 5, "Things Best Left Unseen: The Problem of Hideyoshi in the Twenty-First Century," considers the implications of Hideyoshi's cultural footprint and the future of his popular legacy by looking specifically at how his history of aggression in East Asia has been handled by two different tourist destinations: Kōdaiji Temple, in Kyoto, and Saga Nagoya Castle Museum, in Saga prefecture. In particular, the chapter addresses how the narratives at these two sites have changed as the curators and docents seek to attract visitors while keeping an eye on the history these sites represent.

CHAPTER I

Toyotomi Hideyoshi and "Taikōki"

A Fictional Hero Emerges

Since Toyotomi Hideyoshi's death there has been no dearth of stories about his life. Of the three unifiers, Hideyoshi (fig. 1.1) seems to have most successfully retained his celebrity in the years since his passing. Yoshida Yutaka, a modern translator of Oze Hoan's *Taikōki*, writes, "Comparisons of the personalities of the three heroes who welcomed the modern era, Nobunaga, Hideyoshi, and Ieyasu, have always been popular, but in terms of overall popularity, as one might expect, Hideyoshi always comes in first."[1] This comment by Yoshida reflects a tendency in Japan to compare these three men, and Yoshida's argument that Hideyoshi was the most popular echoes a widely-held opinion about them. The following well-known poem notes how the three men were thought to be different and begins to explain what makes Hideyoshi such an enduring figure:

> If the song bird won't sing, kill it—Nobunaga
> If the song bird won't sing, make it—Hideyoshi
> If the song bird won't sing, wait—Ieyasu[2]

Though he is perceived to have lacked the brutal strength of Nobunaga and the cunning mind of Ieyasu, for many Japanese Hideyoshi represents the everyman, who, by his sheer charisma and grit, was able to rise to the pinnacle of power. His example became a beacon of hope for many people seeking to make similar climbs to success in subsequent centuries.

FIGURE I.I   A portrait of Hideyoshi. Copyright KODAIJI.

To understand the role that tales Hideyoshi told about himself and the way Oze's *Taikōki* and other related stories promoted his long literary afterlife, we must have a better understanding of received history about Hideyoshi, his tendency toward self-promotion, and the vagaries of early historical narratives about him. From the start, he was the perfect protagonist for future tales about him.

The Life of Toyotomi Hideyoshi

To better situate this discussion of Hideyoshi's literary afterlife, we need to start with a more complete outline of Hideyoshi's life as we understand it. Hideyoshi was born in Nakamura in 1537 and originally called Hiyoshimaru.[3] He was the son of Kinoshita Yaemon, a foot soldier for Oda Nobuhide (1510–51), the lord of Owari (the present Aichi prefecture) and father of Oda Nobunaga.[4] Having left home while still a boy to pursue his dream of becoming a daimyo's retainer, Hideyoshi returned to his home province after several years away and became a foot soldier for Nobunaga in 1558. He fought with Nobunaga at the Battle of Okehazama in 1560, Nobunaga's first major strategic victory in his quest to consolidate his rule and become the ruler of the realm (*tenkabito*). In 1573, Hideyoshi became the lord of Nagahama Castle (in present northeastern Shiga prefecture) (fig. 1.2).[5]

Starting in 1577, under orders from Nobunaga, Hideyoshi embarked on a campaign in western Japan during which he invaded Bitchū province (the present Hiroshima prefecture) and besieged Takamatsu Castle to defeat Mōri Terumoto (1553–1625). Nobunaga died unexpectedly when he was betrayed by his retainer, Akechi Mitsuhide (1528–82) at Honnō-ji Temple in Kyoto in June 1582. Hideyoshi and his troops avenged Nobunaga by defeating Mitsuhide's forces at the Battle of Yamazaki. Hideyoshi pursued his quest for dominance by manipulating the succession debate at a meeting of the major players among Nobunaga's men known as the Kiyosu Conference, just over a month after Nobunaga's death. By acting as supporter, protector, and promoter of the young Sambōshi (Oda Hidenobu, 1580–1605)—the son of Nobunaga's eldest son, Nobutada (1557–82), who perished at the same time as Nobunaga—Hideyoshi maneuvered his

FIGURE 1.2   A page from Yada Sōun's illustrated *Toyotomi Hideyoshi: Hashiba Chikuzen no maki* (Toyotomi Hideyoshi: The Hashiba Chikuzen volume), published by Kōdansha in 1938. Image from author's collection.

way into a position of power and neutralized threats from Nobunaga's second and third sons, Nobukatsu (1558–1630) and Nobutaka (1558–83).

After the Battle of Yamazaki, Hideyoshi controlled five provinces. Following his defeat of Shibata Katsuie (1522–83), he annexed four more. By 1587, his rule extended all the way to Kyushu. Odawara Castle, the stronghold of the Hōjō family, was surrendered to Hideyoshi in the summer of 1590, and in 1591, he defeated the final resisters in northern Honshu, completing the military reunification of Japan with all territories being held by either Hideyoshi or his vassals.

As Hideyoshi unified the provinces that made up Japan at the end of the sixteenth century, he also enacted administrative policies that continued in some form into the Edo period. His Great Sword Hunt (*katana gari*) in 1588 prohibited anyone who was not a warrior (farmers, merchants, and monks) from using arms. His policy of reducing the number of castles (*shirowari*) sought to minimize opposition by consolidating power in the strongholds of territorial lords he had chosen. His redistribution of fiefs (*kuniwake*) ensured that his generals moved to areas where they had no established authority of their own. These initial changes gave him more control over potentially dangerous allies. His separation of farmers and warriors (*heinō bunri*) and subsequent freezing of the social order by enforcing class distinctions, restricting movement, and requiring people to remain in the group to which they were originally assigned helped establish the class system imposed under Tokugawa rule, reduced the threat of attack from disenfranchised peasants and farmers, and gave him greater control of armed warriors.

As a leader, Hideyoshi was known as a keen strategist and politician, and his tendency to show a conciliatory and generous attitude toward his enemies is considered to be uncharacteristic of warriors of his time. His social and political reforms for unification ultimately failed to solidify the hegemony of his family line, but they became the basis for more than 250 years of relative peace and unity during the subsequent Edo period. Hideyoshi's cadastral surveys (*Taikō kenchi*), which required the measurement and classification of all parcels of land, marked the first consistent multiregional land registration project. These surveys made it possible to calculate the value of land in terms of yield (*kokudaka*) and led eventually to the establishment of universal standards in measurement. Perhaps most significantly, they led to the registration of individual cultivators for each plot of land, thereby paving the way for improved assessments, taxation, and reapportionments and providing a mechanism for taking censuses.

After dominating Japan, Hideyoshi turned his attention to the Korean peninsula, which he hoped to overrun handily on his way to subjugating China. Ultimately, though, the invasions he ordered on the peninsula in 1592 and 1597 became military quagmires, and when he died in August 1598, he left troops stranded there on the brink of defeat. The final years of his life and rule were marked by increasingly rash behavior, particularly following the death of his infant son Tsurumatsu in 1591. Besides the attempts to take over China and Korea, Hideyoshi also required his trusted tea master and advisor Sen no Rikyū to commit suicide and ordered the death of his nephew and heir Hidetsugu. In addition, in 1597 he sentenced twenty-six Christians to death as a way of suppressing tensions between competing groups of missionaries. In the weeks and months preceding his death, Hideyoshi became obsessed with ensuring a smooth transition to the rule of his young son Hideyori, creating a council of Five Great Elders (*gotairō*) and insisting that they swear absolute loyalty to the boy.

When he died at the age of sixty-one, Hideyoshi had managed to unify Japan, but he spent his later years pursuing his interests in Noh and the tea ceremony and involving himself in elaborate building projects. Instead of dying gloriously in battle, he died of illness on his native soil, far from the front lines where his men fought and died.

Hideyoshi, Emplotment, and the Enticing Blanks of History

In thinking about why Hideyoshi has been such a popular subject in historical fiction, Hayden White's writing on narrative discourse and historical representation proves useful. The blanks and discrepancies in the historical record about Hideyoshi leave plenty of room for "emplotment," to borrow White's term. In *The Content of the Form*, White writes: "Any given set of real events can be emplotted in a number of ways, can bear the weight of being told as any number of different kinds of stories. Since no given set or sequence of real events is intrinsically tragic, comic, farcical, and so on, but can be constructed as such only by the imposition of the structure of a given story type on the events, it is the choice of the story type and its imposition on the events that endow them with meaning."[6] Using this idea from White, we could argue that, in a sense, all history is narrative, requiring choices by the historian to determine not only what to do with missing information but also how to piece together the available historical data. For White, even annals contain choices made by the historian (narrator) that influence both the meaning and the interpretation of the "facts" being presented.[7] The writers of historical fiction take this notion a step further and argue that they are simply extending the boundaries of the narratives that already exist—adding and taking away details to meet the needs of their stories.

Narita Ryūichi notes that the question of history versus literature has been discussed in Japan since the beginning of historical fiction writing in the late nineteenth century.[8] According to him, it makes little sense to pursue the distinctions between historical fiction and the study of history (which he defines as historical writing based on source materials) because both require the authors to fill in missing information and to make interpretive moves based on their knowledge of the material and their own historical perspectives. Narita notes that because the distinction between history and literature is much less clear than one would expect, scholars in Japan have taken up this debate approximately every ten years—going all the way back to Mori Ōgai's 1915 essay "History as It Is and History Ignored."

The blanks in the historical record along with Hideyoshi's self-fashioning and his ability to speak to the common man (as a former lowly peasant himself) make him a particularly adaptable figure. Because so little is known about his early life and because there are often discrepancies in the sources that provide insights into his later life and military and political careers, the historical narrative surrounding Hideyoshi has blanks and incongruities that have also made him appeal to the imagination of authors, politicians, and journalists from Oze's time onward.

Hideyoshi started appearing in the records of Nobunaga's conquests in the 1550s, when he was in his late teens and early twenties. Other than stories he told about himself, however, very little about his life before this has been documented. The years leading up to Hideyoshi's first appearance in the Nobunaga records provide ample opportunity for writers of fiction to shade their stories of Hideyoshi in any number of ways. For example, in *Shinshi Taikōki* (The new historical Taikōki), Shiba Ryōtarō's young Hideyoshi works hard to peddle whatever he can to make his way up out of poverty, giving readers a young and energetic entrepreneur who was an appropriate model for people experiencing years of high economic growth. And in *Shinsho Taikōki* (The new Taikōki), Yoshikawa Eiji's protagonist is younger and smaller than the other boys but also fast and cunning, Japan's David to the Goliath of its World War II foes.

As Hideyoshi begins to appear more regularly in the historical record in accounts such as *Hideyoshi jikki* (A true account of Hideyoshi), *Ikeda kafu shūsei* (The complete Ikeda genealogy), *Mōri-ke nikki* (Diary of the Mōri clan), and *Kuroda kafu* (The Kuroda genealogy), the inconsistent ways that various documents record these events provide new possibilities for interpretation. Even when Hideyoshi's later years are being recounted by his near contemporaries, their accounts diverge. These conflicting details about his career appeal to fiction writers because, like the blanks in his early years, they give authors a degree of creative license they might not have otherwise.

Oze's analysis of a famous turning point in Hideyoshi's career and the springboard to his rise to become ruler of the realm—the days immediately following the death of Nobunaga—serves as an instructive example. In particular, a comparison of how the fate of the lord of Takamatsu Castle, Shimizu Muneharu (1537–82), was handled in these various accounts illustrates how nuances in the way a story is told can influence subsequent retellings of it. The general contours of what happened are these: Hideyoshi learns of Nobunaga's death while in the midst of a water siege at Takamatsu Castle. His men keep this news from the Mōri clan by intercepting Mitsuhide's courier. Realizing that he must act before word of Nobunaga's death reaches the castle, Hideyoshi immediately concludes his campaign against the Mōri with a swiftly brokered peace treaty. Unaware of Hideyoshi's real motivation, the Mōri negotiators agree to his offer without delay. Muneharu commits suicide, and Hideyoshi turns his attention to an attack on Mitsuhide. In some accounts, the Mōri knew about Nobunaga's death before completing their agreement with Hideyoshi, but in others, they didn't. In any case, they did not try to delay him by refusing his peace offer or resuming hostilities.[9]

Even in accounts written by people who lived around the time of the events they are describing, the details vary, and readers are left with the same questions they started with: How did Hideyoshi learn of Nobunaga's death? Was he able to keep this knowledge from the Mōri? And what role did Muneharu play in the final conditions of the peace treaty? At the beginning of the section of *Dai Nihon shiryō* that covers the days following Nobunaga's death, there is a brief summary: "Hideyoshi keeps Nobunaga's death a secret and brokers a peace treaty with Mōri. Shimizu Muneharu kills himself."[10] More than two hundred pages from historical source materials—including various diaries, family histories, and *Taikōki* by Oze and Kawasumi—follow. A cursory sampling of the information found in these and sources such as *Hideyoshi jikki*, *Ikeda kafu shūsei*, *Mōri-ke nikki*, and *Kuroda kafu* reveals discrepancies in the way these events were recorded. Clearly, each writer of these historical sources is writing from his own perspective, and the historical and literary accounts of the days immediately following Nobunaga's death at Honnō-ji shows how varied the interpretation of this well-known event can be. Many sources discuss how Muneharu's ritual suicide was a condition of the peace treaty insisted upon by Hideyoshi after Nobunaga died. Other sources argue that Hideyoshi purposely delayed the resolution of conflict with the Mōri to deceive them about Nobunaga's death. In some accounts Hideyoshi tells the Mōri of Nobunaga's fate, but in others he does not. A lengthy analysis of the differences in these accounts, though interesting, is a project for another time. What one should note for the purposes of this argument is that even the earliest sources "emplotted" these events in specific and often very different ways.

In order for Oze's narrative of Hideyoshi as a righteous leader to work, the Hideyoshi who wrested power from Mitsuhide needed to be a man blessed by heaven yet unsullied by the self-centered and brash behavior of his final years. Thus, when Oze tells the story of Hideyoshi's actions following Nobunaga's death, he creates a narrative that helps demonstrate how Hideyoshi's rise and fall represent what can happen when a leader loses sight of Confucian ideals and begins to rule selfishly. Oze's interpretation of these events emplots them in a way that is particularly useful for moral instruction. According to Oze, Hideyoshi learns of Nobunaga's death from a courier sent to him from Kyoto. After mourning for an evening, Hideyoshi wakes up the next morning and inspects his troops as usual, to give his enemy the impression that all is well. That day, even though he knows Nobunaga is dead, he rejects the treaty proposed by the Mōri. The next day, he sends his negotiators with a message telling Mōri Terumoto (1553–97), the Mōri leader, that Nobunaga and his son have been killed and that Hideyoshi is willing to agree to peace if the Mōri will accept the treaty suggested the previous day without amendment.

Whereas many of the Mōri see this as a perfect opportunity to take advantage of Hideyoshi, in Oze's tale Kobayakawa Takakage (1533–97) convinces them not to do so by giving three reasons. First, he notes that before Nobunga's death, Hideyoshi was obviously consolidating power and therefore likely to defeat Mitsuhide, and if the Mōri do not agree to Hideyoshi's condition, they will incur Hideyoshi's wrath once the Mitsuhide affair is resolved. Second, even though Hideyoshi could have signed the same treaty with them the day before, keeping Nobunaga's death a secret, he did not. This implies he is brimming with confidence and has no fear of defeat. Third, Hideyoshi's rule is clearly ordained by heaven, and he will not be defeated by mere men.[11] After hearing Kobayakawa's argument, Terumoto agrees to accept the treaty as it is. And again upon the advice of Kobayakawa, he offers his troops and guns to help Hideyoshi in his battle with Mitsuhide in the hope of securing future support from the man destined to rule over Japan. The third point made by Kobayakawa again reminds readers of Oze's primary goal—to emphasize the importance of virtue in leaders. Through Kobayakawa, Oze is arguing that Hideyoshi's successful negotiation of the treaty with the Mōri proves that he was a righteous ruler.

Furthermore, Oze suggests that even before the news of Nobunaga's death reached Hideyoshi, Muneharu and three others offered to commit seppuku in exchange for the lives of the others in the castle who are near starvation. Moved by their sacrifice, Hideyoshi agrees and prepares the items they requested—in exchange for this sacrifice, they asked for a small boat, sake, fish, and tea. In Oze's account, the four men commit suicide before the Honnōji news reaches Hideyoshi. Like Kobayakawa's speech, this act becomes an example of what a righteous ruler looks like and proof that Hideyoshi's rise was ordained by heaven. Even if Nobunaga had not died, Hideyoshi would have successfully negotiated the peace treaty.[12] To Oze, a Confucian scholar, Hideyoshi's rise and fall represent what can happen when a leader loses sight of Confucian ideals and begins to rule selfishly: the Hideyoshi who wrested power from Mitsuhide was a man blessed by heaven and as yet unsullied by the self-centered and brash behavior of his final years.[13]

Whether the blanks in Hideyoshi's story result from differing perspectives in firsthand accounts or a lack of historical records from the start, the elusive nature of his legacy has helped make him a popular topic for writers of historical fiction from the seventeenth century to the twenty-first. An analysis of how authors such as Yoshikawa, Shiba, Tsutsui Yasutaka, and Nagai Michiko and others talk about their writing process illuminates the fluid relationship they have with the historical source material and helps further explain why Hideyoshi is such an appealing subject.

These authors understand, as White and Narita point out, that no historical narrative is free of interpretation, but they also find ample opportunities to be creative and mold the story of Hideyoshi's life in ways they believe will be most appealing to their readers. Yoshikawa, known as a meticulous researcher, would spend months digging through historical sources before sitting down to write his novels. In his theories regarding the relationship between history and fiction and his obligations as a writer of historical fiction, Yoshikawa argues it is a writer's duty to do the historical research—but it is equally his job to fill in the "blank spaces" of history, which are of the greatest interest to him.[14] In an article called "Taikō o kataru 14: Ningen Taikō no idaisa" (Talking about the Taikō 14: The greatness of the human Taikō), he explains: "Hideyoshi is larger than life, and it is hard for an author to get a grip on him from head-on. . . . If we try to do this by focusing on the facts[,] . . . for example . . . take the Battle of Yamazaki, there are blank spaces in the story. Even with extensive research, there are still pieces missing in between what we know. If there is a lack of clarity on certain points, the historian has no recourse, but for the novelist it is impossible to leave the blank spots blank, so he uses his imagination to construct the story."[15] Yoshikawa's distinction between the responsibilities of a historian versus those of the fiction writer echoes White's argument about the possibilities and limitations of historical narratives.

Although Yoshikawa finds the blanks of history to be the most exciting part about writing historical fiction, Shiba finds the hindsight gained over time to be the greatest advantage of writing about the past.

For this reason, he prefers to write about people whose lives are complete and the results of whose actions are already clear. He calls this omniscient perspective the "bird's-eye view" (*chōkai*). In "Watashi no shōsetsu sahō" (My approach to fiction, 1964), he writes: "People die. Time passes. The more time passes, the more we are able to view a person's life from a high, bird's-eye view. This is what is interesting about writing historical fiction."[16] Knowing how the story ends makes it easier for him to fill in the blanks and create rich characters. Shiba is particularly attracted to writing about characters like Hideyoshi, whose stories fully reveal themselves as their successes and failures become increasingly evident over time.

Shiba's view of the relationship between historical fact and embellishment—like Yoshikawa's—reflects an approach in which he lets the facts and blanks speak to him. The literary scholar Shimura Kunihiro writes: "Shiba's historical fiction does not simply reproduce history as it was, nor does it simply focus on the paradoxes of history. After firmly grounding himself in the available sources, Shiba develops his own original take on figures from the past."[17] In the March 1997 commemorative issue of *Purejidento* (President) magazine titled "Shiba Ryōtarō ga yuku" (Shiba Ryōtarō sets out), Shiba is quoted as saying, "I read and read the historical sources through and through, and then I write the one or two drops that clearly emerge from the materials."[18] For his well-known *Ryōma ga yuku* (Ryōma sets out), he claimed to have gathered more than three thousand sources, which collectively weighed a ton.[19] As he noted, "When I line up as many of the facts as possible on top of my desk and stare at them, the information that rises up like vapors of inspiration from the facts before me, that is the truth."[20] Whether an author is like Shiba, who prefers to let stories emerge almost mystically from the historical source material, or like Yoshikawa, who finds the blanks in the historical record to be particularly appealing, Hideyoshi proves to be an ideal subject.

Whereas Shiba and Yoshikawa tend to stick fairly close to mainstream interpretations of historical sources, other writers take those same materials and pull harder at the seams. Tsutsui's historical fiction, for example, demonstrates an unwillingness to rely on contemporary sources as he questions the motivations of the recorders of those sources. In contrast, Nagai highlights the way Hideyoshi manipulated his own biographers and challenges the notion that history is always told from the perspective of the male in power. Like Yoshikawa and Shiba, Tsutsui, Nagai, and Ariyoshi Sawako rely on the same set of historical sources to tell their tales. However, the latter three are much less willing to let those sources dictate the stories they tell. For them, the so-called blanks highlight the unreliable nature of history told only based on the sources. As Narita notes, the question is not whether or not fiction writers and historians are writing history but why they are writing it the way they are.[21]

Hideyoshi as Self-Fashioner

The multiple blanks and discrepancies in the historical record about Hideyoshi have made him an engaging figure for writers of historical fiction, but these blanks might have been considerably less intriguing if he had not attempted to fill them in various ways during his life. It is the combination of blanks in the historical record and Hideyoshi's tendency to fictionalize his own story that helped pave the way for works like *Taikōki* to endure. The first person to fictionalize Hideyoshi was Hideyoshi himself. Born into a peasant family, with no money or status, Hideyoshi used a combination of hard work, innovative leadership, and myths he created about himself to achieve court and military ranks well beyond his original station in life. More important than the final court rank Hideyoshi achieved is the mythmaking he undertook. His accounts of his birth are filled with stories of an immaculate conception, an extraordinarily long gestation period (presumably so he could be born on the most auspicious date possible), and diviners who predicted his absolute rule for years to come. Hideyoshi was so persistent in producing these accounts that even early European missionaries and early biographers recounted them verbatim. Therefore, before launching into a discussion of Hideyoshi's afterlife and the ways in which his legacy has been maintained and manipulated over the past four hundred years, we need to take a closer look at how he consciously developed a framework that effectively structured the way he would be remembered. Before biographers and historians analyzed and commemorated him and novelists fictionalized him, he worked hard to fashion a version of himself that elevated his standing in Japanese society by creating a story about his life that was both memorable and enduring.

Hideyoshi was an adept "self-fashioner," to use the term of the literary scholar Stephen Greenblatt. In *Renaissance Self-Fashioning*, Greenblatt analyzes how selves were created and represented in sixteenth-century England. He argues that this was the first time in history that the sense of human identity was open to being shaped by the individual as well as by society. As a result, members of the upper class began to pursue the process of self-fashioning, whereby they attempted to construct their identities based on idealized standards. Implicit in this process is the idea that a person can increase their social and sometimes even political capital by creating fictions about themselves that manipulate their place in the social structure of the day.[22] Hideyoshi may well have been one of Japan's earliest and most successful self-fashioners.

Once he established himself as ruler of the realm, Hideyoshi undertook a process of self-deification that he hoped would compensate for what he knew to be his two biggest weaknesses: a paltry lineage and the lack of a viable heir. Before embarking on the process of self-veneration, however, he had to undergo a process of legitimation. Since it was well known that Hideyoshi came from a family of low rank and lacked the credentials necessary for the type of role he envisioned for himself, he had to create an ancestral line more suitable to his station in life. He did this by having an aristocratic pedigree created for himself. As John W. Hall explains, "Instead of abolishing the court, Hideyoshi assimilated his military organization into the court system, using court titles and ranks—the awards of which he controlled as a way of rewarding and ranking his own men."[23] Unlike Nobunaga, who manipulated his relationship with the emperor while refusing to adopt various titles such as shogun, Hideyoshi pursued rank and title advancement within the court structure.[24] By being adopted into the imperial aristocracy and posing as a Fujiwara, Hideyoshi employed what George Elison refers to as "the force of personality, the judicious use of historical precedents, and the application of cultural cosmetics" to advance himself.[25] Though Hideyoshi briefly considered wresting the shogunate from the much weakened Ashikawa Yoshiaki (1537–97), he sought what he perceived to be greater heights, and after careful orchestration, he realized his dream of ruling the court when he was named *kampaku* (imperial regent) and then *taikō* (retired imperial regent).[26]

Even as he was establishing his greatness within the aristocracy, Hideyoshi began to create a pseudohistory of his life that superseded the highest court rank by inventing an image of himself as a godlike hero of imperial status who was able to gain fame and power due to his innovation and hard work.[27] As Nagai's account so colorfully depicts, it was an image Hideyoshi freely shared with biographers, foreign visitors, and anyone else who would listen. Mary Berry aptly notes, "It is difficult to find in Japanese history a more self-conscious, self-promoting ruler, impossible to find a more ambitious one."[28] An example of how Hideyoshi's self-fashioning found its way into print can be seen at the beginning of Takeuchi Kakusai's *Ehon Taikōki* (Illustrated Taikōki):

> And one night in a dream she saw the wheel of the sun enter her womb and immediately she became with child. After thirteen months of pregnancy, a boy was born on New Year's night of Tenbun 5, the year of the fire senior and the monkey, at the hour of the tiger.
>
> And at that time, there appeared above the roof of her abode a mysterious star, and its light was like that of the noontime sun. After the child grew up, this star would without fail appear in the heavens above at times of desperate battle in order to ward off disaster and turn it into good fortune.[29]

This was not the product of a biographer's larger-than-life recollection of a hero; these were stories Hideyoshi perpetuated himself. As St. Pedro Bautista Blanquez (d. 1597), a Franciscan missionary to Japan in the sixteenth century, corroborates in his description of an audience he had with Hideyoshi at Nagoya Castle in 1593: "He next approached nearer to us, and . . . made the following speech, 'When I was born, a sunbeam fell on my chest, and when the diviners were asked about this, they told me that I was to be the ruler of all that lies between east and west.' Then he added, 'During the 104 reigns that have passed, there has never been a king who has ruled and governed the whole of Japan—and I have subdued all of it.'"[30] These stories that he told about himself left an impression on many of his visitors, who subsequently repeated them. Although the visitors seem not to have believed the tales, the fact that the accounts have lived on in their records highlights how far these stories Hideyoshi told about himself spread.

In addition to rewriting his origin story to convince listeners that he was ordained by heaven to rule, Hideyoshi sought to associate himself with great leaders of the past such as Prince Shōtoku (574–622), Emperor Shōmu (701–56), Taira no Kiyomori (1118–81), and Minamoto no Yoritomo (1147–99). He did this by pursuing endeavors that recalled the actions of these early leaders and then implying that his actions were similar to theirs.[31] Hideyoshi's construction of the Great Buddha statue at Hōkōji temple in Kyoto was meant to parallel Emperor Shōmu's commissioning of the eighth-century Great Buddha statue at Tōdaiji in Nara to indicate his intention to "succeed Shōmu as secular sponsor of the deity and of the foremost religious architecture in the realm."[32] He may also have hoped to capitalize on an idea that entered Japan in the sixth century: that a ruler who followed Buddhist precepts would succeed not only in ruling the realm but also in keeping his people free from hardship. At the very least, Hideyoshi took advantage of the peasants' knowledge of these Buddhist ideas and of the history of the Nara Great Buddha when he appealed to them to turn in their swords for use in the creation of the project in Kyoto.[33]

Finally, Hideyoshi also sought to establish an image of himself as an unparalleled great leader by pushing outward the boundaries of the territory he controlled. By sending troops to the Korean peninsula and by banning philosophies that were considered deleterious to the newly unified realm (such as Christianity), he not only solidified his domestic hegemony but also sought to extend his power beyond Japanese shores. The following account by Luis Frois (1532–97), a Jesuit missionary, demonstrates Hideyoshi's motivations for outward expansion. After a visit with Hideyoshi in 1586, Frois wrote: "He also said that he has reached the point of subjugating all of Japan; when his mind was not set upon future acquisition of more kingdoms or more wealth in it, since he had enough, but solely upon immortalizing himself with the name and fame of his power; in order to do which he was resolved to reduce the affairs of Japan to order, and to place them on a stable basis; and this done, to entrust them to his brother Midono (Hidenaga), while he himself should pass to the conquest of Korea and China."[34] Indeed, Hideyoshi's goal was to become king of the known world and to establish his incontrovertible control over Japan and beyond, in the hope of leaving a legacy strong enough to withstand the jockeying for power that he knew would follow his death.[35]

In spite of Hideyoshi's attempts to establish such a legacy, the Toyotomi reign lasted less than three decades, giving way to Tokugawa rule when Tokugawa Ieyasu emerged as victor in the Battle of Sekigahara. But what Hideyoshi failed to do in terms of establishing a dynasty that would rule Japan for generations, he managed to do in terms of carving out a space for himself in the Japanese imagination. Greenblatt describes power's "quintessential sign" in sixteenth-century Europe as "the ability to impose one's fictions upon the world: the more outrageous the fiction, the more impressive the manifestation of power."[36] According to this definition of power, Hideyoshi was the most powerful man in Japan in the sixteenth century. He not only created a past for himself that was much more noble than his humble beginnings, but he also made sure that stories about himself and his successes were recorded and shared over and over again. Always aware of his public persona, Hideyoshi even commissioned Noh plays in which he was the main character and played the leading role. In short, Hideyoshi stands out due to the persistence with which he fictionalized himself, fictionalizations that ultimately left him open to further interpretation. His acts of self-interpretation in pursuit of self-legitimation had a significant impact on the way he was perceived and written about in the Edo period, and the Edo-period texts become the foundation for much of the modern fiction and films produced over the past century.

Taikōki *and Hideyoshi's Long Literary Afterlife*

The story of Hideyoshi's long literary afterlife starts with Oze's 1626 *Taikōki*. One of the earliest biographies of Hideyoshi, Oze's text has played a significant role in influencing subsequent *Taikōki*.[37] Not only was Oze's account of Hideyoshi's life written by someone with close connections to Hideyoshi's inner circle, but it was also the first *Taikōki* published after Hideyoshi's death, and it has continued to be influential. Starting with Hideyoshi's birth and continuing into the final year of his life, Oze's account is also considered to be one of the most thorough. Perhaps most important for this discussion, Oze's *Taikōki* establishes a pattern of fictionalization about Hideyoshi that continues to this day. As Tsuda Saburō notes, in a considerable understatement, Oze "wasn't always faithful to the historical record."[38]

The preface to Oze's *Taikōki* ends with a cautionary statement that highlights Oze's desire to use his biography of Hideyoshi as a moral tale:

> Not only absolute monarchs (*kunshu*) but average people (*ippan no hito*) as well need to be concerned with whether or not they are acting justly. Whether a government is good or bad depends on whether a leader's actions adhere to the way of heaven. It is entirely up to one's own heart.
>
> The reason people suffer is because they veer from the righteous path and give themselves over to their desires. When one yields to avarice, his descendants are ultimately brought to destruction. This is why all must learn to follow the righteous path.[39]

Before any mention of Hideyoshi's strength in battle and his rise to the top, before any hint of the series of events that would ultimately lead to the demise of the Toyotomi family line, and in fact before Oze even mentions Hideyoshi by name, he gives the readers of this biography a strong warning and a clear sense of how this particular story will end.

According to Oze, people suffer when they "veer from the righteous path," and yielding to avarice will doom one's descendants. In 1626, more than ten years after the last member of the Toyotomi clan was silenced in the Osaka Summer Campaign, readers understood Oze's warning clearly. By then, Hideyoshi had been dead for nearly thirty years, and his family had been decimated.[40] Kuwata Tadachika describes Oze's text as part moral teaching (*kyōkun*) and part historical treatise (*shiron*), emphasizing its general unreliability as historical source material and noting that because of Oze's desire to use Hideyoshi as an object lesson, "there are more than a few places where it is difficult to trust [Oze's] analysis."[41] Indeed, by starting his account of Hideyoshi as he does, Oze signals to his readers that though he is writing the story of Hideyoshi's life, he is also—and more importantly for him—providing readers with an allegory that highlights the pitfalls inherent in living a life marked by egoism and greed.

The discussion of how Hideyoshi has been reimagined in popular historical fiction necessarily starts with Oze's text—and his preface, in particular—for two reasons. First, Oze's *Taikōki* heavily influenced subsequent Hideyoshi narratives. Though a multitude of texts have been published with the word *Taikōki* in the title, only Oze's text is synonymous with the term. It is the most widely read of those texts and is still readily available today as part of the Shin Nihon koten bungaku taikei (The new survey of traditional Japanese literature) series that Iwanami Shoten began publishing in 1989. Furthermore, many historians and writers of historical fiction view the work as a particularly thorough account of Hideyoshi's life. Twentieth-century writers such as Yoshikawa, Shiba, and Fuji Kimifusa (b. 1914) explicitly acknowledge that Oze's work influenced their understanding of the history surrounding Hideyoshi while others, including Kasahara Ryōzō, Tsutsui, and Ariyoshi, clearly draw from either Oze's *Taikōki* or other works influenced by it.

Second, as Oze's preface so clearly demonstrates, from the beginning the story of Hideyoshi has been subject to multiple narratives that, as in this instance, reflect the contexts from which they emerge. Oze wrote his story of Hideyoshi in 1626 with the knowledge that the Toyotomi clan had been destroyed. Given Oze's proximity to Toyotomi power, the rise and fall of the clan would have impacted him greatly. Before Oze became a Confucian scholar, he was a doctor from Owari who served as a vassal to Hideyoshi's nephew Toyotomi Hidetsugu (1568–95), a man made infamous by his brutal treatment of his subordinates and by his untimely death under Hideyoshi's orders. No doubt Hidetsugu's cruel leadership, followed by his early demise, reinforced for Oze the belief that unjust leaders are destined to fail. After Hidetsugu's death, Oze remained without a lord for several years. During that time he wrote Confucian instructional texts and a well-known biography of Nobunaga, *Nobunaga-ki* (Nobunaga chronicles). By the time he wrote *Taikōki*, he was sixty-one and had land worth two hundred and fifty *koku* in Kaga-han. (A *koku* is approximately the amount of rice it would take to feed a person for an entire year, or approximately 180 liters.) He was then serving Maeda Toshitsune (1594–1658), the fourth son of Toshiie (1538–99), one of Hideyoshi's most loyal followers. Oze's proximity to important figures on the Toyotomi side gave him ready access to information about Hideyoshi.[42] It also made it easy for him to write about the dangers of unbridled greed.

Thinking about Oze's *Taikōki* in the context of Tokugawa rule helps us understand the impact of these early narratives about Hideyoshi. Oze's *Taikōki* and subsequent *Taikōki* produced in the Edo period played a role in keeping Hideyoshi's legacy alive when the Tokugawa hoped to downplay it. By the Battle of Sekigahara (1600), Tokugawa Ieyasu had emerged as the most powerful daimyo. However, he could not claim complete sovereignty over the Toyotomi family.⁴³ Indeed, the Tokugawa were forced into a sort of ambivalent alliance with the Toyotomi not only because the Toyotomi were well situated, but also because they were as legitimate as the Tokugawa in terms of their station within the court. Though Hideyori was just a boy, his rank and office were parallel to those of Ieyasu, and Ieyasu's position made it impossible to challenge Hideyori's rank without compromising his own.⁴⁴

In addition to court backing, Hideyori was supported by a cohesive and ambitious entourage—including his mother, Yodogimi—whose members worked hard to assert their post-Hideyoshi legitimacy. In many ways, the surviving members of the Toyotomi clan were as adept at manipulating the system and controlling their own images as Hideyoshi had been. One way they helped ensure Hideyoshi's continued significance was to start the process of deifying him as soon as he died.⁴⁵ They aligned themselves and Hideyoshi with the sacred in two notable ways. First, they supported massive temple rebuilding campaigns throughout Japan. Second, and more relevant to this discussion, they immediately embarked on the process of deifying Hideyoshi by constructing Toyokuni Shrine and enshrining him there. The shrine became the center of Hideyoshi worship.⁴⁶ Emperor Go Yōzei gave Hideyoshi the posthumous name Toyokuni Daimyōjin (Most Bright God of Our Bountiful Country), and Hideyoshi was worshipped at the shrine with great fanfare until the Tokugawa closed it in 1615, after the Toyotomi clan's final defeat.⁴⁷

In the intervening fifteen years, however, the shrine not only remained a poignant reminder of the power of Hideyoshi, and by extension of the Toyotomi, but it also served as a psychological anchor for the Toyotomi resistance to Tokugawa. Furthermore, because of Ieyasu's inability to completely usurp power from the Toyotomi, the shrine became a liminal space where the Toyotomi clan still held sway. Starting in 1599, the shrine was home to a semiannual festival meant to honor Hideyoshi and draw large crowds to celebrate his memory. Besides the large festivals held at the shrine twice a year, there was also a remembrance ceremony held on the eighteenth day of the other ten months. The larger of these festivals attracted Kyotoites from all classes and all sectors of society. Not only did Ieyasu allow observances of Hideyoshi's death to continue, but he attended the ceremony for the first anniversary in 1599.⁴⁸ And though Ieyasu did not attend the 1604 special festival, which was "the most ambitious and conspicuous declaration of the Toyotomi's ambition to remain a strong presence in Japan," he stayed informed of the proceedings and spoke no words in opposition to the deification of Hideyoshi.[49] Ieyasu's tacit acceptance of these activities is additional evidence that the Tokugawa were not yet securely dominant.[50]

Another way the Tokugawa continued to legitimize the impact of Hideyoshi's rule was by its ambivalent response to the publication of Oze's *Taikōki*. Due to a rise in literacy and a subsequent increase in commercial publishing, more townspeople found the means and time to read, and Hideyoshi and the Momoyama period[51] became a popular nostalgic reference point for those who were living through the Edo period and longing for the feelings of novelty that they believed had accompanied the peace and prosperity of Hideyoshi's time.[52] Following the publication of Oze's text, various versions of *Taikōki* quickly emerged, successively building in popularity and attracting a highly developed bourgeois readership whose members were drawn to the rousing tales of heroic deeds. As Tokugawa consolidated power and settled into what would become centuries of rule, stories of Hideyoshi's bravado became more and more popular.[53] Though the Kansei reforms of the late eighteenth century reflect the Tokugawa government's awareness of the need to mitigate the impact that popular publishing had on its readership and led to the banning of various stories recounting Hideyoshi's exploits, this was not enough to stem the flow of popular Hideyoshi-related titles. After the Kansei reforms were finally loosened, the resurgence of interest in works about Hideyoshi—despite the fact that he remained a challenging subject for the *bakufu*—indicates the continuing power of this particular story.

The Tokugawa-Toyotomi relationship was strained when Hideyori was alive. And the continued success of Hideyoshi's biography, in spite of attempts to censor it, forced the Tokugawa to continue to deal with the Toyotomi legacy long after Hideyoshi's death. The fact that tales of Hideyoshi could fare so well at a time when they were most likely to be met with resistance speaks to the resilience and potential for longevity of Hideyoshi's story. Indeed, ever since restrictions on publishing works about Hideyoshi were lifted, beginning at the end of the Edo period, there has been a steady stream of published *Taikōki*. In fact, the only other time works about Hideyoshi were banned was during the Occupation following World War II, when all works about warriors were briefly censored.

Tsuda describes three *Taikōki* booms that occurred during the Edo period. The first followed the publication of Oze's *Taikōki* in 1626. Other works that took advantage of *Taikōki*'s popularity at that time include Takenaka Shigekado's *Toyokagami* (Reflections of a glorious past, 1631), Hayashi Razan's *Toyotomi Hideyoshi fu* (The genealogy of Toyotomi Hideyoshi, 1642), Tsushiya Tomosada's *Toyotomi Taiko Sujōki* (The lineage of Toyotomi Hideyoshi, Edo period), and Ōhara Takekyo's *Shinsen Toyotomi Jitsuroku* (The new and authentic account of the Toyotomi, Edo period).[54] After Oze's *Taikōki*, new versions such as *E-iri Taikōki* (Taikōki with illustrations, 1698)—which, due to its popularity became the first *Taikōki* banned by the *bakufu* (the reason given was that the depiction of the deaths of Hidetsugu's family was too cruel)—and *Genroku-ban Taikōki* (The Genroku Taikōki, 1698) continued to be published, particularly around the semicentennial and centennial years after Hideyoshi's death.[55] The Tokugawa response to this initial boom and *Taikōki*'s popularity was surprisingly muted, but as Julie Davis and others note, Oze intentionally avoided topics that would attract attention from the censors.[56] By 1710, *Taikōki* had been reprinted four times.[57]

The second *Taikōki* boom followed the publication in 1797–1802 of the eighty-four-volume *Ehon Taikōki* (Illustrated Taikoki) written by Takeuchi Kakusai (1770–1827) and illustrated by Okada Gyokuzan (d. 1808). According to Kuwata, *Ehon Taikōki* was intended to be an entertaining fictional account of the life of Hideyoshi, and it was designed to give the reading public more access to stories about the history of Hideyoshi.[58] The boom for *Ehon Taikōki* led to spin-offs in the form of popular historical narratives (*kōdan*), puppet play narratives (*jōruri*), and Kabuki pieces, as well as other printed texts based on it.[59] *Ehon Taikōki* attracted so much attention and gained so much popularity for Hideyoshi-related texts that it was banned in 1804 on the basis of a recent edict banning all works referring to warriors who were active from 1573 on. The author and illustrator were punished, and the publisher had to pay a steep fine.[60] The result was a stifling of the future possibilities of *Ehon Taikōki*.

The third *Taikōki* boom followed the publication of *Shinsho Taikōki* (The definitive Taikōki), published by Kurihara Ryūan (1794–1870) in 360 volumes between 1852 and 1868. The timing of this publication, beginning just a year before the Tokugawa government was challenged by Commodore Matthew Perry's so-called black ships to open its ports to trade and ending with the dawn of the Meiji Restoration, worked in

Kurihara's favor: the *bakufu* no longer had time to concern itself with censorship issues. Kurihara's work is considered the first *Taikōki* to pull together all of the popular (*tsūzoku-teki*) legends about Hideyoshi. It was also the first *Taikōki* to describe Hideyoshi's death. Kuwata argues that unlike the illustrated *Ehon Taikōki*, however, it was full of complicated sentence patterns and on the whole less accessible to the general public.[61] Kurihara based his version solely on secondary sources, including a popular *kōdan* called *Taikō shinken ki* (The definitive biography of Toyotomi Hideyoshi), as well as on *Ehon Taikōki*.[62] By combining these popular works and publishing them just as the Tokugawa regime was falling from power, Kurihara created a *Taikōki* that led to another flurry of *Taikōki*-inspired works such as *Ehon Toyotomi kunkōki* (Picture book of the exploits of Toyotomi Hideyoshi, 1857), written by Ryūsuitei Tanekiyo and illustrated by Utagawa Kuniyoshi.

The story of Hideyoshi continued to grow in popularity after the Meiji Restoration in 1868. There were nearly a hundred different versions of *Taikōki* published in the late nineteenth and early twentieth century, including many illustrated versions (fig. 1.3). Furthermore, plays like *Tsuruya Nanboku IV*, *Katami gusa yotsuya kaidan* (Souvenirs of grass Yotsuya ghost tales, 1884), and Takeshiba Kinsaku's *Hanamiji hisago Taikōki* (The Taikōki of the cherry-blossom viewing vessel, 1885) reveal that the story of Hideyoshi's life was a subject for popular culture in other formats as well.

Along with *Chūshingura*, *Taikōki* also played well with international audiences. One 1883 Japanese newspaper mentions *Taikōki* and *Chūshingura* as two plays that saw repeated success in America and Europe.[63] Furthermore, the continuation of this connection between the two influential stories into the modern era highlights the power of these two texts to speak to a broad audience over many years and through multiple media. The versatility and potential of these texts as *sakuhingun* is obvious from the beginning and shows why both continue to be popular today.

As this chapter has shown, Hideyoshi's literary afterlife demonstrated resilience from the beginning. Despite various pressures that should have curbed the vibrancy of tales about him, Hideyoshi's image in the popular imagination made it through the early modern period relatively unscathed. The persistence and popularity of his story results from blanks in the historical record, his own attempts to refashion his past, and the resilience of Oze's *Taikōki*. The result is centuries of texts, Hideyoshi-*den*, that promote everchanging interpretations of Hideyoshi's life while also

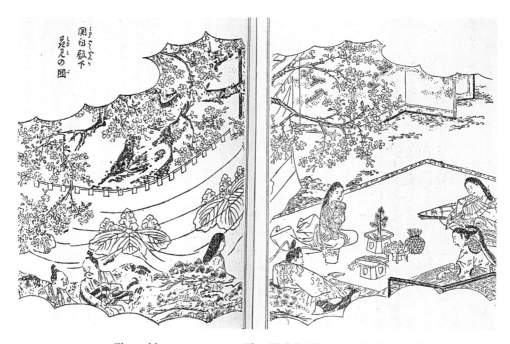

FIGURE 1.3   Cherry blossom viewing in *Ehon Taikōki* (Illustrated Taikōki), edited by Tsukamoto Tetsuzō and published by Aritomo dōshoten in 1927. Image from the author's collection.

allowing for the discussion of the role historical narrative plays in the development of a shared historical memory that is defined in specific ways at specific moments in Japanese history. By studying these various Hideyoshi texts, we can see the role popular culture has played in rewriting history and, more importantly, how history can be mobilized in popular culture for a number of often contradictory purposes.

Chapter 2 moves this discussion of the reimaginings of Hideyoshi's history into the twentieth century. It contextualizes the process of rewriting and reinterpretation within the framework of a Japan at war by looking at how Yoshikawa's serialization of *Shinsho Taikōki* in *Yomiuri Shinbun* from 1939 to 1945 engaged in the larger discourses of total war and Asian expansionism. In the process, Yoshikawa and *Yomiuri* forged Hideyoshi into a distinctly World War II–era hero who served as an important symbol of Japanese identity in the late 1930s and early 1940s.

CHAPTER 2

Hideyoshi's War

Yoshikawa Eiji's *"Shinsho Taikōki"* and Hideyoshi as World War II Hero

> I believe that the figures from our history, the heroes of old, never really die. When a cry goes out calling them in response to circumstances in contemporary society, they return from the land of the dead and offer their services to Japan.
>
> —Yoshikawa Eiji, "Sensō bungaku" (War literature), in *Yoshikawa Eiji zenshū* (The collected works of Yoshikawa Eiji), vol. 47

The serialization of Yoshikawa Eiji's popular *Taikōki* (The records of the Taikō) ended abruptly on August 26, 1945, eleven days after the Japanese surrender at the end of World War II, with a one-line notice buried on the back page of the morning edition of *Yomiuri Shinbun*.[1] The statement was barely noticeable and most likely missed by most of the newspaper's readers: "The serialization in this newspaper of *Taikōki* will, for the time being, cease publication due to the circumstances of the author, Mr. Yoshikawa Eiji (*sakusha Yoshikawa-shi no tsugō*)."[2] It was a single-sentence ending to a six-and-a-half-year enterprise by the newspaper that aimed to inspire the warrior spirit of its World War II readership, an ending quite different from the trumpeted beginning of the serialization in early 1939. Because of this anticlimactic conclusion, the changing representation of this work in *Yomiuri Shinbun* makes it difficult to see the text's sudden and incomplete conclusion as simply the whim of the author, as the notice tried to imply. Indeed, the text's rise and fall in *Yomiuri* was very much tied to the course of Japan's war experience.

Although numerous tales based on Oze Hoan's original *Taikōki* had been published before Japan's entry into World War II, with the Japanese incursion into China in the 1930s and the ensuing hostilities, Yoshikawa was tapped to create a story about Hideyoshi intended to support the war effort by contributing to the mobilization occurring at the time.[3] In the hands of Yoshikawa, and with the support of *Yomiuri Shinbun*, a well-known national newspaper, Hideyoshi was characterized as a benevolent leader and unifier of East Asia, despite the fact that his failed invasion attempts indicate the need for a much different reading of him.

Wartime iterations of Hideyoshi sponsored by *Yomiuri Shinbun* such as Yoshikawa's *Taikōki*, articles based on a roundtable discussion, and other special events that coincided with the beginning of the newspaper's publication of Yoshikawa's serial consistently painted a picture of a man who was a kind, intelligent, hardworking, and persevering leader intent on creating a strong and unified realm whose borders extended well beyond the Japanese coast. As this chapter shows, Yoshikawa's writing in and about *Taikōki* demonstrates how well he understood the role he was playing in manipulating narratives from the past for contemporary audiences, so he and the paper could create a Hideyoshi perfectly suited to Japan's wartime goals. By focusing on Hideyoshi's reputation as a humane leader, a decisive military strategist, and a common man who achieved uncommon success, Yoshikawa and *Yomiuri* collaborated effectively to publish a story that was not only loved by readers but that also supported the war effort.

The context of Yoshikawa's novel within *Yomiuri Shinbun* illustrates the degree to which the newspaper sought to take advantage of the author's popularity, his text, and his subject. The Hideyoshi whom Yoshikawa created for his serialization of *Taikōki* embodies an impressive ability to negotiate; compassion; ingenuity; cheerfulness; sincerity; and, most importantly, hard work. Though this image of a benevolent and humane Hideyoshi stands in stark contrast to the violence often associated with the sixteenth-century samurai, Yoshikawa's Hideyoshi thrived and attracted a wide and enthusiastic readership that did not seem to mind the way that the past was being manipulated for the sake of the nation (fig. 2.1).[4]

Newspapers during the War

Newspapers' involvement in Japanese war propaganda was two-sided. On the one hand, papers found an enthusiastic audience for any stories

FIGURE 2.1 The second installment (approximately two-thirds of the way down the page) of Yoshikawa Eiji's *Taikōki* in *Yomiuri Shinbun*, January 2, 1939. Image from the author's collection.

that kept readers abreast of Japan's overseas successes. On the other hand, knowing how effective papers could be in reaching individual readers, military and government leaders relied on them to promote messages of unity and mobilization for war. In many ways, the perspectives of newspapers at the time were largely those of the military authorities.[5] Papers like *Yomiuri Shinbun* played a significant role in spreading propaganda regarding the war and in seeking to unify thought within Japan about the country's military endeavors. Along with all other major newspapers, *Yomiuri Shinbun* rushed to publish the most sensational breaking war stories, often going to great lengths to do so. These papers owned their own airplanes with which they shuttled correspondents to and from distant fronts, and they put out not only morning and evening editions but sometimes up to three special news bulletins in a single day.[6] As Benjamin Uchiyama notes, the major newspapers were "driven by commercial ambitions to expand circulation into rural areas and dominate the national news market," so they sought to "[mobilize] the public into war frenzy."[7] And as Haruko Taya Cook explains, newspapers competed intensely to "report on the progress of the war and to sustain and develop support for what soon became a huge national effort in Japan."[8] War propaganda drove increases in readership, and in turn, the desire to meet readers' increasing appetite for sensational stories from the front drove papers to produce more propaganda.

Newspapers in particular were at the vanguard when it came to sensationalizing what was happening on the front and promoting various propagandistic stories. In her discussion of media-inspired "war fever" in Japan in the 1930s, Louise Young describes the mass media as a key channel for the dissemination of government propaganda to the public, but she notes that it also became a means for the government to measure public response to events and policies.[9] Thus, as a buffer between the government and the people, the media often portrayed current events in a way that redefined their significance. Uchiyama points out that wartime in Japan was not "an inert, oppressive period in which the state unquestioningly ruled over most facets of daily life and [in] which smooth, harmonious collaboration between public and private actors defined the experiences of total war."[10] In fact, individual wartime experiences were varied, and the way individuals internalized various messages was unpredictable. Still, the major newspapers played a significant role in trying to promote a positive, pro-Japan image of the war throughout.

Actions by *Yomiuri Shinbun*'s president Shōriki Matsutarō (1885–1969) indicate that the paper was fully committed to supporting the war and using the influence of propaganda. In September 1940, *Yomiuri* donated 50,000 yen to support the study of propaganda at the Teidai Newspaper Research Center. Around that time Shōriki noted: "I believe that propaganda is simply spinning things in the best light. It is not only imperative for the nation, but it is also absolutely necessary for helping each individual know his place within the nation."[11] This definition of propaganda was reflected in how the paper approached its coverage of the war and helps explain the enthusiasm with which the paper promoted Yoshikawa's serial. Always the adept businessman, Shōriki saw the newspaper's support of Japan's war effort not only as a method of producing propaganda for the war but also as another way to attract readers.[12]

Shōriki took the helm of the paper on February 25, 1924, not long after resigning his position in the Tokyo Metropolitan Police Department in response to his role in the Toranomon Incident, when the attempted assassination of Hirohito was seen as a failure on his part.[13] Though Shōriki had no experience in mass media, he received the financial backing of Gotō Shinpei (1857–1929), who saw excellent potential in the thirty-eight-year-old Shōriki—a potential that was quickly realized.[14] Within a year of taking over the newspaper, Shōriki had employed a combination of frugality, strict human resource management, and progressive marketing to turn the paper's monthly deficit of two thousand yen into a profit of three thousand yen.[15]

When one considers the controlled environment produced by increasingly stringent censorship laws, it is clear that Shōriki demonstrated an incredible ability to know what would sell and how to get it published. His paper consistently managed to balance providing sensational coverage that drew a consistent audience and not running afoul of censorship guidelines. Gregory Kasza describes how the Home Ministry began to use prepublication warnings and so-called consultation meetings to proscribe certain types of news immediately following the Mukden Incident and beyond.[16] Kasza includes a list of forbidden content as outlined by the Home Ministry at the time, excerpts of which illustrate the types of challenges newspapers faced. A sample of these prohibited items includes:

1. Differences of opinion with the government or military on the nation's basic China policy.

3. Indications that we have territorial ambitions in China or that the new states in central and northern China are Japanese puppets, or doubts about the significance of this as a holy war.

4. Contents fostering a tendency toward peace or weakening public resolve to sustain a long war.

10. Indication that Japan lacks natural resources, stories of bank failures or any other weak points creating uncertainty about the country's ability to wage war.

13. Stories of problems faced by the families of draftees, such as those related to livelihood, chastity, government compensation, or inheritance squabbles, or reports on the private lives of soldiers returning home if they tend to engender unrest or dissatisfaction among troops departing for the front.[17]

Given this environment, it is impressive that, under the direction of Shōriki, only seven issues of *Yomiuri Shinbun* were banned between the beginning of the war with China in 1937 and July 1941. Five of these bans applied to prefectural editions when local papers published the names of soldiers and regiments that were being deployed, since the inclusion of such information was believed to be akin to revealing military secrets.[18] Only two issues of the Tokyo edition were banned: the September 17, 1940, issue was banned for an advertisement for gonorrhea medicine, which was deemed too vulgar; and the October 31, 1940, issue was banned for an article about rice rationing.[19] In other words, publication records demonstrate just how well Shōriki and his newspaper maneuvered in the changing landscape of World War II–era journalism, satisfying readers' interests while also adhering to increasingly narrow government restrictions.

The paper was quite intentional in spinning the war to put it in a positive light, a fact revealed in the articles surrounding installments of *Taikōki* and the accompanying roundtable discussion articles about Hideyoshi called "Taiko o kataru." Next to these articles ran a series called "Letters to My Husband/Letters to My Wife" (*Otto e no tegami/Tsuma e no tegami*) that featured letters from wives to their husbands who were serving in the military and the responses. Besides the empowering and encouraging messages embedded in these letters, the idea that husbands and wives separated by the trials and distance of war could correspond so readily for all to see made the war experience seem much less traumatic than it actually was.

A similar effect occurred when the paper published pictures such as one on the front page of the June 16, 1945, edition. In this picture, high school girls sit primly in rows, smiling widely as they participate in a class at school. The girls do not sit on chairs at desks but kneel on the dirt ground, below blue sky. Other than a lone door frame, nothing of their school or of the surrounding buildings remained. Despite the barren, horrifying landscape around the girls, the caption reads: "Fun Open-Air Classes in the Burned-Out Landscape" (fig. 2.2). This article was published six months after the United States renewed its bombing campaign on the Japanese mainland, a campaign involving sixty-five air raids on Tokyo between December 1944 and August 1945. The most devastating raid occurred on March 9 and 10, 1945, and killed well over a hundred thousand people—providing a much different image from what the paper showed. Students who had been bombed out of their classrooms had likely also lost family members and friends in the raids.[20] The brief article accompanying this picture talks about how these girls' perseverance proves that they do not need chairs or chalkboards to learn. The smiles on the girls' faces serve to further the illusion that war did not weigh too heavily on the Japanese. As the paratext of the *Taikōki* installments—such as the letters between wives and husbands and stories about the resilience of youth—highlights, the narratives being told in the newspapers at the time remained focused on keeping the public mobilized in support of the war.

Yoshikawa and Yomiuri Shinbun

The collaboration between Yoshikawa and *Yomiuri Shinbun* likely would not have happened without the ingenuity and persistence of the newspaper's president, Shōriki, whose idea it was to recruit Yoshikawa. Perhaps another author could have created an equally compelling account of Hideyoshi's life, but it would have been difficult for Shōriki to find another writer to whom the public could so readily relate. Shōriki thought Hideyoshi would be an especially good topic for Yoshikawa because he saw numerous parallels in the lives of the two men: both started out poor and suffered and struggled greatly on their way to success. Shōriki believed this pairing of an underdog author with an underdog historical figure would draw a large audience of sympathetic readers.

FIGURE 2.2   Aozora kyōshitsu.

Yoshikawa Hidetsugu was born on August 11, 1892, in Yokohama, and had overcome crippling poverty as a youth to become one of Japan's best known writers. His family originally socialized with the *nouveaux riche* of the city before his father's drinking and poor business acumen forced them into poverty. Yoshikawa had been working for several years to support his family when, at the age of eighteen, he was involved in a dock accident that nearly took his life. This near-death experience gave him the impetus to leave his backbreaking blue-collar existence and eventually pursue writing. Due to the various challenges of his youth, Yo-shikawa felt connected to his readers throughout his career and claimed to be writing for common people like himself. Because readers could iden-tify with his background as an elementary-school graduate from a poor family who had to work hard just to survive, his writing attracted a wide audience whose members were also surely moved by his passion for the war and his rousing tales of samurai heroes.[21]

Given that Yoshikawa had long been associated with *Tokyo Asahi Shinbun*, *Yomiuri*'s rival newspaper, and had published successful fiction there, Shōriki knew that any work the author serialized in *Yomiuri* would likely draw a large following. Demonstrating the persistence that led *Yomiuri* to a twentyfold increase in circulation during the first fifteen years of his presidency,[22] Shōriki pursued Yoshikawa relentlessly de-spite early resistance by the author.[23] Furthermore, he realized that a focus on Hideyoshi, a hero from Japan's past who was known as a great unifier with visions of expanded Japanese borders, would be timely for the pa-per's World War II readership, whose members were in need of a model of fortitude at home and expansionism abroad. Familiar with Yoshikawa's work, Shōriki expected him to produce a story that would promote na-tionalistic sentiments in the newspaper's readers to support the growing war effort.

Shōriki's persistence with Yoshikawa was not unlike his doggedness in turning around the paper. Faced with the challenge of radio, for ex-ample, he introduced a number of innovative measures aimed at bolster-ing the paper's readership and sought to cash in on the popularity of ra-dio by publishing full-page radio guides and analyses of programs.[24] With the backing of the paper, he created newsworthy events that could then be reported on in great detail, such as a world championship go match in 1926 and exhibition matches in 1931 and 1934 between leading American Major League Baseball players of the day.[25] By 1937, when Japan invaded China, *Yomiuri Shinbun* had developed a solid base of readers who would be faithful consumers throughout the war years.

Yoshikawa was one of the most productive writers of the time, simul-taneously serializing novels and publishing articles in the *Tokyo Asahi Shinbun*, so when Shōriki initially approached him about rewriting *Taikōki*, he declined.[26] He was in the middle of a very popular serializa-tion of *Miyamoto Musashi* (1935–39), his best-selling work to date, and he had never really considered the merits of Hideyoshi as a protagonist. At least this is the impression he gives in *Sōshidō zuihitsu* (Jottings from Sōshidō), a 1936 collection of his memos. In an entry titled "Kakitai jinbutsu" (People I want to write about), Yoshikawa explains that he is drawn to writing about characters who are quintessentially different from Hideyoshi—men who make the wrong choices and end up failing instead of succeeding.[27] In "Kyōmi no aru jidai" (Time periods that interest me), he writes that while he finds sixteenth-century Japanese warfare interesting, it is too tedious to try to write a novel about it because it would be too dull to provide the background information necessary for the audience to be able to understand such a work.[28] Ultimately, however, Yoshikawa was persuaded to write the novel for reasons he outlines in an article published in *Yomiuri Shinbun*, and serialization of *Taikōki* began on January 1, 1939.[29] He later joked that if it were not for Shōriki's persistence, *Shinsho Taikōki* would have never been written.[30]

Yoshikawa, Popular Writers, and the War

Despite his seeming resistance in early negotiations with Shōriki, Yoshikawa appears to have been an active supporter of Japan's war endeavor. Besides serializing popular war novels, Yoshikawa served as a war correspondent and participated in the Patriotic Association for Japanese Literature (Nihon bungaku hōkoku kai),[31] which he helped found and which he directed.[32] The association was established on May 26, 1942, but it actually stemmed from the Patriotic Writers' Convention that had been held on December 24, 1941, just over two weeks after Japan bombed Pearl Harbor.[33] This rushed meeting seemed to ride the wave of nationalism that hit Japan with news of the successful attack on the United States. Yoshikawa notes that with the bombing of Pearl Harbor, the Japanese public was invigorated, and people rushed to donate money to the military. In fact, on December 8, 1941, alone, people donated two million yen (the equivalent of eight billion yen today) to the military as "thank-you donations."[34]

The degree to which novelists and poets had succumbed to war fever following Pearl Harbor is apparent in the literary scholar Yoshino Takao's description of the meeting, for which Yoshikawa had served on the planning committee. After starting with statements of commitment to the emperor and patriotic testimonies from several writers, the group set about formalizing its "writers' declaration" and "convention resolution":[35]

The declaration:

> [Written] with deep appreciation for the imperial declaration of war on December 8, 1941.
>
> The China Incident, with its objective of bringing lasting peace to East Asia, and the Greater East Asian War,[36] has changed the way we write about world history and the present. We Japanese writers, unified here as one, faithfully offer our services for the successful execution of this Great War.
>
> We believe that the Greater East Asian War, [fought] to strengthen this imperial nation for all eternity, will not only secure eternal peace, but it is also a chance for our country to realize the ideal of prosperity for all nations. Therefore, this wave is rushing throughout the world as well, and the crowning glory has been reached. Until that day, as loyal subjects born into this patriotic land, and as writers who live and breathe in East Asia, we solemnly swear as one to do our best to achieve patriotic enlightenment.

The resolution:

> - We, all writers of Japan, pool our talent, bring the war to a satisfactory conclusion, [and] in response to preparation for general mobilization, establish this Japanese writer's association.
> - We bring together all categories of literature and form this new organization, which will put to use all of our strengths.
> - Establishing that we are high-minded Japanese writers, we seek to use our skills to elevate the spirits of this wartime nation.
> - We, through this organization, cooperate on internal and external cultural activities and strive to create a new greater East Asian culture.
>
> December 24, 1941
> The Patriotic Writers' Convention[37]

After agreeing upon the above, the whole group "got into ranks and marched to the imperial palace to pay their tribute to the emperor, where they were not the only group bowing and yelling 'Long live the Emperor!' They remained prostrate there for a long time."[38] The image of these writers making a heartfelt declaration to write for the sake of the nation before marching in ranks to pay their respects to the emperor is a powerful one that leaves little room to question their commitment. When Yoshikawa later claimed to have been ambivalent about Japan's war effort, his role in the promulgation of this declaration makes it hard to take him seriously.

According to Yoshino, Yoshikawa's interest in contemporary history and the political system increased dramatically with the May 15 Incident,[39] and he became active in various meetings held to promote writers' support of the war.[40] Ozaki Hotsuki concurs: "When we trace Yoshikawa's steps at this time, we record a representative example of how one Japanese lived in wartime Japan. . . . As a writer, he worked until the very end to meet the needs of the time; he sincerely believed in his 'service to the nation.'"[41] As a leading voice in the Patriotic Association for Japanese Literature, which sought to "[gather] all of the power of all Japanese writers [to] create Japanese literature which manifests the imperial nation's traditions and ways of thinking, taking as [their] purpose the enhancement of the emperor's culture in support of the war,"[42] Yoshikawa appears to have been quite committed to Japan's war endeavor. And because he was one of the most prolific novelists writing at the time, his work had a strong impact on his broad readership.

Yoshikawa was also active in his capacity as a war correspondent, providing numerous articles from the front and analyses of the war and its terrain once he returned to Japan. Soon after the outbreak of hostilities in Manchuria, Japanese writers began to be sent to the Chinese mainland as war correspondents.[43] The first to go were magazine writers, followed by newspaper contributors such as Yoshikawa. By 1937, thirty writers had been sent to the front under the auspices of the Department of Information. Though popular fiction writers were not the only writers to go to the front, they were in the majority because their work appealed the most to readers and tended to attract a wider audience.

In October and November of 1942, Yoshikawa contributed a thirty-nine-part series to *Tokyo Asahi Shinbun* called "A Flight around the Southern Theater" (*Nanpōken o isshō shite*), which combined culture, history, and geography lessons about the nations of East and Southeast Asia for readers. By the time he began writing *Taikōki*, he had spent a considerable amount of time in China as a member of the government-supported Pen Corps (*pen butai*) and a war correspondent for the *Asahi* and *Mainichi* newspapers. He took his first trip in the late summer and early fall of 1938, traveling with a group that included other famous writers such as Kikuchi Kan (1888–1948), Satō Haruo (1892–1964), and Yoshiya Nobuko (1896–1973).[44]

It is clearly with a desire to serve the nation that Yoshikawa presented *Taikōki*. In his introduction to the serialized version of the novel, he articulates these intentions:

> The origin of the creation of a new *Taikōki* began suddenly with my role as war correspondent.
>
> I don't think there is a time in history when the people have shown greater continental resolve than now. If we look for a time with a similar feel, it would have to be the Eiroku [1558–70], Genki [1570–73], and Tenshō [1573–92] periods when Toyotomi Hideyoshi was living. When I was commissioned to write *Taikōki* in this newspaper, the first thing I thought about was the dual problem of how people today would "read" *Taikōki* and how I as an author would deal with the problems of this text.[45]

Echoing Narita Ryūichi, Yoshikawa seems to be thinking in terms of the three time axes here. He notes that the time of Hideyoshi was truly inspirational (axis 1), recognizes the necessity to adapt his tale to the current environment (axis 2), and wonders how best to appeal to his readers (axis 3). Yoshikawa understands the impact that powerful stories from the past can have on readers in the present, and he hopes to take advantage of that impact to provide a rich, multilayered tale for his readers. The introduction continues: "When we talk about *Taikōki*, since there are the popular editions such as Hoan *Taikōki*, Kawasumi *Taikōki*, and *Shinsho Taikōki*, as well as several modern versions of it, people will think that it is unnecessary to use the same approach to the text today, and as I face these well-used materials and start to create a *Taikōki* for a new era, I have to be prepared for the fact that this task will be more arduous than creating something from scratch."[46] Yoshikawa understands that to take up *Taikōki* is to become part of an ongoing conversation and join a series of interpretations of a particular moment in Japan's past. He also knows that rewriting such a well-known text can have pitfalls, particularly since he seeks to rewrite it in a way that resonates with a nation fighting a modern world war.

His introduction continues: "For several months while President Shōriki was soliciting me to write this work, I remained undecided, but recently, as I climbed through the Yangtze River valley as a war correspondent, I fondly thought of the life on the front for our Japanese soldiers as being like the lives of samurai warriors of old. The rivers, mountains, grass, trees, culture, and entertainment all have some resemblance to Japan, and since returning from my trip to China, a new *Taikōki* has begun to take shape right before my eyes. I turn toward the citizens, during this, what can be called the brilliant second epoch of Japanese history, and resolve to write a daring and bold manuscript."[47] Yoshikawa makes a direct connection between the experiences of Japanese soldiers in the 1930s and the samurai of old. By claiming that the Yangtze River valley provided the inspiration he needed to face the daunting challenge presented by more than three hundred years of *Taikōki* history and "fondly" connecting the bucolic valley to samurai, Yoshikawa ties his endeavor to Japanese expansion into Asia. Furthermore, his conflation of the troops from the Japanese Imperial Army on the Chinese front with sixteenth-century samurai symbolizes the degree to which he seems to have committed himself to the Japanese enterprise on the continent. By calling the 1930s "the brilliant second epoch of Japanese history," Yoshikawa makes the grandeur of his plans for his *Taikōki* apparent before a single installment of it has appeared in the paper.

He ends the introduction by explaining how he will proceed: "I plan to break the work into three parts, starting with the story of the Tokichirō's youth.[48] Past *Taikōki* have had material which is lined up and told as war tales. But I believe new historical fiction writers find the greatest meaning of their work in being like detectives who create the pieces that are missing and fill in the margins of history. Historical fiction has crammed into it the undercurrents of contemporary society, the wishes of the public at that time as well as the emotional strength of giant heroes. I want to write something that energizes the common people who encounter it today and becomes the basis for the construction of culture on the continent tomorrow."[49] In synthesizing the "undercurrents of contemporary society, the wishes of the public . . . [and] the emotional strength of giant heroes" of the past, Yoshikawa promises to create a novel that "energizes the common people" and "becomes the basis for the construction of culture on the continent tomorrow." Again, Narita's three-axes framework is beneficial here, as Yoshikawa uses links between Japan's great past and the challenges of the present to emphasize the potential influence of the work he is about to create. Not only do his lofty plans for the story of Hideyoshi clarify that he expects his novel to inspire a nation once again at war, but he also seems to agree with other scholars of the day when he notes that his story of Hideyoshi will also inspire readers in the colonies and influence colonial culture for years to come.

Though this introduction and the ensuing serialization clearly illustrate Yoshikawa's support of and compliance with the war effort, the question of his and other popular (*taishū*) writers' war guilt is a tricky one. In his 1964 article "Japanese Writers and the Greater East Asia War," Donald Keene argues that practically all Japanese writers supported the war and that there was no tendency in Japan, as there was in Europe, to show peaceful resistance to it.[50] After all, he argues, it was not as easy for the Japanese to take asylum in another country as it was for their European counterparts, and except for the most famous writers, who could live on their royalties from earlier publications, refusing to write what the government asked was financially infeasible. Furthermore, given that Yoshikawa was a popular historical fiction writer by trade, it would have been very difficult for him to keep writing what he was so good at without turning his reflections of the past to Japan's current situation.

Ozaki has accused Yoshikawa of succumbing to what he calls "conversion syndrome," due to what he judges to be an increasingly fascist tone in Yoshikawa's fiction.[51] Though Yoshikawa never directly admitted fascist leanings, it appears he was aware of the potential problems with his writing as he censored *Miyamoto Musashi* and stopped working on *Taikōki* for several years after the war to avoid any issues with the Occupation government.[52] He nevertheless disagreed with Ozaki's charge of conversion, arguing that he was patriotic but not overzealous and famously claiming in a 1938 essay ("Sensō bungaku" [War literature]) that he nodded to "neither [to] the left nor [to] the right."[53]

Though Yoshikawa claimed to have been neutral during the war, critics like Ozaki and Keene point out the impossibility of such a position at that time. Furthermore, Yoshikawa was much more involved in activities that supported the war than many of his compatriots were, making his claims of neutrality hard to believe. In "Sensō bungaku," for example, he wrote: "If the current situation becomes more threatening, if the day comes when my pen, my books, and my desk fall under the fires of war, I, too, as a war correspondent, will go to Manchuria, not denying the chance to abandon my meager self [for Japan]. Exchanging my pen for a sword, in my love of country, I don't intend to be inferior to Byron who was killed in the Grecian wars, though I lack his stylish appearance."[54] Despite the significant role he played in inspiring fellow writers and general readers to support the war effort, Yoshikawa later demonstrated an ambivalent and inconsistent attitude toward the war and his role in it, and it is this ambivalence for which he is best remembered. Suzuki Sadami explains: "During the war, Yoshikawa supported the war effort. He stopped writing briefly after Japan was defeated. Starting in 1950, *The New Tales of the Heiki* (*Shin Heiki monogatari*), which was created over the span of three years, became widely popular and became known as 'national literature' that hoped for peace. But because debate questioning writers' responsibility regarding the war lingered for a long time, it is only natural that people doubted Yoshikawa's lack of opinion about history."[55] Yoshikawa consistently denied having fallen victim to Japan's war mania, but the body of his writing from this time seems to contradict that claim. His denial of war responsibility, when read in the context of the situation that confronted writers who lived through the war, reflects the complexity of his position as a successful popular historical fiction writer during World War II.

In the eyes of the Occupation government, Yoshikawa, like many others, was deemed to have been complicit in war efforts and was prohibited from publishing for several years.[56] In fact, two years into the Occupation, the historical fiction genre as a whole was banned for praising the "feudalistic samurai spirit and incit[ing] a militaristic tendency."[57] This ban was not strictly enforced, however, and many writers kept writing historical fiction. Yoshikawa was one of them, publishing *Shinsho Taikōki* in 1950 and beginning the serialization of *Shin Heike monogatari* in the same year. A few years later, he started his serialization of the best-selling *Shihon Taiheiki* (My Taiheiki). He continued to publish until his death in 1962, and it is clear that, whatever his leanings, he ultimately emerged from World War II relatively unscathed.

Yoshikawa often stated that the masses, represented by the common reader, were a source of great knowledge, and that all the world was his teacher.[58] He frequently used his association with the common reader as a way to legitimize his writing. During the war, his self-proclaimed ability to hear the voice of the nation in the form of his readership served the added role of validating his increasingly nationalistic rhetoric.

Yomiuri Shinbun *and* Taikōki

Previous sections of this chapter have demonstrated how newspapers like *Yomiuri* geared its readership up for war and highlighted what made Yoshikawa and Hideyoshi ideal for this endeavor. This section explores what representations of Hideyoshi looked like in the paper by analyzing round-table discussion articles and other articles as well as Yoshikawa's text. In particular, interpretations of Hideyoshi at this time emphasize his humane leadership skills that reached beyond the borders of Japan, his ability to strategize effectively, his perseverance, and his ability to motivate others to do what is necessary to support their lord—and by extension their realm.

Though it ultimately published the most about Hideyoshi during World War II, *Yomiuri* was not the only publication trying to capitalize on his legacy. He was also portrayed as a model warrior or citizen in other newspapers and even in government sources. The *Tokyo Asahi Shinbun* ran several articles mentioning him—including one in the December 12, 1937, evening edition that dealt with the recent fall of Nanjing, when the paper invoked Hideyoshi's invasion of Korea to remind Japanese youth to persevere through what could be a long and tough war. There are also numerous references to Hideyoshi in the multivolume *Gendaishi shiryō*, a collection of materials on Japanese history from 1921 to 1945. These likewise link Hideyoshi to Japan's World War II efforts. "On the Mission of the Imperial Army" (Kōgun honzen no ninmu ni tsute), written in 1933 by young military officers who hoped to redefine the army's role in an attempt to promote nationalism, argues that the Imperial Army's primary role was not to protect Japan but to strengthen it by extending Japanese power throughout East Asia.[59] As a result, Hideyoshi and his invasions of Korea were presented as the ideal of what the army and its leaders should strive to achieve.

What makes this argument so striking, however, is that in the figure of Hideyoshi, the young officers called on a distant past whose example did not further their cause: "The appointed task of the Imperial Army is to bring the entire world together under one rule. The emperor is attempting to do this, but for the past 3,000 years, the Imperial Army seems to have lost its awareness of this task. Even so, over the years, there have been a few, such as Empress Jingū, Hideyoshi, the Meiji Emperor, and those who carried out the Manchurian incident, who have been able to execute this mandate. Others have forgotten this appointed task and are career soldiers who think only of the struggle for power, self-protection, or riches. Because of this, they have missed the opportunity."[60] However—unlike Empress Jingū, who is said to have come before him, or Emperor Meiji, who came after him—Hideyoshi was unsuccessful in his bid to conquer land beyond Japan.[61] While it may seem puzzling to see Hideyoshi listed as a hero from the past who successfully expanded the Japanese empire, this was not the first time his invasions of Korea had been used as an example of Japanese military strength.[62] During the Edo and Meiji periods, there were multiple references to Hideyoshi's military prowess and his success in Korea. Here, the sixteenth-century invasion of the Korean peninsula is used as an example of the warrior spirit and forward thinking necessary to make Japan into a great nation. Similar rewritings of national memory about Hideyoshi occur throughout the 1930s and early 1940s and enable the image of Hideyoshi to be used alongside others who were ultimately more successful in Japan's colonizing endeavors.[63]

No publication remained as committed to using Hideyoshi as a symbol to motivate readers as *Yomiuri* did. During its six-and-a-half-year run from 1939 to 1945, *Taikōki* appeared in daily installments in the paper almost without interruption. Except for what can be assumed to be holidays scheduled by the author, the newspaper, or both, the only two days where the serial was noticeably absent were December 8, 1941 (which was marked by glorious headlines about Japan's successful surprise attack on Pearl Harbor), and August 15, 1945 (the day Japan announced its surrender).

Throughout its serialization, *Taikōki* maintained a seemingly contradictory existence in *Yomiuri Shinbun*, insofar as Yoshikawa's serial entries were constantly present and yet seemingly detached from the headlines of war surrounding them. But given how much space each installment of *Taikōki* took, the value of Yoshikawa's tale—to the readers, the paper, and the war effort—seems clear. Even when *Yomiuri* was printing only a total of four pages (a spread made from a single broadsheet), Yoshikawa's serial took up a full sixth of a page every day. Although the serialization of *Taikōki* appeared to take readers to a past that had little to do with Japan of the 1930s and 1940s, the opposite was true, of course. The first notice of the upcoming serialization made on November 5, 1938 (and published at the same time as Yoshikawa's article described in the previous section), titled "*Taikōki* sanbu saku" (Taikōki in three parts), sheds much light on the thinking behind the choice of author and story line. From the first sentence of this unattributed article, it is clear that *Yomiuri* intended to use Yoshikawa's novel to resurrect Hideyoshi as an unsullied hero for a nation in need of a shared touchstone. The notice begins: "Taking advantage of recent events and in support of Japan's actions on the Asian continent in the name of the imperial cause there, we have something that will vividly recall the 'hero' Toyotomi Hideyoshi. Leading popular fiction writer Yoshikawa Eiji will bring this hero back from the grave and pass on the full account of his life."[64] Here, the goals of the upcoming serialization are set forth in clear terms. The link between the hero Hideyoshi, Japan's great past, and the situation on the Asian continent is unequivocal. Though Hideyoshi's failures in Korea and his inglorious death from illness far from his battling troops should have been well known to the early twentieth-century reader, in the hands of Yoshikawa and *Yomiuri Shinbun* these shortcomings are forgotten. One has to wonder how Hideyoshi, who died before realizing his dream of Asian conquest, can stand proudly for the imperial expansionist cause in 1938. This, of course, is a question that remains unanswered (indeed, untouched) throughout Yoshikawa's novel and *Yomiuri*'s coverage of it. Since Hideyoshi was a national icon during World War II, his image was by necessity only partially drawn, but the parts of his life and story portrayed in the *Yomiuri* serialization offer readers a well-defined framework for reading him as a war hero and altruistic leader.

The notice continues: "A three-year serialization of *Taikōki*, one of the most monumental works of recent years, will begin with the start of a new year. Dividing the work in three sections: 'The Tōkichirō Era' of Hideyoshi's youth, 'The Hideyoshi Era' of his prime, and 'The Taikō Era' of his mature years, Yoshikawa will devote his heart and soul to this work, and he will cover thoroughly the interesting aspects of Hideyoshi's life which have been missing from other versions of *Taikōki* written up to now."[65] It must have been tantalizing for readers to think about what Yoshikawa would bring to his *Taikōki* that had not been seen before.

Taikōki ran for more than twice the length promised in the introductory notice, stopping only with Japan's defeat in August 1945. Since neither *Yomiuri* sources nor Yoshikawa's writing provide any explanation as to the reason for this forty-four-month discrepancy, we can only speculate. Perhaps the text was more popular than originally expected; perhaps Yoshikawa, having gotten into the swing of it, was no longer hesitant and therefore was willing to produce more than anticipated; or perhaps Japan's entry into the Pacific War with its bombing of Pearl Harbor on December 8, 1941—less than a month before the end of the proposed three-year period—produced a need to keep the serialization going. The fact that Yoshikawa stopped writing as soon as he heard the emperor's August 15 radio announcement of Japan's surrender (the story ran until August 23, 1945, only because Yoshikawa had worked ahead and the paper decided to publish all the installations he had completed) seems to indicate that the continuation had much to do with the extension of the war itself.

In the next paragraph, "*Taikōki* sanbu saku" notes that Hideyoshi's ability to do "great things" during an "unusual time" in Japanese history is not unlike what the late-1930s readers of *Yomiuri Shinbun* were being asked to do for the sake of their nation at war: "Toyotomi Hideyoshi, who rose from humble origins to eventually rule the entire realm, is the greatest person to have ever lived in Japan. Using his ingenuity and heroism, Hideyoshi was able to devote the entire sixty years of his life to achieving great things during a very unusual period in Japan's history."[66] The hyperbole in this statement is obvious today, and the fact that the newspaper published it is an example of how the mass media played an important role in creating a "fascist public sphere" that readers engaged with regularly.[67] According to this notice, Hideyoshi was not only the greatest Japanese person to have ever lived, but he also spent every one of his sixty years achieving this greatness. The paper fully expected readers to overlook the troubling decisions that characterized the last ten years of Hideyoshi's life and instead follow his example in trying to overcome the increasingly challenging hardships they were encountering as Japan's war efforts expanded. Even though the claims in the notice are exaggerated, many readers willingly accepted this image of Hideyoshi as a reliable hero and model citizen. The parts of Hideyoshi's life that did not fit with this discourse of courage, sacrifice, and benevolence in East Asia were ignored to promote Japanese national pride and a sense that expansion into East Asia in the 1930s and 1940s was necessary and good.

The idea that Hideyoshi was a hero and a model citizen becomes controversial when the topic is Asian dominance, but this dissonance did not deter the *Yomiuri* staff writer from making the connection between Hideyoshi and success in Asia, despite the fact that Hideyoshi never successfully asserted control over another Asian country. The notice concludes by reemphasizing the greatness of the source material, *Taikōki*, and the man chosen to write the new version, Yoshikawa:

> Without a doubt, the person to write about the hero Hideyoshi is Japan's very own Yoshikawa Eiji. Mr. Yoshikawa possesses an exquisite writing style, and he has been quite determined in writing this story, beginning to write this story only after spending several months going over all the historical source materials he was able to gather.
>
> The writer's resolve regarding this work is unparalleled as a look at his words suggests.[68] He hopes to pour his heart and soul into the piece and won't give up until he has created a masterpiece that will leave readers speechless. This newspaper, in this present time, this "period of hero-longing," hopes that this work of literature will help make sense out of this difficult time.[69]

The final sentence unequivocally connects Yoshikawa's novel and the Japanese wartime reader. Readers are assured that Yoshikawa will delve deeply into the historical source material to (re)create a hero who can help guide Japanese citizens through the trials of war. This linking of present and past serves to legitimate Japan's actions in East Asia and encourage readers to take strength from those who helped create the Japanese nation.

By touting the author and the text, this notice appealed to the commercial tastes of the paper's readership. Many readers had grown up with Yada Sōun's version of *Taikōki* that was serialized in *Hōchi Shinbun* from 1925 to 1934. They were also quite familiar with Yoshikawa, whose breakout success *Jonan kennan* (Women troubles, sword troubles)— serialized in the first issues of *Kingu* magazine in 1925—and his current best seller, *Miyamoto Musashi*, made him one of the most widely read historical fiction writers of the time. By claiming that this *Taikōki* would follow in the tradition of other versions but improve upon them, the author of this notice makes clear that *Yomiuri* hoped to capitalize on the popularity of the Hideyoshi legend, which had found renewed vigor following Yada's serialization of it.

The notice introducing the upcoming serial was the first step in an extensive advertising campaign that the newspaper ran in support of Yoshikawa's novel—a campaign that helped redefine Hideyoshi for World War II readers. *Yomiuri Shinbun hyaku nijū nen shi* (The 120-year history of the *Yomiuri* newspaper) describes the "multifaceted plan" by which the newspaper would promote *Taikōki*.[70] First, the paper sponsored a roundtable discussion with several Hideyoshi specialists on January 25, 1939. Second, it created a "Hō Taikō" (His Highness Taikō) exhibit that included a panorama of Hideyoshi's life and portraits, as well as a collection of his treasures, and was open from February into March at the Shiroki-ya department store in the Nihonbashi district of Tokyo. According to the paper, the exhibit opened February 26, 1939, to "a surging wave of famous admirers" and welcomed people to come see the man who "experienced war on the continent 340 years ago."[71] Finally, in December of that year, Kikugorō VI (1885–1949) performed the leading role in a Kabuki play based on *Taikōki*.[72]

Aside from the serial itself, the most significant publicity related to Hideyoshi provided by *Yomiuri Shinbun* was the roundtable discussion the paper hosted, called "Let's Talk about Taikō" (*Taikō o kataru*), with Japan's "seven great authorities": Yoshikawa, Tokutomi Sohō (a journalist, historian, and critic; 1853–1957), Masamune Hakuchō (an author; 1879–1902), Shirayanagi Shūko (a critic and author; 1884–1957), Itō Masanosuke (a major general in the Imperial Army; 1877–1963), Yamamoto Eisuke (an admiral in the Imperial Navy; 1876–1962), and Watanabe Yosuke (a historical materials editor at Tokyo University; 1874–1957) (fig. 2.3).[73] The roundtable discussion took place in the first month of the serialization of *Taikōki* and led to a series of print articles. The participants offered well-articulated views of Hideyoshi in 1930s Japan that reinforce Yoshikawa's depiction of him, indicating that there was broad agreement regarding what Hideyoshi represented for readers and scholars during the war.[74]

The most vocal of these participants was Tokutomi, who served as the moderator and promoted Hideyoshi as a benevolent leader in East Asia. Once a proponent of Western democratic ideals, by the 1930s Tokutomi had become an ultranationalist who strongly supported Japan's

盛り上る"太閣熱"

七權威が座談會

徳富蘇峰翁ら作者吉川氏中心に

得難き好資料を發表

松坂屋美容室

FIGURE 2.3　"Moriagaru *Taikōnetsu*" (Taikō fever builds), the introductory roundtable article in *Yomiuri Shinbun*, published on January 27, 1939. Image from the author's collection.

mission in Asia. In his well-known draft of the "Basic Plan for Establishment of Greater East Asia Co-Prosperity Sphere," Tokutomi argued that
Japan must exhibit "courage, knowledge, and benevolence. If Nippon
should lack even one of the three, it will not be able to become the Light
of Asia."[75] As the moderator of the roundtable discussion, he emphasized
the traits that make Hideyoshi a prime example of a humane warrior supporting the quest for a universal Asian identity. As a model representative of "the Light of Asia," the Hideyoshi described by the discussants
demonstrates benevolence, the ability to rise in spite of past hardships,
an unwavering commitment to his cause, a persuasiveness directly linked
to his passion for his domain (or, in the 1930s, nation), and an ability to
act quickly and decisively to advance his cause. These same attributes are
highlighted in Yoshikawa's novel.

On February 12, 1939, a few weeks after the roundtable discussion,
"Hideyoshi, Japan's (Historical) Figure," the first of nineteen spin-off articles based on this discussion, was published in the paper. The last article appeared on March 10, 1939. Other titles included "The Dawn of Modern Japan: Hideyoshi and Legal Tender," "War and the Problem of
[Inadequate] Provisions," "The Dawn of Modern Japan: Hideyoshi and
Legal Tender," "War and the Problem of [Inadequate] Provisions," "The
Battle of Hideyoshi's Life," and "For the Sake of Nation."[76] The titles
point to the link between Hideyoshi and the newspaper's support for the
war effort, and each of the articles centers on an aspect of Hideyoshi's
legacy that could help readers understand and perform their roles as loyal
and frugal citizens.

The first roundtable article emphasizes two themes that ran throughout the discussion and that highlight the particular biases with which
the participants approached their analysis of Hideyoshi in 1939: the concept of humane war and the notion of a universal Asian identity. In the
first article, Tokutomi proclaims, "Hideyoshi is not only a hero all of Japan can stand behind, but a hero for all of Asia as well."[77] This notion
drives the Japanese imagination of Hideyoshi during World War II and
was therefore a fitting metaphor with which to launch the articles. Tokutomi explains that Hideyoshi is a "hero to us all" thanks to his demonstration of proper filial piety toward his mother and acceptable behavior
toward his wife—all without the cruelty so common in his day between
lords and retainers.[78] Tokutomi concludes by saying, "He wasn't incor-

rigible, so we can say he was on the humane side."[79] The point here, which is repeated throughout the roundtable articles, is that Hideyoshi was fallible but behaved humanely even toward outsiders or enemies, and it is this combination of traits that made him a great leader. By interpreting his failures (in this case, his infidelities) as symbols of his humanity, Tokutomi and the other participants create a logically coherent argument for why Hideyoshi should serve as the ideal model from Japan's past.

In one particularly memorable roundtable article, when Tokutomi provides details regarding the differences between Hideyoshi and Nobunaga and Ieyasu, another theme emerges. In that article, Tokutomi argues that Hideyoshi is not only a modern hero but also the quintessential Japanese person, a model for all Japanese to emulate. Tokutomi explains that first, because Hideyoshi understood what it meant to have nothing, he did not cling to material possessions, which enabled him to work quickly and lightheartedly. Second, Hideyoshi was able to compromise. Third, he always maintained a cheerful demeanor, even when suffering. Fourth, he had proper understanding of *mono no aware*, the evanescence of things, and could therefore appreciate true beauty. Thus, not only did Hideyoshi have good leadership skills and the right personality, but he also understood the fleeting nature of all things (material and nonmaterial) and was the ideal model for the Japanese reader. Tokutomi goes on at length about Hideyoshi's superior qualities and drives home the point that Nobunaga and Ieyasu could not even compare: "If we were to hold an exhibit of Japanese people, Hideyoshi would be the perfect representative because he demonstrates so many characteristics of Japaneseness."[80] For Tokutomi, Hideyoshi's ability to overcome adversity and rise to the top while also being relatable and exhibiting the traits of the ideal Japanese person—who is humane, diligent, and altruistic—made him stand out among his sixteenth-century peers and set him up to be the ideal model for the wartime Japanese readers of *Yomiuri Shinbun*.

One of the first scenes of *Shinsho Taikōki* demonstrates that Yoshikawa characterizes Hideyoshi using similar language and ideas. This scene opens with six-year-old Hideyoshi (then called Hiyoshi) trying to be the first of a group of young boys to find a cache of honey. As the smallest and youngest of the bunch, he incurs jealously when he secures the prize and is taunted with calls of his nickname, Monkey. He is disappointed when his friend Ofuku, nicknamed China Boy, joins the others

in jeering him. Hiyoshi censures Ofuku for his lack of loyalty and reminds him that, were it not for Hiyoshi's support, the other kids would
bully him instead:[81]

> There had never been a time when Hiyoshi got upset by being called Mon-
> key, but when Ofuku joined in the taunts, Hiyoshi glared at him.
>   "Have you forgotten that I always stand up for you, you sissy?"
>   Hearing Hiyoshi say this, Ofuku could say nothing. His face crumpled
> and he began chewing his nails. Worse than being called a sissy, in his
> childish heart, he felt ashamed at being called ungrateful. . . .
>   [Upon seeing troops returning from battle] one of the kids said, "Let's
> go watch," and the group excitedly ran off in the direction of the troops.
> Only Hiyoshi and Ofuku were left behind. Ofuku wanted to join the
> others, but the weakling was unable to break free from Hiyoshi's glare, and
> seemed to waver between going and staying.
>   ". . . I'm sorry."
>   Ofuku timidly approached Hiyoshi and placed his hand on his
> shoulder.
>   "I'm sorry, okay? . . . Okay?"
>   Hiyoshi's face turned red and he pulled his shoulder away, but when he
> saw Ofuku was on the verge of tears, he softened.
>   "It's just because you ganged up on me and said mean things to me," he
> said, still not satisfied.
>   "They tease you, calling you 'China boy' all the time. But have I ever
> joined in their teasing?"
>   "No. . . ."
>   "I always tell them that if you are one of our friends, you can't be a for-
> eigner, don't I?"
>   "Yes."
>   "Right, Ofuku?"
>   "Yes. . . ."
>   Rubbing his eyes, tears turned the dirt on Ofuku's face into round
> splotches.
>   "You dummy! It's because you always cry that they call you China boy!
> Let's go watch the soldiers. Come on, we have to hurry!"
>   Pulling Ofuku along, Hiyoshi ran in the direction of the soldiers.[82]

Yoshikawa's use of the word "China boy" (*tōjinko*) to refer to Hiyoshi's
bullied friend, who has recently returned from living in China with his

father, is intended to alert readers to Hideyoshi's compassion and concern for even the weakest and most outcast of his group. While the term *tōjinko* was in use during Hideyoshi's time, it referred to someone who was either exotic or ridiculous or strange.[83] By the 1930s, however, the term was clearly derogatory. For the 1939 reader, who was well aware of Japan's expansion into China and the rhetoric of Japanese superiority in Asia, using China as an insult—as the children do in Yoshikawa's story—would have been effective. And when Hiyoshi easily accepts Ofuku into their group by saying, "If you are one of our friends, you can't be a foreigner," this can be read as support for a unified Asia in which all people are peaceful allies.[84]

This scene is also significant because from this early point in the novel, it is clear that Yoshikawa is painting Hideyoshi as a person of exceptional strength, wisdom, and generosity. Even as a boy, he is portrayed as a benevolent ruler and great conciliator, unwilling to let the betrayal by a weaker friend provoke him. Ensuing scenes show how his childhood trials make him both strong and determined, and it is clear to the reader that Hideyoshi is destined for the greatness that only such beginnings can produce. Throughout Yoshikawa's text, Hideyoshi is a stalwart and magnanimous leader.

Hideyoshi demonstrates similar magnanimity when dealing with enemies in battle. The section describing the events following Oda Nobunaga's death and leading up to the Battle of Yamazaki focuses on Hideyoshi's singleness of purpose, which is tempered only by his generosity and compassion. When Hideyoshi learns of Nobunaga's death, he weeps, recalling how "his head had been patted by the man's hand, and his own hands had carried his master's straw sandals."[85] Even his crying serves to emphasize how Hideyoshi synthesized the ideals of sentimentality and nationalism. As his emotional side weeps, his rational side issues orders. Hideyoshi tells his men to stop all suspicious travelers to keep the news of Nobunaga's death from spreading and then forces the successful completion of a peace treaty with the Mōri clan.

Yoshikawa's exaltation of Hideyoshi as the ultimate benevolent Japanese hero prevails even when his Hideyoshi demands that one of the Mōri clan's most powerful generals, Shimizu Muneharu, take his own life as part of the peace agreement. Instead of being seen as ruthless, this demand becomes another example of Hideyoshi's calculation and compassion. As

Muneharu sits in a boat that has been rowed to the middle of the castle moat so people on both sides can see his suicide, a messenger from Hideyoshi rows out and makes the following speech: "Peace could not have happened without your consent. . . . The long siege must have been difficult for you, and my lord Hideyoshi would like you to accept this gift as an expression, however inadequate, of his feelings. You should not be concerned about us if the sun climbs too high. Please take your time making a thorough farewell."[86] The messenger then presents Muneharu with a final feast of sake and fine food, and Muneharu is allowed to commit seppuku in style, partaking of the food and drink and doing a farewell dance before slitting his stomach open. In Yoshikawa's hands, Muneharu's death, an event that has been described in conflicting terms in other sources, becomes one more example of the theme of generosity in difficult circumstances.[87] In Yoshikawa's interpretation, Hideyoshi's ability to combine benevolence, conciliation, and cool calculation under pressure enables him to successfully avenge Nobunaga's death.

The notion that Hideyoshi was a compassionate warrior who was a hero for all of Asia reflects a common discourse in the 1930s that sought to promote Japan's aggression in Asia as a necessary means to a much-desired end. Japan was fighting a just war, acting not in a base attempt to spread its empire and satisfy its lust for power, but to ensure peace and prosperity for all Asia. In other words, Japan was fighting a humane war, and as Japan's most humane warrior, Hideyoshi was the perfect hero for a unified Asia. Just as the seven roundtable participants emphasize Hideyoshi's humaneness, Yoshikawa's text focuses on his benevolence. When passages like the ones describing Hiyoshi's childhood kindness toward a friend turned traitor or the dignity allowed to an enemy before his death are considered in the context of their original serialization, they take on a second layer of meaning. Hideyoshi's goodwill toward those around him can be read as similar to Japan's goodwill to the rest of East Asia.

Besides being a symbol for altruism and humanity, in the *Yomiuri* roundtable articles Hideyoshi also becomes a symbol for the ability to overcome adversity. Throughout the modern era, Japan had experienced firsthand the failure of and frustration with unfair treaties with the West, and this image of the slightly built, uneducated Hideyoshi breaking free from his past and taking control of the realm was an appealing one for a country in the midst of fighting to assert its own power on the international stage. The roundtable article titled "High Position without Lineage: Fast Action, Broad-Minded Spirit" is another one that seeks to explain what sets Hideyoshi apart from his predecessor, Nobunaga, and his successor, Ieyasu. Tokutomi argues that Hideyoshi's greatness is a direct result of the fact that he made his way out of such lowly beginnings.[88] Ultimately, it was his ability to leave such great adversity behind and to forget the insults of the past, particularly when disadvantaged because of his small stature and birthright, that was expected to resonate with Japanese readers.

In this article, Tokutomi points out Hideyoshi had many appealing qualities that made him popular with the public, but it was his relentless perseverance that set him apart:

> Hideyoshi is unparalleled. Nobunaga is great (*erai*) but his father was a considerable man, and Nobunaga inherited his good fortune. Ieyasu suffered significantly, but even so, he did so as a Mikawa samurai. . . . But Taikō-sama had no castle and no retainers, just himself alone,[89] and even so he broke free of those restraints to achieve great rank. . . . On this point alone, I think we have to say [Hideyoshi] is the greatest of the three. This man was not ensnared by history, by his background, or by his environment. And because he is someone who is willing to strike out on his own in the world, it was only natural that nothing could stop him.[90]

The Hideyoshi who is not "ensnared" by his past and who would "strike out on his own" is a very modern hero and a model for how Japan could secure its position once and for all in the company of great nations.

The participants in the roundtable agreed that another trait that set Hideyoshi apart was his strong leadership ability, which was evident in his decisiveness, effective strategizing, and ability to motivate his men. They noted that one way Hideyoshi demonstrated these traits was in battles. The roundtable article called "The Battle of Hideyoshi's Life: The Battle of Yamazaki against Mitsuhide" focuses on these skills by analyzing how he got revenge on Mitsuhide. Itō pointed out that with only ten thousand troops against Akechi Mitsuhide's sixteen thousand, Hideyoshi should have lost the Battle of Yamazaki—despite the popular belief that Hideyoshi somehow had the upper hand: "It is often written that Hideyoshi's victory at Yamazaki was assured, but I don't believe this is the case. Akechi was a formidable opponent, and the two men were evenly matched as warriors. But Hideyoshi was so determined, he would have killed the entire clan himself. . . . Up to this point, Hideyoshi had gone to battle between thirty and fifty times, but this was the most decisive he had ever been."[91] Itō maintained that Hideyoshi should have lost at Yamazaki, an outcome that would have changed the course of history. Instead, Hideyoshi's ability to guide and motivate his troops contributed to his victory. In the next article in the series, Itō continued: "Why wasn't Akechi able to defeat Hideyoshi despite the fact he had sixteen thousand troops to Hideyoshi's ten thousand? He fell victim to Hideyoshi's hypnosis. Toyotomi Hideyoshi was a famous hypnotist. . . . He was able to make people live or die with a single movement of his hand."[92] In Itō's view, Hideyoshi's decisions ensured that the battle would be fought in the narrow area of Yamazaki, lessening Mitsuhide's advantage in army size. Furthermore, Hideyoshi's seemingly nonchalant attitude lulled Mitsuhide into a sense of complacency that eventually led to his defeat. According to Itō, Hideyoshi had an almost supernatural ability to control those around him due to his superior leadership skills.

In World War II reimaginings of Hideyoshi, he often persuades his adversaries to support his cause without resorting to unnecessary force. In both his words and actions, he is depicted as inspirational—or, as Itō put it, hypnotic. According to the roundtable participants, Hideyoshi inspired people to follow his orders. Yoshikawa's Hideyoshi demonstrates this ability over and over again when he carries out seemingly impossible tasks while also giving motivational speeches to those around him. These moments in the novel when Hideyoshi's seemingly hypnotic negotiation skills go to work for the sake of his province (Owari) and his lord (Nobunaga) highlight how Yoshikawa's *Taikōki* was intended to mobilize readers for the sake of the war.

Hideyoshi's motivational speeches and exceptional planning are highlighted throughout Yoshikawa's novel and often enable the author to make connections that resonate with World War II readers. Two specific examples of Hideyoshi's early successes illustrate how Yoshikawa used dialogue he attributed to Hideyoshi to rewrite well-known incidents in his career so as to promote wartime diligence and national solidarity. In Yoshikawa's *Taikōki*, Hideyoshi is always a model of the ideal citizen—

frugal, hardworking, and totally committed to the greater cause—and he does not hesitate to inspire others to be like him.

The first example of Hideyoshi's diligence and resultant success is when he is promoted to the position of head of the kitchen, a duty that was considered a demotion by most warriors. Instead, Hideyoshi (then called Kinoshita Tōkichirō) is excited by the challenge and goes about the task in his usual diligent manner. He reorganizes the kitchen and analyzes the way goods are purchased and consumed. Soon he is able to streamline kitchen duties, reduce waste, and improve overall morale. His knowledge and common sense make him more than equal to the task. As one of his suppliers notes, "Up against you, Master Kinoshita, a merchant is put to shame. You know the going rate for dried vegetables, dried fish, and grains! You've got a good eye for wares, too. It makes us happy that you're so skilled at bargain hunting."[93]

Such compliments are common in Yoshikawa's text, as are the sentiments expressed in Tōkichirō's reply:

> Life comes from what one eats, so the survival of this castle depends on the food prepared in the kitchen. Our job is to give them the best that we can. . . . All you merchants think about is profit. Well, this has everything to do with profit. What would you do if the castle fell into enemy hands? Wouldn't you lose years' worth of billing in principal and interest? And if a general from another province became the lord of this castle, wouldn't the merchants he brought with him replace you? If you think about it, in these terms, with the lord's clan as the root and all of us as flowers and branches, we will prosper as long as our lord prospers. Isn't this how we should think about profit? Thinking in terms of profit on the supplies you bring to the castle is actually shortsighted.[94]

Tōkichirō's earnestness in the kitchen serves as an entreaty to the Japanese people to work hard no matter how menial the task. More significantly, however, his speech encouraging the suppliers of Nobunaga's food to remember the importance of their seemingly irrelevant role in the success of the province can easily be read as an appeal to readers early in the Shōwa period (1926–1989) to remember the importance of being frugal and forward thinking in all they do and never forget their own value to the nation.

A second example of Tōkichirō's diligent leadership, accompanied by an impassioned speech for the sake of his province, clarifies the link between Hideyoshi's province and the Japanese nation. When Tōkichirō is still employed only in the stables, he notices that a damaged section of Nobunaga's castle wall is not being repaired quickly. In a fit of youthful impertinence, he confronts the foreman and calls attention to his negligence. Such an insult to his superior is punishable by death, but Tōkichirō is saved by the logic of his argument. The following day, Nobunaga reprimands him for overstepping his boundaries. When Tōkichirō claims that he can complete the castle repair in three days, Nobunaga promotes him to overseer of building on the understanding that Tōkichirō's failure to complete the task will mean certain death. When his superior and ally Maeda Toshiie, here called Inuchiyo, asks Tōkichirō whether he has any chance at succeeding, he replies, "I know nothing about building walls. . . . [But] the construction workers are men just like me, so if I use all of those men and get them to work to their full potential, I believe we can do it."[95] Yoshikawa's Hideyoshi believes even the most monumental task can be overcome when people work together toward a common goal. Here, the reader is expected to see a link between Hideyoshi's sixteenth-century castle repair and Japan's twentieth-century military engagements. Whether through kitchen management or wall building, readers are being shown the importance of industriousness, unity of purpose, and commitment to a shared goal.

To succeed at his task, Tōkichirō divides the wall into sections and puts workers into groups that will compete with one another, reminding them that they are not to leave their stations: "A worker in the workplace is the same as a soldier facing the enemy. He should never leave his post. Whether he is a carpenter, a plasterer, or a mason, his tools should never leave his hand. That would be the same as a soldier who throws away his weapon on the battlefield."[96] The subtext here is obvious: Yoshikawa argues that all Japanese are warriors in the nation's divine cause. When Tōkichirō realizes that the men are only pretending to work hard while secretly harboring resentment toward him, he tries to motivate them with food and drink, and when that does not work, he gives the following moving speech:

"Foremen, you aren't drinking! Perhaps you think that you, like generals, have responsibilities and therefore shouldn't drink, but don't be so anxious. What can be done, can be done. What can't be done, can't be done. If I was wrong, and we can't do this in three days, it will be resolved with my suicide. . . . If it's that you are worried, this particular construction project and even my own life don't really concern me. What worries me is the fate of this province where you all live. Like I've said over and over, taking over twenty days to do this little bit of construction, with spirit like this, the province will perish. . . . Provinces rise and provinces fall. I imagine that all of you have seen this, too. And I imagine you know the suffering of people who lived in provinces that fell. After all, it's something that can't be helped.

"It's no surprise that our lord, his generals, and those of us who are the lowest samurai do not forget about the defense of even the slightest part of the province. . . . But the rise and fall of a province is not in its castle. Where is it, you ask? It's right here, in you. The people of a province are its stone walls. They are its moats. As you construct this castle, you may feel as though you're plastering the walls of somebody else's house, but you are quite wrong. You're building your own defenses. What would happen if this castle burned to the ground one day? Surely it would not stop with the castle. The castle town, too, would be engulfed in flames, and the province would be destroyed. . . . If the province fell, it would really be the end. Children would cry for parents, and the elderly would search for their kin. Young daughters would flee raising cries of terror. . . . You must never forget what will happen to your parents, your children, your wives, your sick ones if the province perishes.

"So why are we at peace today? First, of course, it's thanks to His Lordship. But you, the people of this province, also protect us with this castle as your very center. No matter how much we samurai fight, if the heart of the people of this province were to falter . . ." Tōkichirō spoke with tears in his eyes, but he was not simply good at acting. He wept from the heart and meant every word he spoke.

Those who were touched by the truth of his words were sobered and watched him in silence. From somewhere came the sound of someone blowing his nose.[97]

The melodrama of this moment—grown men crying over the possibility of losing their province and family members—is intentional. Hideyoshi ends his speech by calling on "the people" to remain steadfast in their support of the army that fights to protect their way of life. He points out the importance of every man's diligence and commitment to the quest to maintain peace and protect the realm. Through this emphasis on Hideyoshi's focus on and commitment to unity, Yoshikawa provides his readers with a sixteenth-century hero who is perfectly suited to the needs of a nation that must commit itself to war. Ultimately, the men complete the wall in time—thanks, of course, to Hideyoshi's sobering yet motivating entreaties that they work together for the greater good.

Reading the entirety of these roundtable articles today, one is struck by their repetitive praise of Hideyoshi, their overly optimistic assessment of Japan's role in Asia, and the surprising fact that seven of Japan's greatest scholars, authors, and military men could sit together in a room for hours and agree so wholeheartedly about the nature of Hideyoshi's legacy. Although the articles fail to shed much new light on knowledge about Hideyoshi despite this ostensible goal, they do provide readers with an articulate and consistent interpretation of Hideyoshi as the ultimate symbol of what Japan should be. In both the roundtable discussion and Yoshikawa's interpretation of Hideyoshi in his novel, a clear link is made between Hideyoshi and the particular inflections of Japanese identity described by Tokutomi and the focus of much propaganda at the time. Hideyoshi symbolizes the "courage, knowledge, and benevolence" that made him the "Light of Asia," and Yoshikawa and *Yomiuri Shinbun* urge their readers to help create a nation that does the same.

Conclusion

Yoshikawa wrote at length on his theories about the relationship between history and fiction and his obligations as a writer of historical fiction, arguing that it is the right and mandate of a writer of this genre to recall the heroes of old, fill in the blank spaces of history at times of need, and offer their services to the nation. There is a certain disingenuity to his claims that the thrill he found in writing came from doing research and filling in the blanks. After all, his interpretations of the events he depicts reflect very clearly the rhetoric of a war he seemed to support. For Yoshikawa, blankness offered an effective strategy for telling the tales he wanted to tell regardless of the historical record.

Beyond filling in the blanks to create a version of Hideyoshi that reflected the image of a Japanese national hero, Yoshikawa also created blankness where none had existed before. He refused to tell the story of the end of Hideyoshi's life and thus avoided becoming entangled in Hideyoshi's more erratic behavior in that period. In a 1938 essay titled "Sakka no sekai" (The author's world), Yoshikawa discusses the "problem" of historiography:

> In history, there are a large number of mistakes. It is dangerous to take everything at face value.
>
> That's why when I view things from an author's point of view, I read history very carefully. I read diligently and with respect, and in turn, I also take history, how should I say it, lightly. That might sound as if I am belittling history somehow, but at first, I view history lightly. That is to say, I don't think all of history is true. After all, it is something that people have written. Historians, for a variety of reasons, have a desire to settle things and give the definitive account.[98]

Echoing Hayden White, Yoshikawa notes that all history is a story someone has told and is thus subject to interpretation. He explains: "The relationship between fiction and historical fact is somewhat problematic and has become an issue with some of my recent works, so I will just say it. When talking about historical fact, no one really knows where the facts end and fiction begins. Even if three people observe the same events, when those three people talk about what they saw, they will each describe something different. . . . When writing a novel, when you take up historical facts, if you think too much about historical accuracy, you really can't write a good novel. But then, if you don't take the historical facts seriously, you can't write a good novel, either."[99] Yoshikawa believed that "one of the missions of a good novel is to convince the reader the story is true, no matter what kind of fantasy the author creates."[100] In other words, successful historical fiction is defined by readers. If they find the story believable, enjoyable, and worth reading, then it has told the history well.

Because Yoshikawa's version of *Taikōki* covers Hideyoshi's life only from age six to age forty-nine, what is left unsaid about his behavior after becoming leader of the realm is another way Yoshikawa emplots Hideyoshi's life and gives it new meaning. At the end of the novel, Hideyoshi and Ieyasu meet in Osaka Castle for a peace conference. Even though Ieyasu has not been defeated by Hideyoshi in battle, he concedes political victory. Hideyoshi celebrates by holding a grand feast before retiring to the inner sanctuary of the castle to drink with his trusted retainers. Yoshikawa's final image of Hideyoshi as "a short man surrounded by his ladies-in-waiting, all of whom surpassed him in height" reminds the reader of his remarkable rise to the top without delving into the more complicated events that characterized the end of his life and career.[101] Having created a vision of an ideal ruler and soldier, Yoshikawa ends his story at the point when the forty-nine-year-old Hideyoshi assumed the role of leader of the realm. In some ways, his silence regarding Hideyoshi's later years, when his actions became increasingly idiosyncratic and despotic, says more than the hundreds of pages that fill the novel. Nawata Kazuo points out that when asked about this, all Yoshikawa said on this topic was that he liked the period of Hideyoshi's struggle to get to the top and was less interested in the years after he took control of the realm.[102] But the reality is that the close relationship between the book and the war effort also explains this ellipsis.

After a four-year hiatus following the end of the war, Yoshikawa resumed serialization of *Taikōki* in a number of regional newspapers and eventually published the work in book form under the title *Shinsho Taikōki* (The new Taikōki) in 1950. With this publication, the somewhat circuitous history of this novel's creation came to an end.

Yoshikawa understood the importance of *Taikōki* in relation to prowar narratives rampant during the 1930s and 1940s in Japan, and he sought to create a Hideyoshi perfectly suited to Japan's wartime goals. While he later claimed to be neutral regarding the war, Yoshikawa speaks to his ultimate objectives as a writer in an essay published in 1931: "The things that are easy to lose are not life or possessions; they are the self and truth. When we lose our true selves, various anxieties and irritations set in. . . . Today people are not just losing themselves, they no longer understand what it means to be Japanese."[103] In his attempt to teach his readers what it meant to be Japanese before and during World War II, Yoshikawa found an ideal vehicle in the figure of Hideyoshi from Oze's *Taikōki* and a willing audience in the form of Shōriki; the military personnel, intellectuals, and journalists who participated in the February 1939 roundtable discussion; and the readers of *Yomiuri Shinbun*.

The image of Hideyoshi was called back from the "land of the dead" to serve the Japanese nation on the psychological battlefront. As a popular source of propagandistic stories, the representation of Hideyoshi provided readers with a clear sense of Japanese national identity during World War II and encouraged them to commit themselves wholeheartedly to the war effort. Military officials, scholars, critics, and authors used Hideyoshi as an example of perseverance, hard work, proper pan-Asiatic thinking, and nationalism to further their various war-related agendas. The popularity of Yoshikawa's *Shinsho Taikōki*, serialized for more than six years despite rampant paper shortages and government censorship of fiction thought to be frivolous or contrary to the war cause, shows just how well suited Hideyoshi and *Taikōki* were to this endeavor.

CHAPTER 3

The Salaryman Samurai

Hideyoshi as Business Model

Given that Japan suffered so greatly during the long years of war, it is surprising how quickly military leaders of the past like Hideyoshi became the focus of popular tales after the country's surrender. Hideyoshi's malleability made it remarkably easy for him to transition from war hero to business icon, and as Japan headed into its economic recovery, his appealing rags-to-riches story made him an ideal role model for the burgeoning middle class and its new sense of economic possibilities. His ascent from impoverished farmer to ruler of the realm resonated with a nation of people intent on overcoming the destruction of World War II.

As a result, as early as the 1950s, works about Hideyoshi flourished in a wide range of formats. The next batch of *sakuhingun* works based on *Taikōki* came primarily in the form of early postwar novels and self-help manuals focused on promoting business success, though he was also popular in magazine articles and films. In almost all of these early postwar rewrites of him, Hideyoshi was reborn as an ideal human resource manager and a commerce leader from whom readers had much to learn. As discussed in chapter 2, stories about Hideyoshi and other similar figures had been mobilized for the Japanese war propaganda effort. However, samurai from the Sengoku period appealed to leaders in the early postwar period as models because the latter felt they themselves were involved in an equally critical effort to rebuild their nation and create a stable foundation for a peaceful future.[1]

By analyzing how several business how-to books and representative historical fiction and business fiction (a.k.a. "business novels," explained below in the chapter) written about Hideyoshi in the decades of Japan's rapid economic growth appealed to an increasingly business-oriented readership, this chapter illustrates how Hideyoshi became a necessary and constructive symbol for a nation in need of redefinition after a lost war. This chapter also demonstrates that once the traits emphasized for Hideyoshi as military leader had been appropriated for use in the business context, issues of violence and war guilt that can be associated with Hideyoshi are harder to ignore. Beginning in the late 1960s and early 1970s, new fissures in his representation point to an increasingly fractured sense of the role that history and the past can and should play in understanding the present. By making Hideyoshi into a pop culture icon to be idolized—or criticized—in the postwar period, these works uprooted him from his traditional historical context and created scenarios that forced readers to confront the social implications of reading the so-called samurai salaryman (the latter word in Japanese, *sarariiman*, means a white-collar company employee) as a modern hero.[2]

Japan's recent and distant military past conflicted with an emerging discourse of peace and economic success. The experiences of total surrender, occupation, and the push for financial recovery led to the creation of a new national identity centered on economic development, rather than one shaped by Japan's military strength and imperial ambitions. In this context, Hideyoshi was mobilized once again, this time transformed to fit the aims of a postwar Japan and a postwar Japanese audience. Traits highlighted during the war, such as his human relations skills, ability to be strategic, and perseverance, were emphasized now as the basis for many positive postwar interpretations of him. Ultimately, he turned out to be a prolific model for the quest for postwar prosperity.

During the war, Hideyoshi was the ideal soldier citizen, but as Japan faced harsh postwar realities, the work done by Hideyoshi's image shifted. In the postwar period, Hideyoshi became a safe space, a touchstone from the past to which readers and writers returned for guidance and strength as they moved into a much different and relatively unknown future. Miyazawa Seiichi writes about how the Meiji Restoration became a mythical point of origin to which people would return as they sought role models to help with present-day challenges.[3] According to him, there was a collective interpretation of the Meiji spirit that intellectuals, politicians, authors, and others relied on to enact a "second Restoration."[4] That restoration helped ground people when Japan faced risky or difficult situations. In a similar way, the multiple facets of Hideyoshi's image and his ability to effectively promote himself when he was alive have made him a point to which people return again and again when in need of a supple figure who can serve as a helpful guide to multiple possible futures. While World War II readers needed a charismatic soldier who "altruistically" subdued East Asia, early postwar Japanese readers were desperately in need of a malleable and reliable figure who could serve as a model for how to succeed in a nation trying to rise out of the ashes of a lost war.

Hideyoshi's rise in contemporary pop culture as a symbol of expansionism and national unity during World War II was followed by a dip in the immediate postwar years, when Occupation censors banned books about samurai. In September 1945, not long after Occupation forces arrived in Japan, the Occupation leaders created the Civil Censorship Detachment and began to censor literature that contained militaristic propaganda, descriptions of fraternization between Occupation forces and Japanese women, criticism of Occupation policies, or inappropriate references to the Supreme Commander for the Allied Powers. As part of this censorship, any works of historical fiction that "praised the feudalistic samurai spirit and incited a militaristic tendency" were forbidden, including all works about Hideyoshi.[5] Though Occupation censorship did not end until 1949, censorship laws were loosened well before then. Despite the immediate postwar ban on historical fiction and the ostracization of writers who were perceived as overly nationalistic then, by the mid-1950s and early 1960s, fiction about Hideyoshi was flourishing once again.[6]

In the 1950s, stories about Hideyoshi began to appear in business novels, self-help books, and business magazines. Many historical and business novels about Hideyoshi were published in the early postwar decades. At the same time, business how-to manuals directed at the growing class of salarymen used Hideyoshi, Oda Nobunaga, and Tokugawa Ieyasu as prototypes for business success. Hideyoshi's popularity in these three distinct genres—business novels, historical fiction, and how-to manuals—illustrates how, at a time when Japan was beginning its economic ascension and simultaneously distancing itself from the Occupation, he provided the origin story readers needed as he became the businessman's hero.

Success in the growing number of salaryman positions meant financial comfort for the employee's entire family, so it is not surprising to see that a new genre of business novels and how-to manuals geared toward this sector of society thrived. Not only did salarymen have more disposable income to spend on books, but many of them also had more time to read as they commuted to and from work. Thus, they became a target audience for publishers and writers of popular literature.

The English term "business novel" is commonly used for *keizai shōsetsu*. These are a type of popular novel that emerged as a subgenre in the 1950s and were particularly prevalent in Japan in the 1960s and 1970s. In 1957, Shiroyama Saburō, one of the earliest authors of business novels, explained why he began writing them: "It seems as if Japanese fiction is often written about a world removed from the business realm. But, if fiction is meant to delve into the way humans live, I found myself very dissatisfied with all the novels being written that separated themselves from the world of business even though questions of how one can survive in the business world or how one should interact are of vital importance."[7] Business fiction writers like Shiroyama saw not only a great niche for themselves but also understood the importance of writing fiction that spoke to the changing needs of their readership. These novels were read not only by company workers but by their wives and other members of society who were eager to get a glimpse into the world of the Japanese salaryman.[8]

Japanese business novels are fictional accounts about businessmen that are meant to convey useful information on various aspects of the business world and company life while also entertaining readers with their highly relatable characters and story lines. In contrast, business how-to manuals or self-help books are nonfiction practical guides for what one needs to do to succeed as a businessman. Self-help books about business often use stories from the past to illustrate the various leadership or management skills they purport to teach. While self-help books focused on success in the business world were a relatively new phenomenon, modern Japan has a long history of self-betterment books that goes back to Samuel Smiles's *Self Help*, a book first published in 1882 that encouraged readers to live upright lives and work hard for national and personal success that was widely read by members of the elite classes of the Meiji period. Given that readers were somewhat predisposed to read self-help publications, business manuals experienced widespread success.

Japan after World War II

To better understand the context for this reimagining of Hideyoshi as a business model in the postwar period, it helps to examine the circumstances in which these stories were being produced. Immediately after World War II, Japan was in ruins. When General Douglas MacArthur, the Supreme Commander for the Allied Powers, arrived in Japan in September 1945, he noted that due to the economic, cultural, and psychological losses that Japan had incurred during the war, it had become a "fourth-rate country."[9] Indeed, at the time of Japan's surrender on August 15, 1945, 3–4 percent of the country's 1941 population had perished in the war, most major cities had been heavily damaged by Allied bombing, as much as a quarter of the country's wealth had been destroyed, and 30 percent of all rural dwellers found themselves homeless. At the same time, roughly 6.5 million Japanese were living overseas, either as expatriates in the far reaches of what had been Japan's empire or as stranded soldiers.[10] For a nation whose desire to be treated as a first-rate country—alongside the strongest Western nations—had helped motivate war with the West in the first place, it was exceptionally difficult to accept the fall in status. Memories of the psychological and physical suffering wrought by the war and subsequent surrender served as a strong motivator for economic growth and recovery.

Starting in the 1950s with the outbreak of the Korean War, Japan entered a period of extended economic growth that would last until the early 1970s, as industries were mobilized to support U.S. forces in the region. From 1950 until 1973, the gross national product of Japan grew at an average rate of 10 percent per year—record growth that eventually became known as the economic miracle. Whereas the war years had been marked by scarcity and want, these postwar years of growth were ones of surplus and possibility. In 1960, more than 70 percent of the population considered itself to be part of the financially mobile middle class, a share that would rise to 90 percent by the early 1970s.[11] By the mid-1960s,

Japan had entered a period now known as the golden sixties. This exceptional economic growth enabled salarymen and their families to become consumers in a way not seen before or during the war. Not only did the Japanese population in general have more spending power, but people's newly acquired middle-class consciousness stimulated higher rates of consumption and increased their desire to own expensive items. In the 1960s, people strove to acquire the "3 Ks" (*kā, kūrā*, and *karā terebi*—car, air conditioner, and color television), and in the 1970s, they sought the "3 Js" (*jūeru, jetto*, and *jūtaku*—jewels, overseas travel, and house).[12] According to the economist Yutaka Kōsai, while only 7.8 percent of non-agricultural households in Japan had televisions in 1957, the share had jumped to 95.0 percent by 1965.[13] There were similar increases in the ownership of refrigerators and washing machines. Families were also able to save more and pursue higher education in ways not possible before or during World War II.[14] In other words, Japan in the 1950s and 1960s saw the emergence of a new national identity centered on national and personal wealth.

Salarymen and their families were the most visible representatives of these hopes of achieving a middle-class life.[15] Though the term "salaryman" was not new in the postwar era, it was only after World War II that the possibilities it represented were mobilized as a symbol for the ideal postwar lifestyle.[16] Though this group made up only part of the emerging middle class and represented only a fraction of the workforce in Japan, and though there were also discrepancies among salarymen in terms of income and social position, the position of the salaryman was one that was aspired to by many families who were drawn to the social and economic security it seemed to represent. In other words, salarymen became a metonym for Japan's economic hopes and dreams.

Salarymen, who worked long hours for the good of their company, came to be seen as a new class of samurai: men who sacrificed for the economic recovery of the nation. They represented industriousness, wholehearted commitment to their company, and a willingness to put their jobs above all else. Japan's rapid economic growth has been attributed in part to the determination and hard work of this growing class of white-collar workers. Thus, not only is it natural that a connection emerged between the samurai heroes of the past and businessmen of the present, but it also makes sense that the same stories about Hideyoshi that during World War II evoked a sense of nationalism in their focus on his singleness of purpose and desire to succeed for the sake of his lord were reinterpreted in the early postwar period to emphasize his business acumen. In the immediate postwar period, Hideyoshi came to symbolize *shōnin no saikaku* (merchant resourcefulness). His successful rise to the top, often attributed to his hard work and creative leadership skills, came to represent the possibilities for a Japanese nation desperate to reinvent itself.

Kasahara Ryōzō's Sarariiman shusse Taikōki *and Hideyoshi as Businessman*

The first author to provide readers with a popular postwar Hideyoshi was Kasahara Ryōzō (1912–2002).[17] His series *Sarariiman shusse Taikōki* (A *Taikōki* of a salaryman rising up in the world) was the first work of fiction to place Hideyoshi in a modern business setting. The resounding success of this series indicates the degree to which the Japanese population was ready to read Hideyoshi as something other than a battlefield hero. Indeed, there was a surprisingly strong market in the early postwar period for stories about samurai as successful businessmen. Kasahara's series, which introduced the idea of Hideyoshi as a salaryman hero, began in the latter half of the 1950s, first as a collection of feature films directed by Kakei Masanori at Toho Studios and then as novelizations of the films by Kasahara based on his screenplays. Kasahara's novels offer an ideal contemporary postwar hero in the guise of an up-and-coming salaryman whose striking resemblance to Hideyoshi serves to emphasize his innate business prowess. Kasahara's reinterpretation of Hideyoshi's stories gave his audience a way to reclaim and relate to warriors of the past and to find new meanings in these familiar tales.

In all, Kasahara turned five films into novels: *Sarariiman shusse Taikōki* (first published in 1957), *Zoku sarariiman shusse Taikōki* (A Taikōki of a salaryman rising up in the world continued, 1957), *Zokuzoku sarariiman shusse Taikōki* (Even more Taikōki of a salaryman rising up in the world, 1958), *Sarariiman shusse Taikōki—kachō ichibankura* (A Taikōki of a salaryman rising up in the world, head of the number one storehouse,

1959), and *Sarariiman shusse Taikōki—kanketsu-hen—hanamuko buchō* (A Taikōki of a salaryman rising up in the world—the final episode—the bridegroom department head, 1960). Two publishing companies, Shun'yō Bunko and Kōfū-sha, eventually published book versions of the entire series, though the titles vary.[18]

Kasahara adeptly identifies Hideyoshi as the type of character who could drive a tale of postwar business success and, like Yoshikawa Eiji before him, emphasizes his protagonist Hidekichi's motivation, hard work, strong interpersonal skills, and willingness to take risks as the keys to his success. Kasahara reimagines the popular sixteenth-century warrior as a young man entering the business world for the first time. *Sarariiman shusse Taikōki* is one of the earlier books in Kasahara's *Shachō* (Company president) series (1956–70), which placed well-known heroes of old in humorous situations that simultaneously challenged them and enabled them to show how their skills could be effectively applied to twentieth-century problems. Although his primary motivation for remaking *Taikōki* as a postwar saga about an underdog from Hokkaido trying to succeed in the Tokyo business world was to entertain, Kasahara's movies and novels also reveal a growing emphasis on viewing Japan's aggressive past as antecedent to the more evolved, nonviolent businessman warrior of subsequent generations.

Hideyoshi was not the only warrior from Japan's past that Kasahara chose to rewrite, but he was one of the author's most fertile subjects, based on the number of films and books the story generated. Other works like *Sarariiman Chūshingura* (The salaryman's treasury of loyal retainers, 1961) and *Shachō Taiheiki* (The company president's chronicles of great peace, 1959), written around the same time as the *Sarariiman shusse Taikōki* series, also display famous warriors from Japan's past placed in modern companies, but the multiple extant sequels to Kasahara's modern take on Hideyoshi highlight the fact that his stories about Hideyoshi were among his most popular and most successful.

The series begins with the young Kinoshita Hidekichi, a Hokkaido native who is in his senior year of college in Tokyo and looking for his first job. Told in the third person by a somewhat meddlesome narrator who repeatedly interrupts the flow of events to add his opinion, the story traces Hidekichi's eventual success in landing a job at Japan's most prestigious company, Japan Motors, and his often bumpy but ultimately triumphant rise to the position of department head. Along the way, he has experiences and encounters characters clearly meant by Kasahara to recall the well-known exploits of Hidekichi's sixteenth-century doppel-gänger Hideyoshi, exploits popularized by the widely read versions of *Taikōki* written by Yada Sōun and Yoshikawa.

Kasahara draws numerous connections between his twentieth-century businessman and the sixteenth-century warrior. For example, the name Kinoshita Hidekichi combines one of Toyotomi Hideyoshi's last names with an alternative reading of the characters that make up his first name.[19] The first impression readers have of Hidekichi is of a small, energetic young man with monkey-like movements—a reference to Hideyoshi's well-known nickname Saru (monkey)—who leads his college cheering section for baseball games. Hidekichi's friends and acquaintances recall for readers various famous sixteenth-century figures. For example, Hidekichi's confidant and *kōhai* (lower-ranking, junior member) in the cheering section is Kuroiwa, a name meant to recall Kuroda Kanbei (1546–1604), one of Hideyoshi's closest allies. His longtime on-again, off-again friend and another member of the cheering section, Maeda Keiichirō, becomes one of his greatest competitors at Japan Motors. This character is clearly a reference to Maeda Toshiie (1538–1599), who served Nobunaga with Hideyoshi but was later affiliated with Hideyoshi's rival Shibata Katsuie before signing a peace pact with Hideyoshi. Oda Nobuta—a name certainly meant to recall Hideyoshi's lord, Oda Nobunaga—was another member of the cheering section and had graduated a year ahead of Hidekichi. By establishing these connections between Hidekichi and Hideyoshi in the first chapters, Kasahara creates a discursive structure that draws the reader into a constant comparison between the sixteenth-century warlord and the twentieth-century businessman. He also produces a character who was widely popular with a general public whose members were intent on succeeding economically in the new age.

By following the pattern of *Taikōki* texts that trace Hideyoshi's rise from peasant farmer to ruler of the realm while describing his various feats of bravery and perseverance along the way, Kasahara's series tracks the life of the promising white-collar company employee Hidekichi. As a result, whereas Yoshikawa's Hideyoshi enthusiastically embraces his menial assignment as kitchen supervisor, Kasahara's Hidekichi eagerly pursues his job as warehouse supervisor, despite the fact that it is a clear demotion. Yoshikawa's Hideyoshi repairs Nobunaga's castle wall in three days, and Hidekichi does an equally impressive task for his era by selling thirty cars in a week. And while Yoshikawa's Hideyoshi goes behind enemy lines to persuade known enemies of Nobunaga to join his forces, Kasahara's Hidekichi sneaks into the headquarters and meetings of rival companies to gain access to top-ranking officials and negotiate new contracts with those companies.

Just as earlier versions of Hideyoshi had many opportunities to demonstrate his superior leadership skills, hard work, and loyalty, so Kasahara's Hidekichi faces similarly challenging opportunities. For example, when he realizes that his grades are not good enough for him to take the entrance exam of his favorite company, he figures out a way to break into the company president's office and leave an impassioned message in the middle of a cassette tape of the latter's favorite *naniwabushi* music,[20] ultimately landing himself a job there. And when his boss refuses to meet with him about a matter of the utmost importance for the company, he devises ways to get close enough to the president to talk to him, disguising himself as a limousine driver, tracking the president down at the barber shop, and even following him into a restroom. In sum, Kasahara portrays a Hidekichi whose determined yet unorthodox methods are intended to recall similarly atypical behavior from the various fictionalized versions of the life of his sixteenth-century model.

Similarly, Kasahara's Hidekichi is prone to enthusiastic speech making, much like Yoshikawa's Hideyoshi. A by-product of his years as the leader of his university's cheering section, Hidekichi's skill in making impassioned speeches enables him to persuade others with the power of his words. In the speech he inserts into the company president's *naniwabushi* music, he exclaims: "For a long time, I have looked up to you, the most famous person from my hometown, and admired your strong company leadership. I have followed the motto 'Boys, be ambitious!' . . . Since I was a boy, I have loved cars. After getting my driver's license last year, I took a job as a taxi driver so that I could experience driving Japan Motors' crown jewel, the Atlas, an experience that has been very moving for me. . . . In the future, I want to stand in Japan Motors' headquarters as an employee and give one hundred percent of myself to the company."[21] Although Hidekichi's methods are unorthodox, Kasahara insists that his protagonist's ability to clearly articulate his commitment to the success of the company repeatedly earns him respect.

Since Hideyoshi's humble origins are a large part of his appeal for a twentieth-century audience, Kasahara creates a Hidekichi who came from equally modest beginnings. As someone from Hokkaido, Hidekichi is marked as nonurban, nonmodern, and disenfranchised. Because of his native Hokkaido's geographical and sociocultural distance from Tokyo, Hidekichi appears as an underdog and an outsider.[22] He is further marginalized by his family background. His single mother is a poor, uneducated farmer, much like Hideyoshi's mother. Though he adapts well to his surroundings, Hidekichi often longs for his mother back in Hokkaido, emphasizing his nostalgia for his distant home and reminding readers how far he has come. Like Hideyoshi, the impoverished peasant who became lord of the realm, Kasahara's Hidekichi is intended to represent a quintessential success story. Hidekichi represents every person who hopes to use hard work, ingenuity, and a positive attitude to rise in postwar Japanese society.

As the word *shusse* in the title indicates, *Sarariiman shusse Taikōki* is a story about one man's climb to the top.[23] Hidekichi never relents in his struggle to overcome his Hokkaido roots and succeed as an employee of Japan Motors. His incantation of "Boys, be ambitious!" throughout the series links him to the sense of integrity, hard work, and entrepreneurial spirit that contributed to the development of Japan into a modernized nation during the Meiji period. Hidekichi reminds himself to work hard and never give up by repeating this well-known phrase at many important junctures in the narrative. For instance, he utters this phrase while recording his impassioned message on the company president's *naniwa-bushi* tape, when he finally gets called back to work at the main office after a period of exile, when his weeks of hard work finally result in the delivery of a much-needed piece of machinery, and when he is promoted to subsection chief (*kakarichō*).[24] In one of the several instances when Kasahara's narrator intrudes on his story, the narrator explains that "Boys, be ambitious!" has become something of a motto for Hidekichi, adding, "It could also be said that he has already made a name for himself (*shusse shita*) [so the phrase is not wasted on him]."[25] The use of *shusse* here emphasizes the link between these famous words and Hidekichi's rise in the company.

This phrase was introduced to Japan by William Smith Clark (1826–86), a science professor at and later president of Massachusetts Agricultural College (now the University of Massachusetts at Amherst), who served as the first president of the Sapporo Agricultural College in Hokkaido. Upon his departure from Hokkaido many years before, he had charged his students with the words: "Boys, be ambitious for Christ!" An abbreviation of this—"Boys be ambitious!"—is perhaps his greatest legacy in Japan.[26] What started as a reminder to his students to work hard and live well in the name of Christ and as promoters of Christianity in Japan metamorphosed into a symbol of Meiji optimism for personal and national success, not unlike this rewriting of the Hideyoshi myth for the same purpose. In other words, Clark's phrase was invoked again in the early postwar period by Kasahara and intended to encourage all members of society, particularly salarymen, to put in the tedious hard work necessary for Japan to once again rise to the top. The phrase certainly would have been familiar to the readers of Kasahara's work and most likely was intended to elicit in them the same kind of determination that it does for Hidekichi.

Constant rewritings of fictionalized versions of Hideyoshi's life serialized in major newspapers and literary magazines during the twentieth century ensured that readers were familiar with common perceptions of Hideyoshi. Like other writers before him, Kasahara is able to instill more meaning into his story by playing with these existing perceptions, reinterpreting them, and creating a rags-to-riches version of Hideyoshi's/Hidekichi's determined ascent that resonated with a salaryman audience intent on following in his footsteps—not only to achieve their own individual success but also to help rebuild their nation. These novels about Hideyoshi as a salaryman provided the first rewriting of him on an entirely new, nonviolent battlefield, giving readers a way to think about the past that did not include dealing with issues of aggression or war guilt. By placing Hidekichi in high-rises and conference rooms, Kasahara makes him palatable to and relevant for a generation of people ready to move on from the traumas of World War II and more than willing to embrace the model of perseverance, hard work, and dedication that Hidekichi represents. Focusing on his protagonist's unorthodox methods, Kasahara emphasizes that Hidekichi's strong motivation and ability to clearly articulate his commitment to the success of the company repeatedly earn him respect. In this way, Kasahara's series promotes a discourse of economic growth through individual hard work and loyalty to one's company that came to replace wartime discourses of military success through living, fighting, and dying for the nation.

Shiba Ryōtarō and Hideyoshi as Merchant

Shiba Ryōtarō's *Shinshi Taikōki* also gave readers a postwar version of a Hideyoshi who demonstrated preternatural business savvy. Unlike Kasahara's Hideyoshi, though, Shiba's was located squarely in the sixteenth century. On the back cover of the *bunkobon* (small paperback) version of Shiba's *Shinshi Taikōki* published by Shinchōsha, the publisher reminds readers once again how agile and relevant *Taikōki* is: "This story, which has been read since ancient times by numerous people over the years and has nurtured Japanese dreams and romance, is a modern *Taikōki* which has been brought back to life for today's society with a cool-headed perspective and a new sense."[27] Like Yoshikawa's *Shinsho Taikōki* before it, Shiba's *Shinshi Taikōki* was intended to be a "new historical" *Taikōki*, somehow different from previous *Taikōki* and better suited for contemporary readers. *Shinshi Taikōki* is Shiba's longest work about Hideyoshi, and with his focus on Hideyoshi's benevolence and his tendency to write about the less controversial early years of Hideyoshi's life and career, it seems, at first glance, far from new or fresh. But by writing at length about Hideyoshi's business savvy and how it prepared him for his push for the top, Shiba gives readers a hero appropriate for the high-growth period of the late 1960s.

Neither a business novel nor a self-help guide to better business leadership, Shiba's *Shinshi Taikōki* can nevertheless be considered merchant literature as it reflects his engagement with the emerging discourse on postwar economic growth that was absent in earlier *Taikōki*. With its focus on what could be best described as Hideyoshi's preternatural business sense, Shiba's portrayal of Hideyoshi illustrates the concept of a merchant's view of history by marking him as business minded from the first words of the first chapter, repeatedly pointing out how Hideyoshi is unlike his contemporaries in his views on money and wealth, and emphasizing the parallel between Hideyoshi's frugality and 1960s Japan.

Shiba uses Oze Hoan's *Taikōki* as a model for writing a story of Hideyoshi's life that attributes much of his success to a seemingly anachronistic set of traits that are best suited to a merchant. Throughout the novel, Shiba uses the terms "*shōnin*" or "*akindo*" (both mean "merchant") to refer to a set of business-appropriate skills that his Hideyoshi seems to possess that set him apart from his peers, and it is this focus on his merchantlike qualities that establishes Shiba's Hideyoshi as the perfect hero for the generation experiencing Japan's economic miracle. Shiba's interpretation of Hideyoshi as a hero with well-developed merchant skills gives readers the type of fiction they have come to expect from him. He also gives them a hero fitting for the 1960s.

Shiba grew up in a merchant family in Osaka, a background that arguably had an influence on his view of the world. His grandfather managed a rice cake shop in the Nanba section of Osaka, and his father was a pharmacist. The literary scholar Matsuo Masashi argues that Shiba's novels provide a "merchant's view of history": "With a nature that leads him to think deeply about matters, Shiba has that particularly Japanese townsman spirit, the root of that modern-day rationality runs deep. When this deep logical thinking emerges in his view of history, we can call it his 'merchant's view of history' (*shōnin shikan*)."[28] And the literary scholar Maari Sumika draws a direct connection between Shiba's writing and what she calls "merchant literature" (*shōnin bungaku*): "Among Shiba's novels, there are ninja and samurai, bakumatsu patriots and military men, even scholars. Shiba's writing truly includes protagonists from all professions and all levels of society, but most of these protagonists are people who had a combination of economic knowledge, sophistication, skill, and accomplishment. . . . Shiba especially embraced 'merchants' who showed high ideals and business savvy."[29] I concur with Narita Ryūichi, who—writing about Shiba's novel *Ryōma ga yuku*—argues that a focus on money and Ryoma's skill with it is intended to make Ryōma a character who resonates with a readership focused on the economic ascendancy of the 1960s.[30] There are similar connections between money and success in *Shinshi Taikōki*. Shiba's personal background influenced his work, as did his desire to write novels that spoke to the social and cultural interests of his readers—many of whom were salarymen. Though Shiba's Hideyoshi has many similarities to Yoshikawa's, in *Shinshi Taikōki* Shiba's decision to fashion Hideyoshi into a type of Sengoku period businessman made Hideyoshi a decidedly postwar hero.

When thinking about the potential impact of *Shinshi Taikoki*, it is helpful to understand the outsize role Shiba has had in historical fiction in twentieth-century Japan. Shiba is often referred to as "the people's writer" (*kokumin sakka*). Narita argues that Shiba deserves this moniker because he had an extremely large readership that continued to grow even after his death, because the influence of his works extends well beyond his novels and into other forms of media, and finally, because his writing expresses a strong sense of the nation (*kono kuni no katachi*) and the people (*kokumin*). The scholar Suekuni Yoshimi posits that Shiba earned this nickname because he offered heroes who gave readers a sense of hope about the future while creating works that were also highly entertaining. The danger, according to Suekuni, comes when Shiba's readers mistake his fictional works for historical fact (*shijitsu*).[31] We see this focus on reader-centered writing in *Shinshi Taikōki*, and when Shiba paints Hideyoshi as a keen businessman, we also have the opportunity to appreciate the ways in which he interprets well-known historical figures using his informed bird's-eye perspective to give readers his own point of view of well-known events. In an article titled "Sōsaku hōhō" (Methods of literary production), Shimura Kunihiro points out that Shiba covered every possible genre and era in Japan and highlights the three primary characteristics of his historical fiction: it was written with the reader in mind; it was written with the advantage of what Shiba referred to as an omniscient bird's-eye point of view—that is, the benefit of hindsight in dealing with figures of history and the opportunity to learn from the past; and it highlights the pathos of defeat by emphasizing the beauty of decay and ruin.[32] Narita explains that Shiba adds his own details to historical source materials to create a particularly "Shiba view of history (*Shiba shikan*)."[33] In *Shinshi Taikōki* we see this focus on reader-centered writing when Shiba offers a Hideyoshi who is a keen businessman, but we also have the opportunity to appreciate the ways in which he interprets well-known historical figures using his informed bird's eye perspective to give readers his own point of view of well-known events.

Shiba's interpretations of Hideyoshi start with his own opinions about Hideyoshi's merit as a historical figure. Shiba's brief 1963 essay "Watashi no Hideyoshi kan" (My view of Hideyoshi) shows that he also made links between Hideyoshi and the everyday reader in 1960s Japan. The essay begins: "I love Hideyoshi, and I especially love the Hideyoshi before he became ruler of the realm."[34] Suekuni argues that Shiba deliberately included certain aspects of Hideyoshi's life and omitted others based on his own opinions about how Hideyoshi should be remembered. For example, Suekuni suggests that Shiba's omission of the last years of Hideyoshi's life was intended to maintain Hideyoshi's stature as a hero: "It wouldn't be wrong to argue that the changes to historical fact that occur in Shiba's novels are necessary for him to maintain the heroism in the characters he is writing about."[35] Although Shiba praises Hideyoshi's sense of timing, he also indicates why he wrote about only part of Hideyoshi's life in *Shinshi Taikōki*. Ultimately more than an essay about how he saw Hideyoshi, "Watashi no Hideyoshi kan" can be read as Shiba's explanation, at least in part, of why he decided to focus only on Hideyoshi's more successful early years, painting him as a model for modern Japanese leaders instead of offering a more complicated and complete account of his life and leadership.

Shiba thought that Hideyoshi was the perfect Japanese hero for two reasons. First, unlike the fourteenth-century samurai hero Kusunoki Masashige (1294–1336) or the so-called last samurai, Saigo Takamori (1828–77), Hideyoshi was a hero who did not quite achieve godlike status. For Shiba, Hideyoshi's utter commonness and sense of humanity led to his possessing a combination of compassion, strong diplomatic skills, and an innate ability to relate to others that made him an extraordinary leader with the capacity to bring people to his side without either overpowering them with his charisma or destroying them with his military might.[36] Shiba's point is that anyone can be a hero, and that, as Hideyoshi proves, one does not have to be perfect to be an effective leader. In other words, Shiba's Hideyoshi is the ideal model for a society painstakingly aware of its imperfections after a failed war.

Second, Shiba argues, Hideyoshi had a flawless sense of timing. Had he risen in the ranks earlier in Nobunaga's quest to take over the realm, he would not have had the opportunity to learn from Nobunaga's mistakes and would have been forced to participate in more violence. According to Shiba, therefore, Hideyoshi's understanding that his job was to promote stability and the reconstruction of a unified Japan, a realization he achieved by watching and learning from Nobunaga, was not only ahead of its time but was also entirely appropriate for a Japan in the midst of becoming a postwar economic power. According to this argument, if

Hideyoshi had come later, he would not have benefited from the general sense of fatigue that people felt for the Tokugawa regime, which turned Ieyasu into a villain and made Hideyoshi's missteps seem forgettable. For Shiba, Hideyoshi represents the perfect combination of excellent timing and inherent relatability for a readership in need of a realistic hero who offers a hopeful model for Japan's rising middle class.

Shiba's tale about Hideyoshi was part of a *Taikōki* boom that resulted from the airing of the NHK *Taiga dorama* (Taiga drama) of a version of Yoshikawa's *Shinsho Taikōki* that ran from January through December 1965 under the title *Taikōki* and ended mere weeks before serialization of Shiba's *Shinshi Taikōki* began in February 1966 in *Shōsetsu Shinchō* (it ran until March 1968).[37] Although a wide range of historical moments become the basis for the annual *Taiga dorama*, a large portion of these televised dramas represent the Sengoku period. *Taiga dorama* have historically had the highest viewership of any NHK program and are usually in the top ten, if not the top three, shows viewed in any given year. The adaptation of Yoshikawa's *Taikōki* was the third *Taiga dorama*, and (ending just before the new year) it garnered the largest viewership of any NHK program aired during 1965. The publication of Shiba's novel was well timed to ride the wave of Hideyoshi's popularity.[38]

Shiba's *Shinshi Taikōki* covers Hideyoshi's early years and career, offering extraordinary details up to the point where he takes control of the realm, while quickly glossing his last ten years in a single paragraph. Like Yoshikawa, Shiba focuses on Hideyoshi's rise to the top, but unlike him, Shiba emphasizes Hideyoshi's unusual ability to use an abacus, his focus on making money, and his understanding and manipulation of the concepts of supply and demand. Not only does Shiba's text focus on Hideyoshi as merchant, but it also ends when Hideyoshi is at the height of his career, once again leaving readers with the rosiest possible interpretation of Hideyoshi.

Reader response to Shiba's text following its serialization demonstrates that his interpretation of Hideyoshi was not only well received but also read as primary historical source material by at least part of his audience.[39] Shiba was always well aware of his audience and the reactions to his work, and over the course of the serialization of *Shinshi Taikōki*, readers sent letters to the editor expressing their thoughts and hopes related to the work. A significant percentage of these letters drew direct links between

Shiba's Hideyoshi and the readers' own society, indicating that they were reading Shiba's novels as he intended. The serialization ran for twenty-six months, and about one-third of the installments elicited reader response. The respondents can be roughly divided into three groups. The first group wrote about how Shiba's *Taikōki* was different from the *Taikōki* that came before it and pointed to his crisp writing style and enthusiasm for his subject as the source of its readability. The second group was also pleased with Shiba's approach to Hideyoshi's story but commented specifically on past events and how Shiba had helped them better appreciate those moments in Japan's history. The final group was drawn to the fact that Shiba was creating a new Hideyoshi, one appropriate for their times. The last two groups are particularly interesting because they clearly read Shiba's work along the multiple axes outlined by Narita and looked to Shiba for ways to better understand their own world.

In August 1966, Sugaya Masayoshi, a reader from Shimane prefecture, wrote: "Starting with the section before Hideyoshi became the lord of Sunomata Castle, the story has gotten very interesting, particularly after he gains the support of the peerless strategist Takenaka Hanbei. This is the tale about Hideyoshi's suffering and ambition and about the power he has to survive; he's like a weed that never loses its vitality. Undoubtedly, this same strength seems to be lacking in those of us who are living today."[40] Sugaya appreciated Hideyoshi's weed-like resistance to the challenges around him and clearly made a connection between the Hideyoshi being presented by Shiba and the type of perseverance needed to succeed in the 1960s. A similar connection was made in the January 1967 issue, when Nishikawa Osamu, a reader from Shiga prefecture, reported that "Shiba's writing, which teaches us that we should apply the same type of resourcefulness Hideyoshi displayed during the Warring States [Sengoku] period, has impressed me deeply."[41] Reader response to Shiba's work was overwhelmingly positive, but more interesting, readers tended to make a connection between Shiba's sixteenth-century Hideyoshi and the condition of twentieth-century Japan. Furthermore, they read Shiba's story of Hideyoshi as a sort of instruction manual for how to live in postwar Japan. As the two readers quoted above demonstrate, many people read Shiba's work as a directive calling for hard work and resourcefulness that, in their eyes, was absolutely necessary for success in Japan in the late 1960s. In other words, Shiba's novel—much like other works about

Hideyoshi discussed above—struck a chord with readers struggling to make sense of the rapidly changing world around them.

Shiba took up the theme of Hideyoshi's business savvy early and revisited it throughout his novel. The first chapter, "The High Priest of Business," starts with the story of the young Hideyoshi (then simply called Monkey) who traveled first with itinerant priests and then on his own as a needle salesman. In contrast to other *Taikōki* discussed thus far, the focus clearly rests on Hideyoshi's business ingenuity. Oze's *Taikōki* includes very little discussion of Hideyoshi's life before he enters the service of Nobunaga, and Yada's *Taikōki* offered more details about his youth but focused on his rise to the top without any mention of the burgeoning entrepreneurial skills described by Shiba. Yoshikawa's *Shinsho Taikōki* focused on Hideyoshi's perseverance and loyalty in childhood, with a passing reference to Hideyoshi's peddling that is glossed over by an emphasis on his confidence and magnanimity. Lest the reader miss Shiba's point, he reminds us that sixteenth-century Japan was a society made up of farmers and samurai, and merchants were only beginning to arrive on the scene. His narrator explains: "Samurai and farmers. In this society where only these two groups existed, merchants were just beginning to appear. As people began to live more freely, Japan was gradually becoming a money-based world."[42] Furthermore, through his narrator Shiba points out that the ability to use an abacus and other merchant skills were not common until the Edo period, and in fact few citizens in the Sengoku period had the basic skills needed for commerce. The narrator interrupts the story to elaborate: "Incidentally, today the Japanese are said to be known for their proficiency in math. In particular, their skills in mental arithmetic are said to be the best in the world, but these are skills that were acquired only after the use of the abacus and arithmetic for commerce became widespread during the Edo period. Japanese of the Warring States period seem to be of an entirely different race due to their lack of these skills."[43] Very early in the story, then, Shiba marks Hideyoshi as different because he has skills suited to managing money and selling goods.

Throughout the text, Shiba's narrator interjects examples of Hideyoshi's distinctive economic sense. In a later scene, the narrator makes a simple but powerful statement: "It seems that Hideyoshi's ideas were different."[44] What follows is a discussion of Hideyoshi's unusual refusal of the money awarded to him by Nobunaga for his hard work: "Oh, this is no good. . . . My lord is wasting money on me. I have to work harder so he will double his money."[45] This idea of multiplying Nobunaga's wealth is repeated, for example, when Hideyoshi's income reaches one hundred *koku* and he says: "This one hundred *koku* is just a seed. I will turn it into ten times the profit for my lord."[46] Hideyoshi's initial response can be read as the grateful and modest response the reader would have expected from a man with a history of loyalty—after all, most fans of Hideyoshi and *Taikōki* were familiar with the story of how he warmed Nobunaga's sandals in the breast of his kimono and how he fought loyally for Nobunaga until the latter's death. But when the narrator emphasizes how unusual Hideyoshi's response to his reward is, the focus shifts away from the common reading of Hideyoshi as extremely loyal and toward a reading of him as a model for a new generation of business-minded readers. Shiba's narrator explains: "On this point, Hideyoshi is more like a merchant than a samurai. . . . This idea that he must work to repay Nobunaga for the income he has received was completely different from the logic of samurai during the Kamakura and Muromachi periods. It seems, indeed, that business ideas have taken root in Hideyoshi."[47] To conclude this episode, the narrator points out that this was also when Nobunaga began to realize that Hideyoshi's new way of thinking—specifically, his ability to see various situations from a fiscally sound point of view—set him apart from other members of his cohort. In this brief account alone, the narrator refers to Hideyoshi as "merchant" (*akindo*) four times and notes his commerce (*shōgyō*) skills twice, further illustrating Shiba's emphasis on this alternative interpretation of Hideyoshi.[48]

Finally, Shiba describes a fairly typical sixteenth-century tactical maneuver as atypical due to Hideyoshi's keen understanding of market economies when he uses starvation tactics to capture Tottori Castle. Employing simple principles of supply and demand, Hideyoshi orders his men to buy all of the crops being sold in the region. Under his guidance, his men disguise themselves as merchants from a nearby province and enter the castle grounds shouting, "Hokuriku is experiencing a severe famine, so we'll buy rice, wheat, soy beans, whatever you have, at twice the usual price here."[49] Local farmers jump at the chance to sell what they have for a healthy profit, and Hideyoshi's troops manage to exhaust most of the local crops, leaving less than a three-month supply for the castle.

Shiba's narrator attributes Hideyoshi's plan to his merchantlike talents: "This novel idea by [Hideyoshi] is something he'd done before, but it's certainly because he was blessed with the mind of a merchant."[50] The fact that Shiba's narrator explicitly emphasizes Hideyoshi's focus on a market economy can be read as another example of Hideyoshi as a business literature hero. This pattern of having the narrator interject comments to analyze a well-known historical moment as a further example of Hideyoshi's superb business skills is repeated throughout the novel.

Besides demonstrating market savvy, Shiba's Hideyoshi also represents the responsibly frugal citizen that the historian Scott O'Bryan argues was representative of the postwar Japanese population.[51] To be sure, the idea of frugality was not new to the postwar era or to Japan in particular, but its importance was emphasized during the years of recovery. Shiba's Hideyoshi reflects this ideal as he works to reduce waste and avoid corruption. Hideyoshi bristles at the reward from Nobunaga precisely because it might not prove to be money well spent. In Shiba's account, this persistent frugality often invites the ire of Hideyoshi's coworkers. While working for the powerful daimyo Imagawa Yoshimoto (1519–60), for example, Shiba's Hideyoshi strictly enforces policies that require his barrack mates to extinguish all candles and fires unless they are completely necessary so as to save money and supplies for the good of the clan. However, those around him criticize his thrifty ways, and his barrack mates become so angry that not only do they refuse to participate in his wedding, but they also try to sabotage it.[52] In Shiba's novel, Hideyoshi focuses on both making and saving money, making him a particularly apt model for Japanese officials working to redefine notions of prosperity and appropriate consumption in the postwar decades.

Shiba's insistence on referring to Hideyoshi as "the merchant from Owari" and Ieyasu as "the farmer from Mikawa" only serves to emphasize his point.[53] To Shiba, Hideyoshi's success resulted, in part at least, from his skills in the ways of business and money, and his actions reflected a leadership style that was creative and forward-looking in comparison to Ieyasu's. Shiba's Hideyoshi is the ultimate symbol of the ideal postwar leader.

Today, the ubiquitousness of books and magazine articles that cite Hideyoshi as one of the best models from Japan's past indicates widespread acceptance of Hideyoshi as a business model. However, Shiba's persistence in emphasizing Hideyoshi's merchant-like acumen and interpreting him as a man with commercial skills as well as a proper attitude toward money is intended to draw connections between the sixteenth-century warrior, whose understanding of the business practices and economics was ahead of his time, and the twentieth-century postwar Japanese citizen who had what it took to lead Japan to economic superiority. This connection distinguishes Shiba's *Shinshi Taikōki* from the historical fiction *Taikōki* that came before it and further reinforces the notion that Hideyoshi could serve as a model for a postwar audience in search of an entirely new type of hero.

The Emergence of Business Guides and Hideyoshi as Business Model

Hideyoshi continued his transformation from warrior to humane business leader and keen strategist by becoming the subject of nonfiction business how-to manuals. Authors of these self-help books relied not only on the malleability of tales about Hideyoshi but also on the fact that there were many of them to draw from as source materials. They knew that their readers were familiar enough with tales about Hideyoshi that he would serve as an instructive point of reference.

Although novels by Kasahara and Shiba were clearly fiction and meant to appeal to people who knew *Taikōki* and wanted to see another version of it, these business manuals take reinterpretations of *Taikōki* in an entirely new direction, by moving Hideyoshi into the nonfiction work of business management resources. In the process, fiction about Hideyoshi is interpreted as fact. These manuals mark an important transition in *Taikōki* and Hideyoshi *sakuhingun* as tales about Hideyoshi. The business manuals are important to our discussion of Hideyoshi's literary afterlife for three reasons. First, since many of the manuals and magazines that started in the 1960s continue in some form today, they demonstrate the staying power of this particular interpretation of Hideyoshi. Second, several of the manuals' authors offer explicit explanations of what makes Hideyoshi such an effective model for business leadership. And third, some of the manuals provide us with excellent examples of what I am calling history of the third degree: analysis of Hideyoshi and his relevance to contemporary Japan based primarily on twentieth-century popular fictional accounts of him.

The main publisher of modern applications of stories about Nobunaga, Hideyoshi, and Ieyasu was Daiyamondo Shuppan-sha and its offspring, Purejidento-sha. With the establishment of these publishing companies and their continued growth, business self-help publications expanded into magazines. *Diayamondo* (Diamond) became a leading economic magazine during the high-growth period of the 1960s and 1970s.[54] In 1963, Daiyamondo Shuppan-sha partnered with the American company Time-Life International and created Daiyamondo-taimu-sha (Diamond-Time Company), which started a magazine called *Purejidento* (President), a large, glossy economics magazine geared toward businessmen.[55] By the late 1970s, the magazine began focusing on gleaning leadership information from "the past, the present, East and West, using real people and history" as sources.[56] In focusing their efforts on an expanding readership of men and women interested in business success and by taking heroes of the past as one of their main topics, *Purejidento* and *Daiyamondo* hit on a publication model that has helped them remain successful for five decades.[57]

The first examples of these how-to business books were produced in the early 1960s by the Nagoya-based publisher Chūbu Zaikai-sha. Its series titled *Sengoku maneejimento shiriizu* (The Sengoku period management series) was sold as part of its *Chūbu Zaikai maneejimento yomihon* (Chūbu Zaikai management readers) collection, and it offered nonfiction interpretations of the three unifiers as models of leadership that could be applied in the business world.[58] *Hideyoshi to ningen kankei: Hyuuman rireeshonzu* (Hideyoshi and interpersonal relationships: Human relations) was the first of this series to portray Hideyoshi as a model for business. Several other publishers of business-related manuals and magazines followed suit, taking advantage of the growing national discourse of Japan's economic ascendancy to repackage figures from the past for a twentieth-century Japanese audience. Though Chūbu Zaikai-sha published a limited number of works related to business management between the 1960s and the 1990s, another publisher, Karuchā Shuppan-sha, produced an impressive number of publications when it was active in the 1970s. These titles focus on self-help and guidance, and many of them—such as annual guides to business hotels—were intended to be useful for businessmen.

As the economy improved in the 1960s and early 1970s, there was a steady flow of new business self-help books that looked to the Sengoku period for guidance. Many of these texts focused on nonwarrior aspects of their models. In the early 1970s, at least three books used Hideyoshi as an ideal example for business success, leadership success, or both: *Hideyoshi to ningen kankei, Sengoku o ikiru: Hideyoshi ni manabu ningen katsuyōhō* (Living in the Sengoku period: Learning human management from Hideyoshi, 1974), *Hideyoshi no seikōhō* (Hideyoshi's path to success, 1973), and *Hideyoshi ni manabu tōsotsuryoku* (Learning leadership strength from Hideyoshi, 1974).[59] In this last work, Naganuma Hiroaki pursues the simple idea that the best warriors were good human resource managers: "During the Warring States period, it was not enough to just win battles. A good leader had to effectively lead his retainers on a daily basis, organizing his human resources as his best weapon."[60] According to Naganuma, Hideyoshi's strongest leadership skill was his ability to manage not only his own troops but also the enemy forces he defeated and the nonwarrior peasants and merchants affected by his military campaigns:

> In Hideyoshi's case, we are not just talking about effectively leading his own troops. He was able to motivate people who were well outside of his group of retainers, and it is this broad influence that is significant.
>
> In his quest to become leader of the realm, fighting and subduing his enemies was just one aspect of what he did, but he was also effective at using his political power to influence others. Two of his greatest assets, Maeda Toshiie and Tokugawa Ieyasu, were drawn to his side because of his persuasive ability as a leader.[61]

In Naganuma's assessment, as a skilled human resource manager, Hideyoshi was able to convince enemy leaders to support his cause, greatly expanding his base of support. Although Naganuma also talks about Hideyoshi's ability to create effective military strategy, the focus is on the nonviolent aspects of his leadership: his resource management. Naganuma anachronistically and ahistorically interprets Hideyoshi's actions during the Sengoku period and applies them to issues pertinent to career salarymen in the 1960s. The conclusion of his reading of Hideyoshi is that no one had the skills of persuasion or human resource management to rival him.

One of the most prolific writers of self-help books who used the Sengoku period as the source of analysis was Fuji Kimifusa (b. 1914). After leading Japan's ground forces in World War II, he joined the Ministry of Labor. There he worked in the Labor Standards Bureau, rising to the position of chief inspector of labor standards before retiring. Between 1968 and 1988, he wrote more than forty books about the Sengoku period and various sixteenth-century warriors, including *Shōgun ni manabu ningen kanri* (Learn personnel management from the shogun, 1972), *Ieyasu "nin" no keiei* (Ieyasu's "endurance" management style, 1978), and *Hideyoshi ni manabu ketsudan to jikkō no ningen gaku* (Learn from the humanity of Hideyoshi's resolutions and actions, 1988). Fuji's earliest work linking Hideyoshi's leadership style to modern management practices was *Sengoku o ikiru*. The fourth printing of this title was issued just two and a half years after it was first published, indicating its popularity. Clearly Fuji's interpretation resonated with readers.

Several characteristics of Fuji's account are typical of how Hideyoshi is written about in these manuals. First, Fuji follows the same narrative pattern as many other accounts about Hideyoshi: he starts by underscoring the depths from which Hideyoshi rose to become ruler of the realm and then goes on to track his rise. Second, he attributes Hideyoshi's success to his charm, human resource management skills, and determination, describing how his combination of compassion and commitment to unifying Japan made him a great leader.[62] Third, he emphasizes Hideyoshi's ability to rise up in the world (his *risshin shusse*), highlighting his ability to climb from humble circumstances and attain unexpectedly high rank. Fuji cites *risshin shusse* as a primary reason for aspiring salarymen to use Hideyoshi as a model. Furthermore, Fuji links *risshin shusse* to his final point: Hideyoshi and *Taikōki* remain popular in the postwar period because they promote the idea of individual success based on hard work. According to Fuji, "Taikō Hideyoshi is the standard bearer (*hatagashira*) of *risshin shusse* in Japan. Ever since Oze Hoan's original *Taikōki* numerous *Taikōki* have continued to be enjoyed by readers. During Hideyoshi's time, the term *risshin shusse* was not widely accepted. Today, however, with numerous *Taikōki* popular in novels, on television, in theater, etc., Hideyoshi has become a popular hero to whom many of us feel a close affinity."[63] Like Sato Tadao in his discussion of *sakuhingun*,

Fuji notes *Taikōki*'s influence in multiple forms of media and hints at the simultaneity that Kuwata Tadachika credited with making previous *Taikōki* so powerful. But rather than engage with *Taikōki*'s influence in the realm of popular culture, Fuji uses Hideyoshi as described in it to highlight the connection between Hideyoshi and the idea of *risshin shusse*. By doing so, he promotes Hideyoshi as an ideal model of business success and upward mobility.

If reinterpreting history from multiple perspectives and in symbolic terms is history of the second degree, then the multilayering of interpretations that happens when one text interprets another text that has already done its own interpretation is history of the third degree.[64] Instead of relying on original historical source materials, authors of self-help books interpret fictionalizations (such as novels by Yoshikawa or Yada) to provide what they perceive to be the best possible analysis of Hideyoshi. This kind of multilayered and intertextual interpretation happens often in popular Japanese history. One excellent example is the *Taiga dorama* television series and its impact on other media. NHK *Taiga dorama*, which are often based on interpretations of recently popular novels, and which inspire a wide range of spinoffs in manga and consumer goods and even impact tourism, trace the history of a significant moment or character from the past. Aired annually since 1963, they remain among the top-rated of NHK programs in any given year. When looking at all of the *Taiga dorama* spinoffs, it becomes difficult to determine what degree of separation a text has from the original sources, but the pattern of intertextuality is clear and highlights how much historical memory pervades society.

As various accounts about Hideyoshi's life get further and further from the historical source material, questions about the relationship among truth, fiction, and historical narrative become harder to answer. The self-help manuals published from the 1950s through the 1970s highlight the way that Hideyoshi's story nimbly moves back and forth between fiction and nonfiction. In the afterword to their 1965 business manual, *Hideyoshi to ningen kankei* (fig. 3.1), Shimizu Sadakichi (1904–69) and Kojima Kōhei (b. 1932) provide a striking analysis of Hideyoshi and *Taikōki*-based historical fiction. In explaining why they had chosen Yoshikawa's *Shinsho Taikōki* as the text on which they based their study, they articulate the connection between Hideyoshi (as depicted by

FIGURE 3.1 The cover of Shimizu Sadakichi and Kojima Kōhei's *Hideyoshi to ningen kankei: Hyūman rirēshonzu* (Hideyoshi and interpersonal relationships: Human relations), published by Chūbu Zakaisha in 1965.

Yoshikawa Eiji) and Japan in the 1960s. As a result, they highlight why Yoshikawa's Hideyoshi is an appropriate model for 1960s readers to emulate.

The second of the three volumes in the Sengoku period management series, this book was preceded by one about Nobunaga titled Nobunaga to ningen kankei (Nobunaga and interpersonal relations) and Ieyasu to ningen kankei (Ieyasu and interpersonal relations).[65] The discussion of Nobunaga focuses on what the authors touted as his "speed in action," "unerring logic in execution," and "ability to swiftly reward and punish those around him."[66] The volume on Hideyoshi focuses on the three ways he was able to overcome hardships: he took a logical, scientific approach to problems; he emphasized diplomacy between people; and he was always willing to listen to advice.[67] The authors wrote, "His strategy, military prowess, and interpersonal relations skills are applied to current management, and his strategic successes and management failures are pursued in a scientific manner and used as an instructive tale for current businessmen in this decisive volume about management."[68] Kojima and Shimizu's decision to highlight his practical, "scientific" approach to problems no doubt reflects their respective backgrounds as a businessman with a degree in the humanities and a scientist with a Ph.D.

It also indicates their desire to link the Hideyoshi of the late sixteenth century to the twentieth-century issues facing a technologically advancing Japan. They hoped to attribute to Hideyoshi skills that contemporary readers could not only relate to but also work to develop. The authors wrote, "Of course, the Warring States period and our scientifically advanced present are quite different, both in environment and in terms of the way people think, but issues of how people feel when they interact with one another have not changed at all."[69] The authors admitted that the two worlds they sought to compare were very different, but they never wavered in their belief that Hideyoshi was a good and appropriate model for business in the 1960s.

In addition to offering a well-articulated argument about why readers should turn to a period four centuries in the past for guidance, Shimizu and Kojima also provide a distinct explanation of how historical fiction can prove more useful, engaging, and relatable than historical source materials alone. In the book, they argue that Yoshikawa's depiction of Hideyoshi in *Shinsho Taikōki* is particularly well suited to a discussion of business practices in the 1960s for four reasons:

> First, certainly, history books are more historically accurate, but where there is no material, these books cannot tell us about the psychological workings of his heart. Of course they can offer conjecture, but they cannot stray from the results of their historical investigation. But with fiction, there is a certain freedom to interpret, so it is possible to write about the protagonist as if he's a living human being, and, of course, include descriptions of his thoughts and feelings. Since this information is vital to a discussion of human relationships, we have decided to use Yoshikawa's novel as a reference.
>
> Second, since little is known about Hideyoshi's youth, even if we look in the historical record, we won't find anything. We accept that what is not known can't be known, but there is still value in searching for information about Hideyoshi in novels.[70]

These first two reasons highlight the way historical fiction provides details and narrative structure for the authors' salaryman guide. Yoshikawa's text makes their examples and analysis more relevant and easier to follow.

Shimizu and Kojima continue: "Third, Yoshikawa's *Taikōki* has been a best seller since the war and continues to be widely read today. Thus, the demand for Hideyoshi's image will only increase, so we would like readers to see our take on Yoshikawa's interpretation."[71] It is interesting to see the authors so readily admit a willingness to benefit from the popularity of Yoshikawa's fiction. As this book has shown, authors and historians alike never hesitate to take advantage of a boom. In some ways, the drive to promote Hideyoshi as a business model is very much a drive to sell books and benefit from his ongoing popularity.

Finally, Shimizu and Kojima explain: "Fourth, we want to avoid difficult language and use images of Hideyoshi found in novels to add to our analysis of him as a humane leader. We presume readers will find that Yoshikawa's analysis lacks nothing."[72] According to the authors, Yoshikawa has provided the ideal vehicle for their writing about business management because his writing is accessible and entertaining, and it appeals to a wide audience. Shimizu and Kojima clearly hope to capitalize on the popularity of Hideyoshi and Yoshikawa's novel about him, which they think "lacks nothing," to sell their ideas about human resource management in Japan.

The success of the various enterprises carried out by Daiyamondo-sha (and the longevity demonstrated by *Purejidento* and *Daiyamondo* magazines), as well as the emergence of several how-to business books indicates there was a growing salaryman readership interested in self-improvement. The goal of the publications was to ensure that these men at the heart of Japan's economic miracle would be prepared to face the challenges of the postwar economic recovery. Although Japan in the Sengoku period was not the only focus of these manuals and magazine articles, this period—and the three unifiers in particular—serves as one rich source for model leadership and management behavior. These works point to a transformation in the discourse about Japan's warrior past. In the late twentieth century, famous samurai leaders like Hideyoshi become popular icons who can teach subsequent generations how to be great leaders. The publishers' determination to turn the warrior Hideyoshi into a model of leadership appropriate for a peaceful twentieth-century Japan indicates just how much discourses on national identity were changing in the middle of the twentieth century and how effective shifting historical narratives were in helping tell these new stories about the past. Furthermore, given the ways both Oze and Yoshikawa molded Hideyoshi's story to suit their narrative and ideological needs, it is clear that business manuals using the works of those earlier authors as the basis for guidance and advice go beyond Nora's history of the second degree.

Tsutsui Yasutaka's "Yamazaki" and the Critique of Hideyoshi as Business Model

Kasahara offered readers a Hideyoshi who was predictable, if not in an entirely new setting. Shiba gave readers one whose surroundings were very much from the sixteenth century but whose thinking had somehow traversed the centuries and was suited to the present. Business manuals and self-help books about Hideyoshi attempted to normalize the appearance of sixteenth-century warrior ideals in twentieth-century spaces. With each example, we have an ideal hero and leadership model for Japan's economic ascendancy but a failure to address the obvious anachronisms involved when a samurai leader from the past is situated in the present. The science fiction and parody writer Tsutsui Yasutaka provides a more sober reading of Hideyoshi that clearly criticizes this seemingly unfettered idealization of the past. As he does so, he uses his counterinterpretation of Hideyoshi to criticize Japan's increasingly technological and economy-driven society. Tsutsui not only deconstructs historical fiction as a narrative approach, but he also deconstructs the notion that heroes of the past can still be heroes in postwar Japan.

In his novella "Yamazaki," first published in April 1972 in the literary magazine *Bessatsu Shōsetsu Shinchō*, Tsutsui asks readers to consider what would really happen if warriors like Hideyoshi were leaders today.[73] Whereas Shiba, Kasahara, and others seem to be playing with images of Hideyoshi in the twentieth century as a way of entertaining their audiences while also exhorting them to bring the same sort of commitment to their endeavors as Hideyoshi did to his four hundred years before, Tsutsui uses bifurcating temporalities in his story about Hideyoshi to articulate a clear criticism of the idealized past apparent in wartime and early postwar popular literature, in which Hideyoshi is always the hero.

By applying what Ozaki Hotsuki refers to as Tsutsui's "science fictional perspective on history," in his novella, Tsutsui creates metahistorical fiction to satirize the idealization of Hideyoshi.[74] His scientific rhetoric dismantles common interpretations of the past to challenge the basic assumptions behind any preexisting historical narrative powering these stories. As a result, Tsutsui's "Yamazaki," which begins just before Hideyoshi learns of Nobunaga's death and ends as he runs into battle against Akechi Mitsuhide, parodies the tradition of representing Hideyoshi as a paragon of the common man. By deconstructing the genre of historical fiction and criticizing the tendency to idealize technology and turn to leaders of the past for guidance in the future, Tsutsui employs the events leading up to the Battle of Yamazaki to undermine the use of Hideyoshi as a hero while also questioning the changes toward a technology-focused society that he sees in late 1960s and early 1970s Japan.

On the surface, Tsutsui's story is simply a retelling of the events leading up to Hideyoshi's victory at Yamazaki, a victory that put him squarely on the path to becoming leader of the realm. But while at first the story mimics a piece of historical fiction, both in pacing and content, it quickly becomes something more. Instead of using conventional strategies and narrative methods, Tsutsui creates a work of pseudohistorical fiction that introduces anachronistic references and second-guesses original source materials to force readers to reconsider the nature of historical fiction and popular tales from the past. Tsutsui's deconstructive references are apparent from the opening lines of the story and become more and more absurd as the story progresses. In the first line, Tsutsui's report on the exact time of Nobunaga's death is followed by the sentence: "At that time, Hideyoshi was in Okayama prefecture."[75] Even the most historically uninformed Japanese reader would know that Okayama prefecture did not exist until several hundred years later.[76] Throughout the story, Tsutsui shifts back and forth between the historical and current names for the places he discusses, sometimes even doing so on the same page to highlight the incongruities between the popular stories of Japan's past and those of contemporary Japan, and as a result he calls into question any tendencies readers might have to use the past as a model for the present.[77]

He further deconstructs the genre of historical fiction by interrupting the story to insert his own opinions and by giving the reader obviously dubious or contradictory information. His interruptions include constantly questioning the sources of information and the believability of certain events even as he describes them. For example, after recording the reaction to the news of Nobunaga's death by Hideyoshi's faithful retainer Kanbei, who exclaims it must be the will of the Christian God that Hideyoshi have this opportunity, Tsutsui writes, "This is apparently recorded in *Mōri ke monjo*, *Tōdai-ki*, and two or three other places, but somehow I cannot believe that Kanbei would say something like that at a time like this."[78] Because these examples appear in the first paragraphs of "Yamazaki," it is clear that although Tsutsui is using standard historical fiction narrative strategies, he does not intend his story to be a typical piece of historical fiction, nor does he expect his readers to buy into the narrative he is choosing to tell. Once he has put his readers on shaky footing in this way, Tsutsui proceeds to further challenge reliance on historical narrative and narrative structures.

Tsutsui's deconstruction of historical fiction is also apparent in his novella *Tsutsui Junkei* (Tsutsui Junkei), which was originally serialized in

FIGURE 3.2   An illustration of the Dōgatōge drive-in restaurant in the original serialization of Tsutsui Yasutaka's "Tsutsui Junkei," November 11, 1968.

Shūkan Bunshun from September to December 1968 and further illustrates his resistance to a glorified reading of the past. In this story, Tsutsui investigates the events surrounding his ancestor Junkei's role at Yamazaki and his alleged betrayal of Mitsuhide. In a poignant scene, the author—who has stepped into his own story as narrator—visits Dōgatōge, the site where Junkei is said to have stood watching the battle between Mitsuhide and Hideyoshi before ultimately deciding to abandon the losing Akechi forces to join Hideyoshi. What Tsutsui finds there is a drive-in restaurant, which has been carved into the side of the famous hill where Junkei once stood (fig. 3.2).

When the narrator Tsutsui tells the owner of the restaurant that all historical sources indicate that Junkei never visited the spot, the owner refuses to believe him despite the overwhelming evidence he presents, saying, "If Junkei really didn't come here, then why is the story of Dōgatōge Junkei passed on even today?"[79] This is precisely the problem Tsutsui seeks to address in "Yamazaki." Why are these stories still told, regardless of their veracity or lack thereof? What role does historical narrative play in our understanding of who we are and what our present situation means?

By switching seamlessly between standard historical fiction narrative structure and parody, he forces readers to reconsider how history is analyzed and mobilized in their era and to grapple with these questions.

In addition to problematizing the sources that inform readers' understanding of the past, Tsutsui's "Yamazaki" is filled with references to modern technology, and two-thirds of the way into the narrative his account seems to lose track of historical time altogether. After a fairly traditional recounting of the events surrounding the peace treaty that Hideyoshi brokers with the Mōri clan—who at the time of Nobunaga's death were under siege in Takamatsu Castle and surrounded by water—the narrative shifts to a fictional version of the technologically advanced twentieth century. The first example of the intermingling of past and present comes after long negotiations with the Mōri, when Hideyoshi finally closes the deal. Instead of turning his attention to preparing the troops for departure, he has a good night's rest, sleeping well into the next day. When one of his men reminds him of the fact that he needs to hurry to secure reinforcements and catch up with Mitsuhide, he laughs: "According to you, everything is a problem of lack of time. . . . Why write a letter when we can use the phone?" Then he picks up a telephone and tells the operator, "Connect me to Nakagawa in Ibaragi castle."[80] Subsequently, the reader is bombarded with references to modern technology such as phones, taxis, bullet trains, and electric shavers. At this point, Tsutsui's parody and social commentary become the center of the narrative.

The parody's use of technology works on multiple levels. It directly alters the type of story Tsutsui tells, reimagining the decisive factors involved in various significant moments in history. For example, Hideyoshi's ability to beat others to Yamazaki to avenge Nobunaga's death has generally been explained as a result of his skillful orchestration of the swift and smooth signing of the peace treaty with the Mōri, followed by his speed in amassing his troops and getting them into position for a showdown with Mitsuhide. Although the details of how this was executed have been contested, Hideyoshi's efficiency at this pivotal moment has been referred to as proof of his leadership skills. In Tsutsui's account, however, technological advancements aid Hideyoshi on both of these fronts. Technology enables him to quickly spread false information and purposely misdirect others, so he can get to Mitsuhide before anyone else. For example, he calls another of Nobunaga's Oda retainers, Nakagawa Kiyohide:

In no time, Nakagawa Kiyohide answered: "Hello?"

"Is this Nakagawa? It's Hashiba. . . ."[81]

"How are you? Did you hear about Honnō-ji?"

"Yes, I know about it, but don't worry. Oda evaded Akechi's evil plans."

"Oh, is that so? I am glad to hear. All right!"

"He has retreated all the way to Ōtsu. I am on my way there now."

"Where are you?"

"I have made my way to Numa."[82]

Of course, all of this is fabricated. Tsutsui's Hideyoshi lies about Nobunaga's fate and location to buy time. This intentional misdirection ensures that Kiyohide does not panic and join the opposing forces of Mitsuhide and keeps him from inadvertently disclosing valuable information to potential rivals. The fact that Hideyoshi was able to perpetrate this ruse so quickly by phone gives him a considerable advantage.

Technology also allows Hideyoshi to move quickly. After talking to Kiyohide, Hideyoshi sets about securing bullet train tickets for the thousands of men who are serving him, and according to Tsutsui's version of events, his ability to get enough tickets for all of his troops is the primary reason he reaches Mitsuhide so quickly. Hideyoshi's coolness under pressure and good strategic planning, not to mention his ability to understand and use the technology available to him, are clear in this exchange he has with Kanbei:

> "If the trains departing from Okayama are all Hikari, I will buy enough tickets for everyone to travel by Hikari, but if the tickets are sold in advance, there are likely none left. To buy thirty thousand tickets, we will probably need to buy all of the tickets available today, tomorrow, and possibly even the day after."
>
> "We will have to be separated. Of course that can't be helped. Hurry and buy the tickets and then send Ukita Tadaie [1573–1655] and Hashiba Hidekatsu [1568–86] and their men on the bullet trains today so their two brigades can serve as the advanced party. . . . We will leave on trains tomorrow."[83]

The strengths typically emphasized in other fictional accounts of Hideyoshi's life are apparent here—he is optimistic and good at making plans and giving orders—but the setting is quite different. The technology Tsutsui describes redefines the way these warriors communicate and do battle. More important, it offers a new explanation for how Hideyoshi was able to carry out his revenge attack so efficiently and effectively.

These references to technology immediately connect Tsutsui's retelling of Hideyoshi's pursuit of Mitsuhide to 1960s and 1970s Japan. While reinforcing the intertextual and accretionary nature of traditional Japanese storytelling, Tsutsui's subtle and not-so-subtle reinterpretations of the gaps in historical sources allow him to make innovative changes to the popular perceptions of Hideyoshi that heavily influence not only his story but also the way his readers think about historical narrative, forcing them to engage with the familiar history of Hideyoshi and his career while simultaneously questioning their understandings of the past.

The sudden appearance of modern technology is both shocking and unsettling, and the juxtaposition of all these modern conveniences with Hideyoshi's rash and often violent reactions to the delays he encounters force the reader to reconsider the meaning of progress and the idea that Hideyoshi should be viewed as a hero and a model for leadership. When Hideyoshi confronts the station manager about the fact he will not be able to get all of his troops on the bullet trains in less than four or five days due to crowded train schedules, "[the manager says,] 'I am so sorry,' and bows so low that his forehead is flat on the floor. 'I feel morally responsible for this situation. As a representative of the national railroad, I express my sincerest apologies.' He then immediately commits seppuku in that very spot."[84] This scene simultaneously refers to Japan National Railway's commitment to absolute precision regarding time schedules in the 1960s and provides a humorous yet critical view of the double-edged nature of technological advancement.

Hideyoshi does not balk at this seemingly archaic and brutal behavior. The irony of this scene in which someone in a very precisely managed, technologically advanced job commits such an antiquated act emphasizes Tsutsui's twofold point: sixteenth-century heroes do not belong in twentieth-century Japan, and unquestioning overreliance on technology will get Japan into trouble. In fact, the more Hideyoshi relies on technology, the more problems he has, and his dependence on unreliable technology leads to confusion and disruption. The electricity goes out not far into the trip, and Hideyoshi and his men are stuck on a dark, motionless train for four hours. When the conductor commits suicide to take responsibility for the delay, "the buffet chef had no choice but to go to his aid. The waitresses clung to him crying, and one of them stabbed herself in the throat with a fork, following him to the grave."[85] This dramatic moment caused by the inefficiencies of technology leaves Hideyoshi unfazed. He nonchalantly says, "We are still in Okayama prefecture. . . . We are not far from Numa Castle. Since it can't be helped, let's get off here and spend the night at the castle. I'm tired."[86] The following day, the trains are running and all seems well until they reach a flooded section of the track. Dissatisfied with the new conductor's explanation for why they are unable to proceed, Kanbei says, "'Stop making excuses and hurry up and get the train running.' . . . He then stood, drew his sword and cut the elderly conductor. 'Gasp,' split through the forehead . . . the conductor collapsed onto the knees of a man who looked like a newlywed groom."[87] Thick with satire, Tsutsui's introduction of a technologically advanced sixteenth century criticizes both the postwar tendency in the twentieth century to glorify new technology and the emerging discourse on sixteenth-century samurai as leadership models.

In Tsutsui's story, even though Hideyoshi makes progress both physically toward Yamazaki and symbolically toward control of the realm, when his actions and those of people around him are placed in the context of a clean bullet train car, they seem unbelievably barbaric. In this way, Tsutsui subverts the business manuals and Shiba's salesman hero, making Hideyoshi instead into a shallow, impulsive accomplice to numerous unnecessary deaths. This ironic reading of Hideyoshi's behavior asks the reader to question what it means to build a modern, technologically advanced consumer society on the shoulders of alleged heroes like Hideyoshi.

Ultimately, Tsutsui argues for a more nuanced understanding of the past that challenges the type of interpretation offered by writers like Kasahara and Shiba. Kasahara's *Sarariiman shusse Taikōki* series introduces the idea of Hideyoshi as a salaryman hero in a way that sold books and movie tickets to a general public whose members were intent on overcoming the past and succeeding economically in a new age. Later versions of this interpretation offered by writers like Shiba develop the idea of Hideyoshi as a model for business leaders without calling into question the potential pitfalls of such an interpretation. It was not until Tsutsui's deconstruction of the historical fiction genre and his counterfactual rewritings of the history surrounding Hideyoshi that this tendency to glorify Hideyoshi as a business model was called into question. Tsutsui's criticism of Hideyoshi, told in an alternative reality, offers the first hints of a discourse in which Hideyoshi appears to be fundamentally flawed and allows for different ways of thinking about the links between history, the present, and Japan's possible futures.

This chapter has traced the unlikely transformation of Hideyoshi's narrative from war hero to business model. Though he was often cited as the ideal model for World War II soldiers and citizens alike, an early emphasis on postwar economic reconstruction and a widespread desire to separate Japan's past from militaristic thought opened the possibility for Hideyoshi to be reinterpreted in the postwar period as an ideal leader and business model for the latter half of the twentieth century. His vibrant presence in business literature, self-help manuals, and even critiques of Japanese society highlights not only the flexibility of narratives about him but also their ability to take on lives of their own—leading to multiple degrees of separation from historical sources and demonstrating the influence that readers and authors have had on his story.

Early postwar renderings of Hideyoshi in fiction and business manuals offered positive interpretations of him that made him an idealized example of loyalty, hard work, and strong leadership. Like Yada's prewar *Taikōki* and Yoshikawa's *Shinsho Taikōki* before them, Kasahara's *Sarariiman shusse Taikōki* and Shiba's *Shinshi Taikōki* build on an image of Hideyoshi as hero. But beginning with Tsutsui in the late 1960s, the possibility of a nonheroic Hideyoshi emerges. Building on this interpretation, chapter 4 looks at two critical feminist renderings of Hideyoshi that further challenge the notion that he can serve as a model for twentieth-century progress.

CHAPTER 4

The Women of the Realm

Hideyoshi as Social Criticism

Tsutsui Yasutaka's work uses parody to challenge the notion of Hide-yoshi as hero and to highlight problems with the belief that heroes of the past should serve as models for the present, but Ariyoshi Sawako's *Izumo no Okuni* (The Kabuki dancer [literally, Okuni from Izumo], originally published in 1969) and Nagai Michiko's *Ōja no tsuma: Hideyoshi no tsuma Onene* (The monarch's wife: Hideyoshi's wife Onene, originally published in 1971) use female protagonists living in Hideyoshi's realm to criticize him directly. Nagai and Ariyoshi interpret Hideyoshi in a way that reflects the time in which they were writing and seek to challenge retellings that make Hideyoshi a hero by questioning patriarchal structures and exposing the drawbacks and discrepancies of histories told about and by men.[1]

Nagai and Ariyoshi portray the lives and struggles of women in Hideyoshi's immediate circle as well as those in his realm, giving new renderings of the often male-centric history of late sixteenth-century Japan. By creating protagonists who are strong women but unable to fulfill their obligation to bear children—Onene (Hideyoshi's primary wife, 1546–1624) in Nagai's novel and Okuni (the founder of Kabuki, died ca. 1613) in Ariyoshi's—the two writers voice complex but parallel criticisms of the plight of women that speak as much to 1960s and 1970s Japan as to the late sixteenth and early seventeenth centuries they describe. Nagai and Ariyoshi write about Hideyoshi from the perspective of marginalized characters to highlight the way women and other disenfranchised members of society such as farmers, itinerant performers, and prostitutes were often oppressed by events heralded in many narratives of Japanese history. By describing Japan's past from the point of view of those whose voices are often silenced, the authors highlight the absurdity of relying on men like Hideyoshi for encouragement and for a sense of what it means to be Japanese.

These novels by Ariyoshi and Nagai offer readers fictions that challenge the construction of patriarchal histories, reflecting a growing resistance to the apotheosis of flawed men like Hideyoshi. At a time when women were seeking to skillfully negotiate the intersections of their increasingly complicated identities as women, wives, and mothers who were expected to be self-sufficient and hardworking subjects in a Japan intent on economic ascendancy, the novels offered fictional narratives that deconstructed heroic interpretations of the past while simultaneously resisting the limiting notions of Japanese womanhood that result from such interpretations. *Ōja no tsuma*, serialized in various regional newspapers from December 1969 until October 1970 and initially published as a novel by Kodansha in 1971, tells the story of the rise and fall of the Toyotomi clan from the perspective of Hideyoshi's primary wife Onene. *Izumo no Okuni*, serialized in *Fujin kōron* (Ladies' review) beginning in 1967 and published in a three-volume set by the same publishing company between 1969 and 1972, depicts the life and times of Izumo no Okuni (born circa 1571), an itinerant performer who is considered to be the founder of Kabuki.

By portraying the difficulties endured by the women in Hideyoshi's immediate circle as well as those in his realm and by focusing on the constraints placed on these characters by their positions in the patriarchal social structure, these novels by Ariyoshi and Nagai provide a feminist critique of the structures that put figures like Hideyoshi in positions of power. Their novels explore the ways in which women sought to find spaces of independence within and outside these structures and, by giving their readers models of strong women who seek to emerge from the shadows of the patriarchs of the past, they simultaneously call into question how and by whom history is recorded and told.

In both novels, the female protagonists are disenfranchised in particular ways that are directly tied to their inability to become wives and/or mothers: Nagai's Onene never gives birth to a potential heir, and Ariyoshi's Okuni prioritizes her passion for performance (her career), forgoing multiple opportunities to settle down into a more socially acceptable lifestyle. These failures are central to the suffering that Onene and Okuni endure in these tales, but they are also the motivation for their moves toward independence. By emphasizing the characters' struggles against the opposition from women around them who are fighting for the affections of men, Ariyoshi and Nagai demonstrate the ways their protagonists move beyond the gendered paradigms of sixteenth-century Japan. In both stories, the initial tension Onene and Okuni feel in relation to other women is gradually transformed into the realization that the men they have been fighting over are weak and far from exemplary, and as Onene and Okuni emerge in control, their survival subverts masculine notions of strength and success.

Through strong female protagonists who are marginalized by their inability to become wives and/or mothers, but who nonetheless offer unflinching views of Hideyoshi, Nagai and Ariyoshi deconstruct narratives about male heroes from Japan's past while also highlighting the ongoing struggle women face in liberating themselves from the often-limiting roles of wife and mother. After briefly providing the context for these novels, including an overview of early postwar discourses about women, this chapter demonstrates how Nagai's and Ariyoshi's protagonists defy expectations and subvert notions of what makes an ideal woman while also challenging history told by and about men to give readers a particularly feminist reading of Japan's past.

Early Postwar Discourses on Women

Women's bodies, and their ability to reproduce in particular, have been the source of ongoing debates surrounding a woman's place in modern Japanese society. The newly drafted Japanese Civil Code sought, in part, to define formally the family network of relationships so as to give the patriarchal head of the family authority over the rest of its members. In this system, a woman had fewer legal rights than had previously been the case, as she was now subject to the control either of her father in the family of her birth or of her husband after she married. During the Meiji period, the phrase *ryōsai kenbō* (good wife, wise mother) became the code according to which women were encouraged to restrict themselves to the domestic sphere. Women were beseeched through educational and other institutions to contribute to the nation's growth and progress by wholeheartedly supporting their husbands, efficiently managing their households, practicing frugality in all things, caring for their elderly relatives, and rearing responsible and hardworking children.[2] This idea continued to be prioritized through subsequent decades. For example, during World War II, women were implored by another government slogan to "be fruitful and multiply" (*umeyo, fuyaseyo*) as a means of increasing Japan's strength and human resource base.[3] Even after the war ended, women continued to find themselves at the center of discussions about the importance of their household responsibilities in Japan's postwar recovery and economic ascendancy.

As Jan Bardsley, Julia Bullock, Andrew Gordon, Kathleen Uno, and others have argued, just as women before and during World War II were called on to mobilize their childbearing selves in service to the empire, women in the 1960s were expected to play a role in the construction of the new nation.[4] And as men worked long hours to ensure Japan's economic success and provide the income necessary for their families to secure a spot within the burgeoning middle class, women were urged to take on additional burdens at home.

However, women did not just sit back and passively watch as others deliberated about their role in the postwar economy. Writing about the "housewife debate" of 1955, Bardsley explains: "Clearly, the labor of [the] housewife contributed significantly to the creation of Japan's postwar 'economic miracle,' and both her usefulness to corporate Japan as well as the societal and institutional pressures on women to become housewives have been much discussed. . . . [T]he postwar invention of this 'modern Japanese housewife' did not happen quietly—or emerge unchallenged."[5] For women writers, one way to fight against prescribed gender roles was to write about women, who, for a variety of reasons, resisted the roles of wife and mother.

As Sharalyn Orbaugh has argued, women authors in the 1960s and 1970s used their positions as writers to create female protagonists who challenged the "economies of power" that subjugated women.[6] And as Bullock puts it, women authors "defied models of normative femininity" by creating protagonists who were "unapologetically bad wives and even worse mothers."[7] Both Bullock and Orbaugh note that during this period, there was a wealth of successful women writers—newcomers such as Kōno Taeko

(1926–2015), Ōba Minako (1930–2007), and Tsushima Yūko (1947–2016), as well as established writers such as Enchi Fumiko (1905–86) and Uno Chiyo (1899–1996)—who were producing compelling and provocative literature that undermined patriarchal discourses about women.[8] In *The Other Women's Lib*, Bullock explains, "Capitalizing on the rich potential of fictional worlds to highlight ironic disjunctions between feminine stereotypes and feminist realities, [writers like Kurahashi Yumiko (1935–2005), Kōno Taeko, and Takahashi Takako (1932–2013)] actively participated in creating alternative discourses of femininity during the 1960s and early 1970s—even as this era of high economic growth seemed to render such gendered distinctions not only inevitable but also necessary to the cause of national and individual prosperity."[9] Yet although there has been increased interest in and focus on how women writing in the 1960s and 1970s created these "alternative discourses of femininity," the unique position of historical fiction writers has been overlooked. Nagai and Ariyoshi participated in this process by creating what might be called herstories that spotlight well-known women of the past and use them both to criticize male-driven historical narratives and to illustrate how women can and should push back against constraints placed upon them by society.

Ariyoshi's serialization of *Izumo no Okuni* and Nagai's serialization of *Ōja no tsuma* place both works at the heart of these ongoing discussions about the role of women in postwar Japanese society. Both Nagai's novel about infertility and the isolating and disempowering nature of competition between Hideyoshi's wife, Onene, and his favorite consort, Ochacha (d. 1615), and Ariyoshi's novel about a disenfranchised dancer who succeeds in using her body to make a living and founding Kabuki but who ultimately fails to establish herself within the family system offer narratives that challenge the patriarchal system and openly criticize the society that created these restrictive conditions for women.

Nagai Michiko's Onene

At a public lecture given in March 2008 at the NHK Broadcast Museum, Nagai claimed: "I am not writing about women because I am a woman. I simply believe there is a lot to learn from seeing history through their eyes."[10] The writing that Nagai has done throughout her career "sees" history differently than does the historical fiction of contemporary male writers like Yoshikawa Eiji and Shiba Ryōtarō. Onene is just one of many famous women in Japanese history about whom Nagai has written, and her prolific writing career has provided numerous challenges and correctives to interpretations of women. Examples of this can be found in her *Rekishi o sawagaseta onnatachi* (Women who disturbed history) and *Nihon no suupaa reidii monogatari* (Stories of Japanese super ladies), a collection of her essays. By writing about and through the perspective of women, she depicts famous events of history in a way that reflects a complex view of the past often overlooked in male-dominated discourses.

Nagai challenges common portrayals of women by rehabilitating the images of maligned figures such as Minamoto no Yoritomo's often-vilified wife, Hōjō Masako (1157–1225), in *Hōjō Masako*, and she often writes about how women were involved in important moments in history, as in the *Rekishi o sawagaseta onnatachi*. *Ōja no tsuma* offers another example of a woman who defies traditional interpretation.[11]

Born in Tokyo, Nagai was raised by her aunt and uncle. In 1941, at the age of sixteen, she entered Tokyo Women's University to begin studies in Japanese. She graduated in three years, and in 1947 she began auditing lectures in the economics department at the University of Tokyo, where she joined the Society for Research on Women (*Sōgō joseishi kenkyūkai*) and the Society for Research on Contemporary Women's History (*Kinsei joseishi kenkyūkai*). After marrying the historian Kuroita Nobuo in 1949, she worked at Shōgakkan, a publishing house where she served as editor for the magazines *Jogakusei no tomo* (The school girl's friend) and *Madomoazeru* (Mademoiselle). Her own writing career was launched in earnest in 1952 when she placed second in a competition for the *Sandei Mainichi* (Sunday daily) Thirtieth Anniversary Prize with her story *Sanjōin-ki* (The history of Lady Sanjō).[12] Her popularity is evidenced by the many awards she has received, including the leading prize for popular fiction, the Naoki Prize, which she won in 1964 for her novel *Enkan* (Ring of fire). She has also won several other major prizes, such as the Women's Culture Prize (1982), the Kikuchi Prize (1984), and the Yoshikawa Eiji Prize (1988).

A large part of Nagai's motivation for writing about Onene was her ongoing desire to question the veneration of male heroes and to demonstrate the value of history told from the point of view of women: "In the foreign expansionism that happened since the Meiji period, there has been a tendency to overly praise Hideyoshi. More than his brilliant advancement, I wanted to give space to the manner in which his humanity collapsed after he completed his rise to the top, and, because I wanted to rethink this modern hero myth being created, there was no other way to go (*hoka narimasen*) [than to focus on Onene]."[13] Nagai believes that her fiction can serve as a corrective to the one-sided accounts so prevalent in Hideyoshi narratives and challenge the notion that men like him can be heroes. It is particularly interesting to note that Nagai refers to the final years of his life and career as the time when his "humanity collapsed," given that Hideyoshi's humanity was touted by Yoshikawa and Shiba as well as the scholars at the roundtable discussion introduced in chapter 2.

Furthermore, Nagai believes that focusing on the point of view of the women closest to Hideyoshi is the best way to challenge the apotheosis of male figures like Hideyoshi. Nagai also argues that only through the point of view of a woman could she begin to tell the full and accurate story of Hideyoshi's rule. She repeats this belief in the value of a woman's perspective in the afterword to the *bunkobon* edition of *Ōja no tsuma*: "Not only did she successfully navigate the turbulent times of the Warring States period as Hideyoshi's wife, [but] Onene—someone who tends to be overlooked—is the protagonist of my story because I wanted to create a historical novel that offered a different take on the accounts of the turbulent sixteenth and seventeenth centuries by looking at them from the perspective of a regular person who was also a woman."[14] For Nagai, a common woman like Onene has the potential to break free from standard narratives: telling her story has the potential to broaden our understanding of history and reveal that certain heroes of the past may have been less heroic than we thought.

Told by an omniscient narrator, *Ōja no tsuma* begins when Onene is a young girl in the 1550s and ends with her death in 1624. Although most accounts of Hideyoshi's life focus on his rise, Nagai's tale gives readers a clear view of the final decade of his life as well as of what happened after he was gone. Her novel describes in detail the succession struggles following his death, emphasizing the significant role Onene played in helping create the Tokugawa peace. In this way, Nagai highlights the power Onene had amassed despite her circumstances as a childless widow.

Nagai's novel also explores the complicated position held by Japanese women in the late sixteenth century as bearers of children and managers of the household. When Onene appears in historical analyses of Hideyoshi, discussions center on how her inability to produce an heir left her disempowered at a time when the continuation of a family line relied on the presence of a son.[15] In her essay "Nihon ichi no 'okamisan': Kita no Mandokoro" (The best wife in Japan: Kita no Mandokoro), however, Nagai subverts this approach by decoupling the roles of wife and mother and arguing that Onene stands out as one of the most ideal wives of all time: "It is common knowledge that Onene had no children. Despite the fact that this was a major strike against women of her time, she continued to assert influence as Hideyoshi's primary wife because she had exemplary character. Furthermore, what really made Onene great was that she not only had authority over Hideyoshi's various mistresses, but she also paid close attention to politics and skillfully offered her husband advice on such matters."[16] Noting that beneath her seemingly docile outer appearance, Onene was "100 percent tenacious and 100 percent indefatigable," Nagai argues that contemporary wives will not find a better model than Onene because she was able to keep her jealousy in check, remain informed about current affairs, and provide wise counsel to her spouse.[17] In other words, Nagai believes Onene recognized better than anyone that her influence as Hideyoshi's wife extended well beyond the domestic sphere and was not contingent upon her ability to give birth to a son.

This image of Onene as a woman who understood the kind of power she could yield is apparent from the earliest depiction of the relationship between Onene and Hideyoshi found in the novel. Nagai takes advantage of the dearth of historical sources about their marriage to focus on Onene's agency, painting her as a woman who controls the relationship. This is not typically how she has been portrayed in popular fiction or on television.[18] She is actively involved in negotiations between her uncle and Hideyoshi's go-between and makes her decision to marry him based on her instincts. In Nagai's novel, when Maeda Toshiie (Hideyoshi's friend and fellow vassal of Oda Nobunaga) comes to negotiate a marriage proposal on Hideyoshi's behalf with Onene's uncle, she is mortified to discover that her suitor is the uncouth and unattractive Hideyoshi and not Toshiie. But because she is able to look beyond Hideyoshi's low rank and homely features to recognize his potential, Onene decides to marry him and demonstrates the flexibility and independent thinking that reveals her to be someone with considerable agency.[19] Nagai stresses Onene's initial negative reaction to Hideyoshi, his vulnerability, and the resulting pity she feels for him to establish the relationship between these two as one of shared power. Though later in the novel the reader sees Onene's sense of control waiver when she is unable to produce an heir, she ultimately maintains a firm grasp on the affairs of Hideyoshi's household as he rises through the ranks and begins to accumulate mistresses.

By writing about Onene's motivations and her thought processes, Nagai highlights the ways women asserted agency, often in the shadows of well-known historical events. For example, in describing the marriage of Nobunaga's sister Oichi to Asai Nagamasa, a powerful lord with whom Nobunaga sought to create strong political ties, Nagai highlights the fact that women in sixteenth-century Japan had more agency than her readers might realize. As Onene watches the elaborate wedding procession, the narrator reminds readers that they should not feel sorry for women like Oichi and Onene because the idea of marriage for nonpolitical reasons such as love did not exist: "People today . . . call [these] marriages 'political unions.' . . . But at that time, in samurai families, there was no concept of love marriage. These political marriages are different than the way we perceive them today in this world of love and free marriage. It would not be a stretch to say that these women could conceive of no other form of marriage. In other words, just as people from the Meiji period didn't know that not having television is inconvenient, women of Onene's time did not feel particularly sorry for themselves because of these marriages."[20] In scenes like this, Nagai explains that these women were well aware of the power they could wield. These types of explanations, scattered throughout the novel, bring readers back to the present and remind them that they share a history of being subjected to patriarchal social structures that connects them to the women in the novel. Nagai layers Narita's three time axes—in this case, sixteenth-century Japan, 1960s Japan, and the contemporary reader—in a way that effectively encourages readers (especially female ones) to break free from the idea that women have always been subjugated and powerless.

Although Nagai's Onene is adept at using her resources to ensure a propitious marriage for herself, she is unable to assert the same kind of agency when it comes to producing an heir. In a society where women amass power by producing male offspring, Onene's inability to bear a child for Hideyoshi puts her at a considerable disadvantage. Her struggles to conceive and then come to terms with her seeming infertility are key to her development in the novel.

Nagai's narrative implies that the couple's inability to produce offspring could also be linked to Hideyoshi's negligence of Onene and to the fact that he spends less time with her than with his mistresses. However, Onene is forced to addresses this issue of reproduction throughout the novel, first bringing her concerns to Hideyoshi's attention early in their marriage when she learns that her younger sister, Oyaya, is expecting her first child. Though the news of her sister's pregnancy hurts and infuriates Onene, who then pressures Hideyoshi to spend more time with her, he responds to her entreaties by minimizing her concerns, telling her that those worries are unimportant and that they can always adopt if necessary.[21] Later, when one of Hideyoshi's lesser-known mistresses gives birth to a son named Otsugimaru, Onene must decide whether to raise the child as her own or to live under the same roof as Hideyoshi's mistress and son. Onene realizes that this tiny baby jeopardizes her position and leaves her no choice but to raise another woman's child if she wishes to maintain her status as Hideyoshi's primary wife.[22] The baby does not live long, but this episode highlights Onene's difficult position. Although Hideyoshi often acts complacent when dealing with the issue of children, the seriousness of this matter becomes apparent in Nagai's description of how the baby's brief life impacts Onene.

In another scene, Hideyoshi's ability to flippantly deal in the exchange of children with a colleague highlights how differently this issue impacts men and women. When a discussion of battle strategy turns to offspring, Hideyoshi casually asks Toshiie to give him a few.[23] This bartering of children and removing them from their birth mothers, though accepted, is done with a striking insouciance on Hideyoshi's part. In fact, his only wish for Onene is that she accepts his profligate ways in the same way that Toshiie's wife seems to have done. When Toshiie exclaims that all of his women "seem to get pregnant right away," Hideyoshi turns to Onene and says, "Did you hear that, Onene? . . . Just because I have two or three women is no reason to be upset."[24] The issue for Hideyoshi is not whether Onene is able to get pregnant but whether she is willing to let him carry on with other women as he pleases. His callousness in carrying out this

exchange in Onene's presence and then in using Toshiie's example to jus-
tify his infidelities emphasizes the breadth of the chasm that exists between them on this issue.

Nobunaga's attentiveness to Onene's concerns stand in stark contrast
to Hideyoshi's ambivalence about her lack of offspring. In both *Ōja no
tsuma* and "The Best Wife in Japan," Nagai argues that the famous "bald
rat" (*hage nezumi*) letter Nobunaga sent to Onene played an important
role in Onene's ability to succeed despite her infertility. In the missive,
Nobunaga refers to Onene's recent visit to Azuchi Castle, encourages her
to be strong in the face of Hideyoshi's philandering, and insists that she
show the letter to Hideyoshi. Nobunaga writes: "That [Hideyoshi] is said
to be ceaselessly dissatisfied is a great wrong beyond words. However far
he searches, this bald rat will never find anyone like yourself. Thus, from
now on be steadfast, become strong as a wife, and do not give in to jealousy. It is best, in your role as a woman, to leave some things unsaid."[25]
This letter is described by Mary Elizabeth Berry as being "the most revealing document concerning Hideyoshi's married life" and "one of the
most candid items in correspondence of the time."[26] For a historical fiction writer like Nagai, this letter provides a wealth of information from
which she can not only speculate on the nature of Hideyoshi and Onene's
marriage but also better understand Onene's motivations. In her essay
about Onene, Nagai argues that the letter highlights what ultimately
makes her a great wife—her steadfastness and unwillingness to let jealousy derail her—while also demonstrating why she was able to succeed
in sixteenth- and seventeenth-century Japan.

In *Ōja no tsuma*, Nagai's narrator instructs the reader to interpret this
letter from Nobunaga in a specific way that places the blame for Onene's
infertility squarely on Hideyoshi. By doing so, Nagai frees Onene from
a sense of guilt for not producing children. In Nagai's interpretation of
the missing details behind this famous document, Nobunaga is unchar-
acteristically compassionate, demonstrating sympathy for Onene's plight
and generously offering to provide Hideyoshi and Onene with an heir.
The narrator notes that by giving Hideyoshi and Onene a child immediately after learning of the death of Hideyoshi's second son, Nobunaga
demonstrates he is as concerned for Onene's well-being as he is for Hideyoshi's: "Onene would no longer have to worry if Hideyoshi had a baby
with a new woman. No matter what happened, Hidekatsu would be the

heir and Onene would be his adoptive mother. The letter Nobunaga wrote that day was not his final act of support for her. It looked like he would always remember their conversation and the promise he made to her, lending Onene some of his strength."[27] Nobunaga's sympathy stands in stark contrast to Hideyoshi's repeatedly insensitive responses to Onene's concerns throughout the novel, and Nagai's interpretation of the events surrounding Nobunaga's letter bolsters her assertion that Onene's infertility is not only not her fault but also something that can be managed, allowing her to move beyond the limiting confines of her role as a bearer of children.

Nagai portrays Onene as benefiting from Nobunaga's support and eventually overcoming her anxieties about her inability to have children, but her ongoing conflict with Ochacha influences much of the second half of the novel. By focusing on the conflict between the two women, Nagai provides a new reading of Hideyoshi's history that shows twentieth-century readers the degree to which women of the sixteenth century were engaged in battles for power that were at least as hard fought as the wars being waged by the men they supported. Nagai's choice to accentuate these struggles for power and to compare them to Hideyoshi's rise and fall creates a perspective in which his successes and failures cannot be interpreted in isolation. Ochacha, Hideyoshi's primary mistress and the mother of his only surviving son, believes that because she is a daughter of Asai Nagamasa and Oichi, she is superior to Onene—who is merely the adopted daughter of a foot soldier. It is in this conflict between Onene and Ochacha that Nagai addresses issues of female agency and the struggle for power between women in a society ruled by men. From the day she moves into the same castle as Onene, Ochacha focuses on asserting her influence by belittling Onene and contradicting her orders. Although Onene never allows Ochacha to undermine her position, when she learns that Ochacha has given birth to a son, Onene laments: "Young, beautiful, pregnant, and now giving birth to a boy! I lose to her in every way."[28] Despite her strength, Onene still feels threatened by Ochacha, and her struggle to maintain her position within the household despite her inability to reproduce provides a critical perspective on the belief that women's value lay in their ability to have children.

Ultimately, however, Onene is able to prevail over Ochacha, and Nagai's final subversion of the paradigm of woman as bearer of children indicates a movement beyond such readings of this limiting view of women. This subversion happens gradually. First, Nagai parallels the birth of Hideyoshi's only surviving heir, Hideyori (1593–1615), with an increased awareness of Hideyoshi's waning grasp on reality and Onene's subsequent independence. By using Hideyori's birth to highlight Hideyoshi's increasingly erratic behavior, the narrative not only offers a nonheroic view of Hideyoshi, it also marks Onene's rise above patrilineal pathways to power. In her thoughts and words, Nagai's Onene provides a critical view of Hideyoshi's second invasion of Korea (1597), his unnecessary castle building while many of his warriors are fighting and dying abroad, and the way he removes his designated heir Hidetsugu by ordering his immediate suicide and the murder of all the women and children in Hidetsugu's family. These details are often missing in tales about Hideyoshi's life and career.

Critical thoughts that Onene had so often kept in check begin to make their way into conversations she has with the men who would help usher in the Tokugawa peace. Talking about Hideyoshi's erratic behavior, for example, she tells her brother-in-law Yahei: "Out-of-control castle building, the cruel murder of his nephew's women and children, and now the attempt to invade China again. . . . I can't call any of these things the height of good sense."[29] With this shift, Onene no longer shrinks from expressing her thoughts about Hideyoshi. Though the old Onene was too timid to confront him about something as personal as his philandering behavior, the new Onene dives headlong into the political sphere, telling her brother-in-law how to stand up to Hideyoshi and chiding his simplistic view of the "great leader."[30] Even without the support of the men around her, Onene emerges as the guardian of the future of the Toyotomi clan.

Nagai's choice to accentuate these struggles for power and align them with Hideyoshi's rise and fall creates a perspective in which his successes and failures cannot be interpreted in isolation. About the end of the Edo period, Sharon Sievers writes, "The family system, whether operating in samurai or peasant households, isolated women from each other in this competition—making them enemies whose energies were constantly turned toward the struggle with other women, rather than toward the system that oppressed them all, irrespective of class and age."[31] Nagai's Onene provides great insight on this point when she comments on the growing number of Hideyoshi's female hostages and conquests: "With every defeat of [Hideyoshi's] enemies, my enemies increase."[32] Later, she admits:

> The role of primary wife is difficult. The cruelty of the war between women is that a woman must fight using only the weapon of her personal strength. This isn't the case with the weapons men use in battle. By disciplining themselves, they are able to use things such as battle strategies or political skill to defeat their enemies. For women, however, the kinds of weapons they can utilize are those that are out of their control. For example, whether a woman is beautiful or ugly is something for which she is ultimately not responsible. The ability to get pregnant is also not something that she alone can control. And on top of that, whether she will give birth to a son or to a daughter, isn't that something she cannot know until the moment the child is born? Traditionally, oh how these weapons that are out of woman's control determine her fate![33]

Nagai extends this analogy by providing readers with a parallel description of the movement of Hideyoshi's troops into battle and the strategizing and fighting going on between the two women living in his castle.[34] In her version of Hideyoshi's story, the battles between the women are just as hard fought and the heroes are just as noble.

The real test of Onene's newfound strength comes after Hideyoshi's death when she faces off with Ochacha, and their final confrontation emphasizes how these women are impacted by their positions within the patriarchal social structure. Following Hideyoshi's death, Ochacha and Hideyori force Onene to leave Osaka Castle, and Onene retreats to a temple where she will spend her final years. Even though she is physically removed from the centers of power, Onene asserts her growing independence against the Ochacha-Hideyori faction by offering advice to several of Hideyoshi's supporters who continue to seek it. She worries not about whether the Toyotomi line will continue but about whether the men she supports are staying true to their potential and whether peace can be achieved.

The events leading up to the Battle of Sekigahara, when Tokugawa Ieyasu's troops defeated supporters of Toyotomi Hideyori to claim supremacy in Japan at the beginning of the seventeenth century, are presented in

Nagai's text as a battle between Onene and Ochacha: "From one per-spective, the Battle of Sekigahara could be seen as the battle of Onene and Ochacha."[35] Nagai describes the final battle between these two women in 1615 as being just as significant as any military battle in the novel. While Onene remains sequestered at her temple in Kyoto, Ochacha and Hideyori, realizing that resistance is futile, kill themselves at Osaka Castle. Onene emerges as the victor in that she is able to out-live her nemesis, but the victory, if it can be called that, is bittersweet. Onene's lament that the two women never had a chance to talk face-to-face and resolve the conflict between them highlights the degree to which women were separated, forcing them to face various challenges alone. In a society where women were isolated from each other and forced to strug-gle against each other instead of against the patriarchal systems of op-pression, neither Onene nor Ochacha really wins.

By linking Ochacha's death directly to her ability to bear children and produce an heir for Hideyoshi, Nagai once again subverts idealized notions of motherhood. When Onene hears about the death of Ocha-cha, she wonders: "What if Ochacha had never had Hideyori? Or what if her life had taken a different path entirely? And what if Onene had had children? Wouldn't it be Onene who burned to death inside of Osaka Castle instead? In that sense, it is natural to say that Ochacha lived that other life that Onene could have had. 'Ochacha, in the end, you and I never had the chance to talk heart to heart.'"[36] Ultimately, Ochacha is unable to overcome sixteenth-century expectations that she bear children and fight against other women for the affections of her man. The resul-tant inability of Onene and Ochacha to band together to fight against these gender stereotypes leads to Ochacha's death, just as Onene's ability to think beyond such structures saves her.

Nagai's final subversion of the masculine ideal comes in Onene's com-plete rejection of Hideyoshi's quest for power, which was demonstrated in his insatiable need to create legitimizing narratives about his origins. By challenging Hideyoshi as he seeks to create grander and grander sto-ries about his past, Nagai's Onene is also undermining the power of his-torical narratives to establish the "truth" about Hideyoshi and Japan's past. Nagai's use of "the monarch's wife" in the title of her novel high-lights Onene's resistance to Hideyoshi's endeavors to alter his identity, while simultaneously emphasizing her fierce independence and criticizing history told by and about men. According to Nagai, as someone "who never lost her ability to see things through the eyes of a commoner, no matter how successful her husband became,"[37] Onene found her husband's quest for historical legitimacy increasingly problematic. Nagai's Onene levels her harshest criticism at her husband's efforts to rewrite history.

In a meeting with Ōmura Yuko, his official biographer, Hideyoshi tells him that he will reveal a secret about his grandfather that no one else knows. Onene, observing the exchange, perplexedly asks, "Oh, do you mean your father's father?"[38] Hideyoshi quickly explains that Onene never met this grandfather. What Hideyoshi then says is for Onene "an experience unlike any other she had had since they got married."[39] Hideyoshi claims that his grandfather was a high-ranking *chūnagon* (councillor), so Onene mistakenly thinks he is talking about his mother's father and wonders how such a high-ranking man could have such an "exceedingly provincial" daughter.[40] When Hideyoshi's tale describes the man's unlikely journey to Owari before ending with a short poem about him, Onene's confusion turns into awe when she realizes how carefully Hideyoshi has fabricated this story about his roots.[41] The fact that Ōmura is able to record this tale without the least sign of blushing at Hideyoshi's obvious lie amazes Onene even more. Ōmura eventually points out that Hideyoshi's story contradicts the earlier tales he has told about himself, and Hideyoshi indignantly replies, "Didn't I just say that this is something I was keeping secret until now?" Watching this episode between her husband and his biographer, Onene is embarrassed by Hideyoshi's "stupid" behavior.[42] In Onene's criticism of the way Hideyoshi creates a heroic past for himself, Nagai is also criticizing the patriarchal hubris that undergirds the creation of these narratives.

Nagai's Onene rejects Hideyoshi's pursuit of past and future greatness. As Hideyoshi seeks higher and higher positions, Onene never allows herself to be swept up in the quest for power that eventually consumes her husband. Onene, "who never lost her ability to see things through the eyes of a commoner, no matter how successful her husband became," found her husband's behavior increasingly "odd."[43] From the moment the couple sets off on this path toward success, Onene is unfazed by it. She refuses to ride in a palanquin when they move into their first castle.[44] She accepts each new abode and name change with increasing discomfort. As Hideyoshi grows more and more extravagant, Onene becomes more and more embarrassed and annoyed by his behavior. When Hideyoshi shows Onene her new sleeping chambers at Osaka Castle, for example, she is befuddled by the raised stagelike object in the middle of the room and wonders aloud where she is supposed to sleep or sit with that in the middle. Hideyoshi tells her that it is a bed much like the one used by the "Queen of Europe." Rather than feeling flattered, though, Onene retorts, "But we are not even royalty!" Hideyoshi insists they will be royalty soon enough, but Onene points out that nothing can change their births.[45] For all his attempts to manipulate the laws of succession and convince his peers that he deserves the positions of power he attains, Hideyoshi never convinces his closest ally, Onene.

Nagai's use of "the monarch's wife" in the title also highlights Onene's ultimate resistance to Hideyoshi's endeavors to alter his identity and establish himself as ruler of the realm. As Hideyoshi pushes to become a monarch, Onene becomes more vocal about her rejection of such aspirations for herself. In Nagai's rendering of Onene's story, it seems as if Hideyoshi's unrestrained quest for power and the widening gap he creates between himself and common people provide Onene with the impetus she needs to set out on her own. The ironic title of this book alludes to both Onene's inextricability from Hideyoshi's household and the absurdity of the task she has been asked to perform. Even as Nagai reinterprets Hideyoshi as a foil for her criticism of the role of women in sixteenth-century Japan, her Hideyoshi constantly reinterprets himself in her text. And just as Nagai's Onene is ultimately unwilling to be defined by common expectations for women of her time, she is equally unwilling to participate in Hideyoshi's attempts to rewrite his own history.

Onene outlives Hideyoshi by more than twenty years, and by underscoring her ability to endure the hardships of being a childless wife who was forced to remove herself to a temple far from the centers of power after he dies, Nagai creates for her twentieth-century readers a heroine who will not be bound by societal expectations. Nagai's protagonist, who refuses to be crushed by Hideyoshi's coldness and who persists in offering a critical analysis of her husband and his policies, also challenges the tendency of scholars and novelists to prioritize well-known male historical figures like Hideyoshi, acknowledging the increasing diversity in the voices used to tell the story of Japan's past.

Ariyoshi Sawako's Okuni

Ariyoshi, known for fictional works that skillfully weave historical details into stories that demonstrate her well-developed sense of social responsibility, starts her tale of Hideyoshi with Omura, the unreliable biographer whose unquestioning acceptance of Hideyoshi's tall tales so shocked Onene. In Ariyoshi's tale, Ōmura is praised by the narrator for his ability "to turn lies into truth."[46] Though he is absent in works about Hideyoshi written by male authors, both Nagai and Ariyoshi include Ōmura in their tales as a way to highlight the dubious nature of tales of the past—both biographies and subsequent historical fictions—that insist on presenting men like Hideyoshi as heroes.

As a writer, Ariyoshi credits her experience growing up in an educated, cosmopolitan family for giving her an open mind and allowing her to develop her own voice. When she was a child, she traveled with her family to Java for her father's work. Her earliest memories of the world were from the perspective of an expatriate living in a Japanese colony, painfully aware of Japanese prejudice toward non-Japanese on the Asian continent. By the time she was in her twenties, she had gone from being a member of the elite expatriate community to being just another Japanese national who experienced the heartbreak and hardship of surrender and foreign occupation. After a failed marriage, Ariyoshi's experiences as a single working mother led her to think even more about the difficult and often tenuous position of women in Japanese society throughout the centuries.[47]

Ariyoshi writes about real and imagined female characters from the past to add a critical voice to discussions of the position of women in society, often associating her premodern female protagonists with twentieth-century issues. Three notable works of historical fiction by her—*Kinogawa* (The River Ki, 1959), *Hanaoka Seishū no tsuma* (The doctor's wife, 1967), and *Izumo no Okuni*—deal with the plight of women by describing how they manage to survive and sometimes even thrive despite the limitations placed on them by societal expectations. In fact, most of Ariyoshi's historical

fiction features strong women who bear up under intense social and emotional hardships. Many of the women who grace the pages of her novels
struggle more and work harder than the men around them, and they somehow emerge triumphant although they have experienced significant pain
and loss. Common themes that appear throughout the novels (conflict
between two generations of women in a family, men who manipulate
these tensions between women to their advantage, and the oppressive nature of feudal conventions regarding the role of women in the household)
are also present in *Izumo no Okuni*.

When he becomes the performing troupe's patron, in an unexpected
turn of events, Ōmura provides the link between Okuni and Hideyoshi.
Without the link between Ōmura and Okuni, the reader would not have
the opportunity to see such a scathing analysis of Hideyoshi through the
eyes of the protagonist. As the troupe members' fortune changes with the
generous support of their new patron, Hideyoshi also rises in status. And
although the members of the troupe never perform for Hideyoshi, they
live for a time with his close strategist, Kuroda Kanbei, and they perform
for his adopted son, Hideyasu, and for his mistress Ochacha. By consistently being in such close proximity to Hideyoshi, Okuni and her troupe
mates are able to offer extensive commentary on the man and his regime.
Furthermore, by starting her novel with Hideyoshi's dubious biographer,
Ariyoshi alerts readers that she, too, intends to question the reliability of
history told by men. In this case, however, she does so by using the critical voice provided by a childless and homeless dancer from Izumo. Ariyoshi uses the story of Okuni to make two major criticisms. First, by looking at the effects (both intended and unintended) of Hideyoshi's policies
through the eyes of peasants and street performers, she gives critical voice
to those affected by the changes wrought by Hideyoshi, calling into question his status as great leader and hero. Second, by drawing consistent
parallels between the relationships Hideyoshi had with women and the
relationships between Okuni's lover Sankuro and the other women with
whom he consorted, Oan and Okiku, Ariyoshi uses her perspective as a
woman writer in the 1970s to make a larger statement about the oppressive nature of sixteenth-century gender roles and, by implication, their
parallels in contemporary Japan.

Her freedom to move beyond standard societal constructs gives
Okuni the opportunity to be critical in unexpected ways. Because she
and her troupe travel between Osaka, Kyoto, and Edo to perform, they

have opportunities to engage in bleak discussions with a wide range of audience members about how Hideyoshi's new laws have impacted them. After one performance, Sanemon, the troupe's original leader, wades into the crowd to try to learn more about the plight of farmers under Hideyoshi's new land measurement and registry system. They have the following exchange:

> "We don't know why, but life has become more difficult than it used to be," said one old farmer.
>
> Peasants in Hideyoshi's realm were particularly susceptible to his policies, but they expressed deep doubt about them.
>
> "Recently we were ordered to turn over our plows and hoes."
>
> When Sanemon heard one of them say this, he was incredulous and asked "What? Why? How will you be able to farm?"
>
> "Every sword, spear, and gun was counted and collected as well. They said farmers can't have things made of iron."
>
> "Swords and spears are not the same thing as hoes and plows."
>
> "I heard that they were going to make hoes and plows out of swords and spears."
>
> "What? That doesn't make sense."
>
> The farmers were very confused.[48]

Throughout the novel, scenes in which Okuni, the members of her troupe, their family members, or people in their audience express grave concerns, if not outright criticism, illustrate how the changes being wrought by Hideyoshi caused great suffering for members of the lowest ranks of society. Several men from Izumo die while helping build castles for Hideyoshi. The performers in Okuni's troupe become unable to return home because they are out of their district and not counted in the new census that simultaneously assigns each person to a fixed social group. Farmers in Izumo and elsewhere are crushed under the weight of taxes that result from the land reforms established by Hideyoshi. All of these changes are seen through the filter of Okuni, and her sharp criticism of these new policies effectively deconstructs the actions of men in power.

However, Ariyoshi does not merely describe these policies and how they impact her characters. She also has her characters voice clear criticism of the changes and of Hideyoshi himself. By having characters of such low

social standing respond so negatively to Hideyoshi's policies, Ariyoshi
writes a counterhistory of him. Sometimes these criticisms are under-
stated. When Okuni hears the decree forbidding farmers from leaving
their fields and samurai from leaving castle towns, as well as threatening to
kill anyone who aids or hides runaways, she voices the concerns of the
troupe when she asks, "What are we?"[49] Because they are not warriors,
farmers, merchants, or servants to a lord, the members of the troupe have
nowhere to go, so they continue to live and work together despite the decree. Eventually, they are run off by elders and farmers in the neighbor-
hood where they settle. The dancers industriously plant wheat near the old
abandoned farmhouse they inhabit, but the residents worry that allowing
them to farm this land goes against the decree and force them to harvest
the wheat before it is ready. The narrator points out the irony, stating, "No
one seemed to notice Hideyoshi's plan [to force farmers to stay on their
land to increase productivity] was having the completely opposite effect."[50]
When Okuni and the other members of her troupe initially set out from
Izumo, they head toward the capital in the hope of making enough money
to support themselves and the family members they left behind, but the
changing circumstances characteristic of Hideyoshi's rule leave them in a
social and economic limbo that makes subsistence nearly impossible.

Other criticisms are not as veiled. Not only are the lower classes in
Ariyoshi's novel, represented by Okuni, dissatisfied with how the constantly changing laws impact their everyday lives, they are also disturbed
and perplexed by how Hideyoshi seems to treat those closest to him. Ariyoshi describes in gruesome detail the murder of the women and children
of Hidetsugu, Hideyoshi's heir.

"It looks like the rumors are true after all. Near Sanjo Bridge soldiers are
guarding a large, square pit with a mound of dirt piled on the east side of
it." . . .

When they heard that Hidetsugu's life alone wouldn't satiate Hideyoshi's anger and that Hidetsugu's mistresses, servants, and children would
also be punished, Okuni and her troupe mates had trouble believing it.
They decided to go see for themselves. . . .

Okuni saw something small that was on display and stared at it
curiously.

"Ah!" she said, the blood draining from her face.

"What's wrong?"

"That's, that's. . . ."

"Yes, it's the regent's head. It's the vengeance of heaven," Sankuro replied evenly.

On the freshly constructed mound, facing west, Hidetsugu's head had changed colors, baked in the searing heat of the summer sun. It looked like a purple chunk of meat. . . .

Hidetsugu's family members were brought out from the luxurious Juraku Mansion crammed in threes and fours on carts, children shoved together with their parents, and taken to the place of execution.

Except for [Hidetsugu's widow] who calmly prayed while steadily looking at her husband's head, the other women were filled with such fear that they became paralyzed even as they got off the carts. . . .

They first grabbed the children, slashing each of them twice before throwing them into the pit. Thus, the pandemonium began. There were some who resigned themselves to join the regent while many others, forgetting they were trapped, blindly tried to flee. Soldiers caught them by their long hair and cut them down with one or two strokes of the sword even as the women still screamed. All who were watching were too shocked to utter a word. . . .

In no time at all, thirty-nine ladies from Juraku Mansion and Hidetsugu's three young sons were slaughtered and dumped into the pit at Sanjo Bridge.[51]

The senseless cruelty of this scene, which is spelled out in excruciating detail, provides readers with a rare glimpse of an event that is either ignored or glossed over in most fictionalized retellings of Hideyoshi's life. By exposing the violence and seeming irrationality in Hideyoshi's leadership at this point, Ariyoshi underscores the cruelty of patriarchal rule and highlights the truncated narratives upon which much of sixteenth-century history is based as being incomplete—or worse, purposefully deceptive.

By inserting stories often missing from narratives that present Hideyoshi as a hero, Ariyoshi subverts the typical approach used when writing about him, an approach that often overlooks his illogical behavior, his overuse of violence, and the many ways he squanders various resources in his quest for greatness. Describing the elite cherry blossom viewing he hosted at Daigo-ji Temple in the spring of 1598, Ariyoshi avoids the praise and sense of awe often used to depict it and instead focuses on the sheer wastefulness and disenfranchisement such behavior caused for many living in Hideyoshi's realm. For this event, Hideyoshi had hundreds of cherry trees transplanted and had all of the gardens and surrounding buildings renovated. He also insisted that a series of checkpoints be established so that the uninvited could not attend.[52] The extravagance and exclusiveness of this event stand in stark contrast to the experiences of the commoners described in Ariyoshi's book and elicits their ire.

Okuni's reaction to and the narrator's description of this elaborate event that occurred even as Japanese troops were fighting and dying in Korea provide equally sharp criticism:

> "Flower viewing?" Okuni asked, frowning. "But what about the war in Korea?"
>
> Okuni wasn't the only one who thought this was strange, for Hideyoshi's behavior was puzzling indeed. Even Kanbei, a faithful supporter of Hideyoshi, was amazed by the Lord's behavior as he watched his cherry trees being uprooted. Kanbei received almost daily reports telling him that they were mired in their second campaign in Korea and likely to lose. . . . Kanbei knew that only Hideyoshi's closest vassals from western Japan were fighting in this second campaign. . . . Kanbei imagined that Tokugawa Ieyasu, who managed not to become embroiled in Hideyoshi's Korea plans, might one day rule. . . . As he said goodbye to his beloved cherry trees, Kanbei was struck with the realization that even this flower won't bloom forever.[53]

By portraying his policies, his actions, and even his most so-called heroic moments as anything but, Ariyoshi systematically and repeatedly questions Hideyoshi's historical significance.

This subversion of a male-dominated narrative is perhaps most obvious when the narrator describes Okuni's impression after seeing Hideyoshi in person for the first time: "He carried a six-foot sword in a gold scabbard at his waist. It was so much longer than his scrawny body that people couldn't help but wonder how he was able to draw it in battle. He was an upstart, a peasant gaudily decked out in gold."[54] This is the only time in the text when the figure of Hideyoshi appears in the flesh, and he is described as too weak and small to draw his own sword. Okuni and her friends are shocked at how meek Hideyoshi seems, and Okuni wonders why they would ever want to perform for such an unimpressive man. This emasculating description of Hideyoshi as he is seen through the eyes of

Okuni shifts the historical narrative away from talks of great battles and powerful leaders and toward this dismantling of gendered narratives of Japan's past.

In Ariyoshi's text, hypermasculine pursuits such as fighting battles and building castles are depicted as frivolous activities completely disconnected from everyday life. Okuni sees some of the best-known battles in Japanese history, but instead of being impressed by their significance, she experiences them as entertainment. When Okuni and her cohort go out to watch Hideyori's troops attack the lightly guarded Fushimi Castle, for example, they experience it much like one might a picnic or festival:

> Early in the afternoon of September 7, 1600 (the seventh month of Keichō 5), they started walking toward Fushimi. . . . In the evening, they arrived at a spot overlooking the Fushimi Castle. . . . Small fires burned here and there making it glow brightly, and the vividness of the scene below took their breath away. Troops in the castle pushed the advancing army back with their spears, and in the glow of the fire, the sight of them being cut down was like something from a children's play. The sounds of gunfire, the crush of attacking soldiers, the beating of battle drums, and the moaning conch shells drifted up to them. . . . The vast crowd of spectators surrounding Okuni and her friends breathlessly watched the scene below from the shadow of a large warehouse.[55]

First Hideyoshi's leadership and then, more generally, men's penchant for fighting and castle building are deconstructed through the lens of Okuni's experience of them. With her troupe members, she discusses who is winning and who is losing, but in the end, the reader is reminded that the change in leadership will mean very little to her life:

> Fushimi Castle burned and fell. After that, Okuni couldn't help but think about how useless castles were. Since coming to the capital, Okuni had witnessed the construction of Yodo Castle and saw it destroyed. She had seen Hideyoshi build Juraku Mansion and then dismantle it. And as soon as Hideyoshi died, Fushimi Castle, even more splendid than Juraku . . . became the sight of another battle as Hideyoshi's men fought and died there with the castle burning to the ground around them. What good do castles do? The first thing a man in power does is build a castle, and when he loses that power, the castle is the first thing that is destroyed.[56]

To Okuni and her troupe mates—who have much more pressing concerns, such as where they will live and how they will make enough money to feed themselves—the creation and destruction of castles seems like nothing but an extravagant game.

Popular with her largely male audiences because of the alluring ways she moves her body on stage, the historical Okuni has often been shunned and treated as a common prostitute. In Ariyoshi's interpretation, however, this is a role that Okuni adamantly rejects, demonstrating her unwillingness to have her body co-opted by her male-dominated society. Okuni is critical of other women who use their bodies to gain favors, a point made clear when the young troupe member she has been mentoring accepts an invitation to give a solo performance for a nobleman. Okuni is equally critical of women from a nearby house of prostitution who open a theater near hers and copy her dance moves in an attempt to lure more customers. Ariyoshi's decision to portray Okuni as a woman who remains faithful to one man not only subverts the common view that the historical Okuni was a prostitute but also enables the character of Okuni to become a voice of criticism for the plight of all women.

Okuni's position as trendsetting artist and outspoken critic of her society creates a situation in which an unmarried, poor, itinerate performer holds power over some of the greatest men of her time. Okuni's troupe advertises her as being the "best in the world."[57] This phrase, intended to attract an audience to the troupe's shows, also signifies just how unusual Okuni's situation is. The theme of Okuni as "best in the world" persists throughout the novel and demands that readers consider the irony in the fact that a woman who is homeless, ultimately unlucky in love, and unable to produce a child (having miscarried) can put Hideyoshi's mistress in her place and reduce his adopted son to tears. The men in this story of Okuni's life often comment on the fact that though she is a woman, she has surpassed them in terms of her success.

The repetition of this theme of a beggar woman as "best in the world" sets up a dynamic in which even those who are of much higher rank feel inferior to Okuni. Indeed, Okuni's strength compels Sankuro to leave her for another woman, and her success drives her subsequent lover, Nagoya Sanza, to leave her to pursue the life of a bureaucrat. When Okuni explains to Sanza how her success brought Hideyasu to tears, he succumbs to similar sentiments of inferiority:

"Sanza, if I've done something to upset you, please tell me what it is." Okuni didn't think she had done anything wrong, but she wasn't sure what else to say. . . .

"It's not a matter of you doing something to bother me or not. You were already the best in the world when I met you," Sanza replied after a long silence.

"What does that mean?" Okuni replied. . . .

Sanza took a deep breath and sighed, saying, "My dream, as a man, is to build a castle . . ."

"A castle?!" Okuni shouted reflexively, surprised to hear those words cross Sanza's lips. . . . She thought only those vying to become the leader of the realm built castles. . . .

Talking to Okuni, Sanza couldn't help but recall how Okuni described the way that Hideyasu wept when she danced for him. Sanza understood Hideyasu's pain at not becoming the best in the world like Okuni. . . . Wasn't he, Sanza, the same? . . . Perhaps he was merely the man who is loved by the best woman in the world.[58]

Several times in the novel, Okuni asks, "What is a lord of the realm anyway?"[59] This question is less about semantics—she understands the words—and more about her inability to conceptualize a "great man." She is questioning how any of the fallible men who populate this novel can claim to rule the entire realm, especially when the distance between the person in power and the real lives of those she encounters on a daily basis is so great. When Okuni and others climb up to the shrine to Hideyoshi (Toyokuni Shrine) following the fall of the Toyotomi clan, they discover that the elaborate gate at the entrance has been dismantled and moved to an island in Lake Biwa—a physical and metaphorical move of Hideyoshi from the center of Japan to its periphery. Okuni notes how quickly Hideyoshi has fallen from grace: "What she discovered when she got to the top of the stone steps leading to the shrine was that Hideyoshi was most certainly dead and gone. . . . Men's minds change with the times as quickly as you can turn your palm up or down."[60] Okuni's dismay at how quickly men's fortunes change is a comment on the absurdity of the hypermasculinity of a patriarchal society that drives men to kill one another to claim more land and build bigger castles.

But this criticism of men's battles and the resultant rapidly changing forces also speaks to the point that Nagai makes when talking about the battles between Onene and Ochacha: if absurd patriarchal norms are bad for men, they are worse for women. Okuni's trouble with men in Ariyoshi's novel highlights the fact that women, no matter what their status, have very little control over their relationships or whether or not they succeed as wives and mothers. Whether a woman is a poor itinerant performer like Okuni or has a high rank like Onene and Ochacha, she is still circumscribed by her sex and subject to the whims of the men around her. Bound by common-law marriage to the troupe leader, Sankuro, Okuni believes that he is as committed to her as she is to him, so she is shocked to learn long into their relationship that he has a wife in Osaka. Upon learning this, Okuni experiences an uncomfortable combination of feelings—jealousy, pity, and superiority—toward Sankuro's wife, Oan. Although Okuni sees Oan as a rival, she also pities her, knowing that both women face the same fate of being abandoned by a man they trusted. At various points in the novel, when Okuni sees men perpetrating evil against women, she visualizes Oan in the midst of the suffering. For example, when Hidetsugu's women and children were brutally murdered, Okuni thinks she sees Oan among them.[61] When Sankuro leaves Okuni for a younger member of their troupe, Okuni is both furious and resigned because she believes that all women are ultimately enslaved by the fickle nature of men.

Ariyoshi used this stereotypical trope of an older woman being supplanted by a younger beauty to illustrate that even the best in the world can fall victim to the injustices that plague all women, and she expands on this theme by drawing parallels between Okuni's struggles and those of Hideyoshi's women. Talking about Ochacha, Okuni remarks that even the mother of Hideyoshi's heir has to worry about other women stealing her man. Throughout the novel, Okuni sees links between herself and Ochacha. News of Ochacha's first pregnancy (with Tsurumatsu) spreads just as Okuni realizes that she is pregnant, too. Although Ochacha's pregnancy is met with celebration and a sense of hope, Okuni's pregnancy is doomed from the start while she struggles to survive and to secure love and support from Sankuro. Okuni is shocked to learn that Hideyoshi is building a castle on the Yodo River just for his concubine and expected heir. "'What kind of castle is built just so a woman can have a baby,' she wondered deep in her heart and suddenly decided she must go to see it for herself."[62] Driven by her need to understand what it would be like to be one of Hideyoshi's women, Okuni sets out in the snow to view the castle under construction. When Tsurumatsu dies not long after birth, Okuni, who has had a miscarriage, believes this is proof of an inextricable link between herself and Ochacha. Although Ochacha eventually manages to have a son who survives (Hideyori), Okuni is convinced that in their roles as wives, lovers, and (potential) mothers, the two of them are bound by a common suffering. Thus, according to Ariyoshi's novel, the powerlessness to break free of the expectations of patriarchal society and to live equally with men does not discriminate based on age, rank, or pedigree.

Conclusion

Nagai's *Ōja no tsuma* and Ariyoshi's *Izumo no Okuni* both end with the death of their eponymous heroines, who have outlived Hideyoshi by many years. Although Onene and Okuni prove to be clever, perceptive, persevering, and brave, they are hampered by their inability to bear children as well as their inability to reach out to and build alliances with other women. Still, despite their marginalized positions, both women manage to rise to the top, Okuni as a "best in the world" performer and Onene as the woman who advised male supporters of Hideyoshi's legacy through the transition into the Edo period. Though at first these characters may not seem as subversive as their 1960s and 1970s literary counterparts, their sustained criticism of Hideyoshi and their society, as well as their ability to succeed outside of a social structure that viewed women primarily as bearers of children, ultimately serves to challenge patriarchal structures while also deconstructing well-known narratives of the past. With these two novels, Nagai and Ariyoshi offer readers protagonists who challenge the economies of power and expose the numerous weaknesses in histories told about and by men. Through their accounts of these two failed mothers, Nagai and Ariyoshi introduce a Japanese past that is no longer dominated by great men but by hardworking, beleaguered women who are able to succeed—not in spite of the fact that they were not mothers but because of it.

CHAPTER 5

Things Best Left Unseen

The Problem of Hideyoshi in the Twenty-First Century

The preceding chapters looked at how Hideyoshi's image was re-shaped and reimagined in wartime and during the postwar period. But, as Tsutsui Yasutaka, Nagai Michiko, and Ariyoshi Sawako show, using Hideyoshi as a symbol for Japanese progress and success can be problematic. All three writers ask what is at stake when people rely on stories of a samurai past for inspiration or guidance. In this chapter, we consider what happens when Hideyoshi's contested figure makes its way to the twenty-first century, a time when Japanese leaders are intent on promoting a positive image to the world in efforts to benefit from in-creased tourism dollars.

Starting in 2002, as Japan headed deeper into its aging and depopulation crisis, the government began to focus on popular culture as a draw for the promotion of domestic and international tourism.[1] In that year, Prime Minister Jun'ichiro Koizumi declared that Japan was an "intellectual-property based nation," encouraging movement away from a focus on industry to a focus on so-called soft power and "Japan's Gross National Cool."[2] Philip Seaton and Takayoshi Yamamura explain the impact of these changes: "In 2003, there was a restatement of an ambitious target to attract 10 million international tourists a year to Japan by 2010, and the focus of national branding began the shift from traditional culture to a blend of traditional and pop culture. Mimicking the 'Cool Britannia' campaign in the UK, Japan started to be promoted with the slogan 'Cool Japan.'"[3] Part of this move to promote tourism has been a focus on how Japanese popular culture and films can attract domestic and international visitors to sites related to well-known manga, anime, and weekly television dramas. This "contents tourism" is a "cornerstone of Japan's economic plan" and is expected to help drive international and domestic tourism.[4]

Koizumi's goal of ten million international tourists annually by 2010 echoes a similar goal set fifty years before, when Prime Minister Hayato Ikeda announced plans to double national income within a decade. Ikeda's plan was meant to boost production and consumption and serve as a revival strategy for a nation in ruins, and Koizumi's proclamation can be read in a similar way. After all, how can a country with limited natural resources and a shrinking and aging population flourish in the twenty-first century if not by heavily promoting its cultural exports?

Given the already significant challenges of representing Hideyoshi's problematic history in contemporary Japan, the national move toward promoting a cool and hip Japan to international tourists makes telling his story even more complicated. Hideyoshi, Japan's first aggressor in East Asia, has not been well received by Japan's neighbors. As a result, the focus on using "cool Japan" promotions to help facilitate more tourism seems to have led to a transition in the way historical narratives are told at places that have a close connection to Hideyoshi. This chapter focuses on two of these sites—Kōdaiji Temple and Saga Nagoya Castle Museum—as they seek to remain relevant and aware of consumers' needs while also managing the challenges caused by Hideyoshi's legacy in East Asia. At both places, the influence that popular culture has on the presentation and representation of Hideyoshi is clear, as they make efforts to reach both younger and international visitors.

Sometimes Hideyoshi's visibility or invisibility occurs in the most unexpected places: at Saga Nagoya Castle, where he launched his two unsuccessful invasions of Korea, his image is all but missing, and at Kōdaiji Temple, with which he was not closely associated (but where Onene spent the years after his death), he seems ever present. In cases like this, it is clear that the image of Hideyoshi is being manipulated in an effort to attract tourist dollars. Over the past ten years or so, Nagoya Castle Museum, in Saga prefecture, and Kōdaiji Temple, in Kyoto, have undergone transformations in the narratives they tell about Hideyoshi, reflecting the ways in which historical sites adapt to address consumers' interests or desires. By drawing upon the government's emphasis on soft power and "cool Japan," as well as on the popularity of contents tourism and the *yurukyara* ("wobbly" mascot) boom, both sites offer an unexpected counternarrative in their efforts to attract young and international tourists as a way of surviving and thriving in a depopulating and aging nation. Furthermore, the ways in which both sites play with visibility and invisibility emphasize the challenges that warrior heroes of the past like Hideyoshi present even today.

Sites to Remember, Sites to Forget

In many ways, the most contradictory rewritings of Hideyoshi have come at sites of remembrance such as his castle museums in Nagoya, Saga prefecture, and Nagahama, in Shiga prefecture, and the Toyokuni shrines built in his honor in Nagoya and Kyoto. Whereas serialized literature, television, manga, and other media allow for a mediated interpretation of Hideyoshi that can be edited to suit the needs of the writer and facilitate the story they want to tell, narratives told at sites of historical significance find it more difficult to modify the story they tell. Although time may help people forget the violent events of sixteenth-century life that occurred at some of these locations, those events cannot be erased or elided from the historical record, just as physical spaces cannot simply cease to exist. In the case of Hideyoshi, this has resulted in increasingly ambiguous representations of him at these sites. As noted above, he is visible where he should not be and invisible where he should be visible.

The story of the decline of the Toyokuni shrine in Kyoto not long after Hideyoshi's death highlights the challenges these sites can represent. As demonstrated in chapter 1, in the years immediately after he died, Hideyoshi was worshipped at the Toyokuni shrine in Kyoto, usually with great fanfare, until the Tokugawa closed the shrine in 1615 after the Toyotomi clan's final defeat. In the intervening fifteen years, however, the shrine served not only as a poignant reminder of the power of Hideyoshi but also as a psychological anchor for the Toyotomi resistance. The story of this shrine is one of many examples of how complicated historical sites can become. In its heyday, the shrine was one of the centers of religious

FIGURE 5.1   Mimizuka (Mound of ears), near the Toyokuni shrine in Kyoto. Photo by author.

and social activity in Kyoto, so the degree to which it has declined is striking.

Today, for example, the grounds at the shrine tend to be desolate, many of the structures are in need of paint, and every time I have been there, I was the only visitor. Furthermore, across the street from the shrine entrance, beside an empty park lined with taxi drivers taking naps and often overgrown by weeds, sits a grassy mound in need of mowing. Occasionally, I have encountered a group of Korean tourists at the mound, but often it is completely abandoned.[5] A plaque commemorating the site as Hideyoshi's famous Mimizuka (Mound of ears) explains that the ears (or, more accurately, the noses) of Koreans killed in battle were buried there at Hideyoshi's order as a way to signify the superior strength of the Japanese during the two invasions of Korea in the late sixteenth century (fig. 5.1).

Like the shrine across the street, the mound appears also to have been largely forgotten. Each year, I give students an assignment in which they

FIGURE 5.2   A child plays at Mound of Ears Park, next to Mimizuka. Photo by author.

have to find little-known places in Kyoto. Using hints, students must locate their assigned spot and determine its significance in relation to local or national history. Mimizuka is always a challenging one. It does not appear readily in tourist information, though it has become slightly easier to find since first appearing in *Atlas Obscura* in 2016.[6] Even when students manage to make their way to the temple area, they often cannot locate the mound. Furthermore, inquiries to passersby about its location tend to yield poor results. People often do not really want to talk about it. Google and Trip Advisor reviews of the site highlight the discomfort it causes Japanese tourists, who call it "Japan's black history," "a well-kept but terrifying memorial," and "a shameful historical relic."[7] One visitor described being too afraid to go near it, as she feared the murderous looks in the eyes of the foreign tourists she saw there, and another described getting lost at twilight in Kyoto and accidentally coming across the mound.[8] The latter visitor writes, "I remember walking away from it half-crying because of a sense of terror I couldn't put into words."[9] Although others describe the site simply as a beautiful spot or just another example of how different the past was from the present, the uncanny nature of the space speaks to the ambivalence of Hideyoshi's legacy in the twenty-first century (fig. 5.2).

At Nagahama Castle Museum, which commemorates Nagahama (located in northeastern Shiga prefecture, on Lake Biwa) as a castle town built by Hideyoshi in 1573, the curator Ota Hiroshi points out the contradictory impulses of visitors to the site: "Even today Hideyoshi is a hero in Nagahama. But the despotic Hideyoshi is not accepted as part of the success story."[10] According to Ota, visitors to the museum often choose not to engage in discussions of Hideyoshi's more despotic years in a way similar to Yoshikawa Eiji's decision to end his novel when Hideyoshi reaches the apex of power and before he starts his spectacular decline. However, Ota argues that in twenty-first-century Japan, the choice not to talk about Hideyoshi's troubled final years is done with full disclosure. Not talking about the past is an option, but ignoring it is not. This change in the way Hideyoshi's life is perceived indicates a larger shift in the way his role in history is understood today. As Ota insinuates, manipulation of the Hideyoshi narrative seems to be necessary for the success of sites dedicated to him.

Virtual Hero

Saga Nagoya Castle Museum (fig. 5.3) is perched precariously on the fine line between its stated goal of facilitating stronger Japan-Korea relations and telling the history of the site upon which it sits. Memorialization at this site risks memorializing the problematic moments in Japanese-Korean relations, including the annexation of Korea in 1910 and the use of conscripted Korean soldiers during World War II. Hideyoshi's relative absence here highlights the complexities of this narrative tension.[11]

FIGURE 5.3   Exterior of the Saga Nagoya Castle Museum. Photo by author.

Nagoya Castle was built in 1591 in Hizen domain just outside of what is now Karatsu City in Saga prefecture. As Hideyoshi amassed a large number of troops there, the castle town became one of the largest and most vibrant cities in the world at the time. On a clear day, you can look from the castle site and see the island of Iki, about one-fourth of the way between mainland Japan and the Korean peninsula. At the site, the only building is the castle museum, which has a well-appointed modern design and a sloping green roof and stone that helps it blend into the hill behind it.

According to the museum's English-language guide, the museum's goal is to foster better relations and exchange between Japan and Korea: "There is a long history of exchange between the people of the Japanese Archipelago and the Choson Peninsula. The Bunroku/Keicho Campaign (Im Jin/Jong Yu Oe Ran, or Hideyoshi Invasion) was a sad event that temporarily severed that relationship. By examining the war and clarifying the role of Nagoya Castle in it, Nagoya Castle Museum aims to promote mutual exchange and friendship between two states."[12] Promoting Japan-Korean friendship at the site from which Hideyoshi's troops set out to attack the Korean peninsula is difficult. Not only is the museum problematic because it touts Japan-Korea friendship on the very site from which Hideyoshi's invasions were launched, but it also risks oversimplifying the relationship between the two nations by describing it as being generally free of tension.

The curators of the museum, all prefectural government employees, have sought to manage the tension between telling Hideyoshi's history and promoting friendship in two central ways. First, the museum narrative expressed in the permanent exhibit centers on the long history of positive exchange between Japan and South Korea. Second, images of conflict are either omitted or contextualized in ways that subsume them to the larger museum's narrative of peace.[13] Though the goals of the museum—to save artifacts and materials related to the invasion of the Korean peninsula and to promote Japanese-Korean friendship—seem contradictory, visitor numbers indicate that the museum is managing to strike a workable balance between the two. Each year, despite its remote location thirty minutes by car from the nearest train station (much longer when traveling by city bus), approximately 90,000 people visit the museum annually. Four percent of those visitors come from abroad, and a significant portion of those (three thousand) come to the museum each year as part of package tours from Pusan or Seoul. Based on an interview with the educational curator, Hisano Tetsuya, in the summer of 2016, I learned that most Korean visitors are drawn to the museum because it is free, it has Korean-language materials readily available, and it is a popular stop for Korea-based trekking tours. The special exhibits and long-term collaboration between this museum and related ones in Korea are also draws.

Though the museum seeks to "promote mutual exchange and friendship" between Japan and Korea by "clarifying the role of Nagoya Castle," any discussion of positive Japan-Korea relations proves complicated for several reasons. First, in the context of later Japanese militarism, Hideyoshi's invasions of Korea have been interpreted over time as Japan's first attempt to gain dominance in East Asia, and the fact that the invasions led to a partial incursion on the Korean peninsula has been seen as having paved the way for nineteenth- and twentieth-century annexation and colonization. Talking about the role of Hideyoshi's castle without attempting to unpack its later significance undermines attempts at openness and reconciliation. Second, by focusing on the archaeological site instead of the people and policies involved in the decision to invade the Korean peninsula at the end of the sixteenth century, the museum becomes another example of how agency and responsibility have been removed from discussions of Japanese wartime agression. This approach has led to international criticism of Japan's ability and/or willingness to properly atone for Japanese aggressions in East Asia—particularly during World War II. Third, even though the castle was built by Hideyoshi, his nebulous role as an icon in twentieth- and twenty-first century Japan is further clouded by his ambiguous presence in the space.

The strategy of minimizing difficult moments of the past by portraying them as if they are only a small part of a much larger story has been employed by many museums. However, in focusing the museum's narrative on the castle's role in history, narrowly defined, its curators essentially remove all of the people who were involved in this history, perpetuating a narrative that removes human agency and downplays the significance of these moments in the history of East Asia. Allowing the historical narrative to speak for itself effectively removes bad actors: a battle was launched and people died, but the site and the actors remain somehow blameless.

This parallels a common refrain regarding Japan's agency during World War II. Talking about that war, Akiko Takenaka notes that when there is limited or no human agency in narratives, it is easier for Japanese people to see themselves as uninvolved—or, worse, as the victims of wars their ancestors helped create. She explains: "This is due, in part, to the structure of the Japanese language that allows for complete sentences without explicit active subjects, but it also conveniently supports the 'being tricked' sentiment shared by a large component of the survivor generation. . . . The war happened, the bombs dropped; war is bad because people suffer as a result. This kind of narrative places the blame on war and weapons, rather than on the people who made the decisions."[14] Nagoya Castle Museum risks perpetuating these types of narratives, first by choosing to tell the story of the castle site without fully explaining the role of Hideyoshi and sixteenth-century Japanese thinking in this history, and second by failing to fully acknowledge the provocative role these invasions played in subsequent decades (particularly up to and including World War II, when Hideyoshi's invasions of Korea were interpreted as exemplary military successes). Look again at the introduction to the museum: "There is a long history of exchange between the people of the Japanese Archipelago and the Choson Peninsula. The Bunroku/Keicho Campaign . . . was a sad event that temporarily severed that relationship." By limiting Hideyoshi's unprovoked invasions of Korea to being "a sad event that temporarily severed" a much longer and generally positive relationship between Japan and Korea, the museum sets itself up to tell a skewed history of the site.

The layout of the permanent exhibit highlights the way that the years of Japanese aggression, including Hideyoshi's invasions, are subsumed into a much larger story. The exhibit hall is a large open space of overlapping diamond-shaped rooms, which visitors traverse in a clockwise direction from the entrance. The space is divided into four sections: "Before Nagoya Castle," "Nagoya Castle in History," "After Nagoya Castle," and "Special Historical Landmark: Nagoya Castle Ruins and the Encampment Sites." In the first section, the focus is on "the history of exchange between the Japanese archipelago and the Choson peninsula from the primitive periods to the middle ages."[15] In this part of the exhibit, visitors can view some of the earliest items exchanged between Japan and Korea. Letters sent between the two countries and travelogues written by early Korean visitors are also on display. This first section seeks to establish the long-standing relationship between the two countries, emphasizing a rich history of positive exchange.

The second section seems to anchor the museum, covering three walls at the far end of the exhibition space. One of the walls is devoted entirely to the specifics of Nagoya Castle, its construction, and the growth of the castle town around it. Another wall covers the Bunroku/Keicho Campaign, with screen paintings of battle scenes, some armaments, missives, and other documents from the time. The third wall underscores the cultural significance of the Momoyama period and displays items that highlight the high quality of pottery and textiles being produced at that time. Despite the fact that this part of the museum is dedicated to the years of the invasion, there is surprisingly little weaponry. Instead, the focus is on the town and culture that rose up around the castle.

Bits of Hideyoshi are present here. A copy of the *Toyotomi Hideyoshi-ga* (Portrait of Toyotomi Hideyoshi), a famous portrait of Hideyoshi in his later years that depicts him with unnaturally small hands and feet in the typical Momoyama style, hangs on the wall, and a replica of his

FIGURE 5.4   Models of a Japanese *atakebune* (left) and a Korean turtle boat at Saga
Nagoya Castle Museum. Photo credit Saga Nagoya Castle Museum.

well-known spiked helmet anchors a corner display. There is a wooden
statue of him as Taikō, and a *jin-baori* (surcoat) worn by him is displayed
as an example of Momoyama artistry. However, this space also contains
artifacts related to Yi Sun-shin, the Korean general whose maritime battle
skills helped hold off and eventually defeat the Japanese invaders. Besides
Yi's writings, the museum displays a painted scroll showing his likeness,
imprints from a memorial marker in his honor, replicas of his battle ban-
ner and weapons, and tributes awarded to Yi by China's Ming emperor.
This focus on Yi makes it seem as if he is somehow equally responsible
for the fact that these battles happened. In this way, Hideyoshi and Japan are once again let off the hook for war responsibility.

   The focus of the Bunroku/Keicho Campaign display, and indeed of
this section of the museum, is the large (one-tenth size) replicas of a Korean turtle ship and a Japanese *atakebune* in the middle of the room
(fig. 5.4).[16] Though the ships are similar in size, when they are placed side
by side, the inferior fighting capacity of the Japanese ship becomes clear

in comparison to the tall sails, dragon-shaped bow cannon, and spiked roof of the Korean ship. Visually, the turtle ship dominates the space, giving the section an even heavier emphasis on Korean representations of the battle and further overpowering any mention of Hideyoshi in the process. Not only is his presence dwarfed by that of Yi's ship, but the imbalance of power the two ships represent seems to highlight Hideyoshi's failures. He is quite literally minimized here.

The overall focus of this section on Nagoya Castle in history is not on the campaign but on the building of the castle town and the impact of Momoyama culture in Kyushu at the time, as well as on the ways that Korean culture positively influenced Japan in the years during and immediately after these invasions. References to Japanese aggression and Hideyoshi's role in it are not completely absent from the museum, but contextualized as they are by being surrounded by a far greater number of display items that are about neither war nor aggression, the overall effect is one of de-emphasis and even erasure.

This trend of de-emphasizing the sixteenth-century battles continues in the section around the corner. "After Nagoya Castle" is devoted to "materials that illustrate the reciprocal relationship between the Japanese archipelago and the Choson peninsula beginning from the arrival of the Choson envoy in Edo period (1615–1868) to modern times."[17] Four hundred years is a lot of ground to cover, and the result is a very cursory history of Japan-Korean relations following Hideyoshi's invasions. This allows (or perhaps causes) the museum to minimize moments of conflict between the two countries. Items displayed here include screens portraying visits by various Edo-era Korean envoys to Japan as well as examples of items exchanged between the two nations. There a single display case devoted to the deteriorating relationship between Japan and Korea in the twentieth century. It holds modern-day Japanese and Korean textbooks as well as textbooks that were used on the Korean peninsula during the colonial period. Looking at them side by side, visitors can compare how this period of time was and is taught in the two countries. Photos include an image of the Korean Imperial Palace with Japanese flags hanging outside and a group of March First Movement protesters in Seoul calling for independence from Japan. Explanations provided in Japanese and English (but not Korean) contextualize these pictures this way: "After the Meiji Restoration, Japan forced Choson to sign a series of unfair treaties: in 1910

Japan colonized the Choson peninsula. People of the Choson peninsula fiercely resisted the Japanese rule, participating in the nationalist independent movements, such as the March First Demonstration. However, Japan oppressed them thoroughly, transforming Koreans into Japanese imperial subjects and mobilizing them for forced labor and military service. The Japanese colonial rule for 35 years left many Koreans deeply scarred."[18] This explanation does important work in acknowledging Japanese expansionism and its impact on Korea in the first half of the twentieth century, but relegating such traumatic history to a single paragraph in a small display case risks alienating the very audience the museum hopes to reach. In a museum focused on improving relations between the two nations, a fuller frank discussion of how the moments of tension between the two nations have influenced and continue to shape East Asian politics seems necessary.

The fourth and final section of the permanent exhibit introduces visitors to the vast network of encampments that were established in Hizen at the time of the Bunroku/Keicho Campaign, emphasizing once again just how populated and strategic this region became at the time of the invasions. Ending with this focus on place and space, and on how Hideyoshi's decision to build a castle here led to the development of a thriving city, moves visitors beyond thoughts of failed exchanges and back to the stated goals of the museum: to preserve the castle's history and to support positive exchange between Japan and Korea.

On the whole, the museum manages to achieve its somewhat contradictory aims. With the predominance of the permanent exhibit space focused on the ongoing relations between the two countries over thousands of years, the implication is that the moments of conflict between the two—during the Bunroku/Keicho Campaign and from annexation in 1910 until the end of World War II—were relatively brief. As a result, the museum presents a narrative that occupies an awkward middle ground: it does not entirely ignore the nations' conflicts, but neither does it address them fully. Unable to completely divorce Hideyoshi from his castle and fearing that any overly positive depiction of him would prevent them from achieving their goals, the curators have left him present, but only as a shell.

Debates about whether or not to reconstruct the castle have been influenced by overwhelming pressure to leave this part of Japan's history

FIGURE 5.5   Saga Nagoya Castle ruins. Photo by author.

covered by the layers of time. On the grounds surrounding the museum, archaeologists work to unearth clues about the footprint of the original structures on the site (fig. 5.5). When I interviewed the head archaeologist about this task in 2006, he told me, "At least once a week, a Japanese visitor tells me to stop because some history is best left hidden."[19] As a compromise, archaeologists continue their work, but rather than reconstruct the buildings that once stood in these spaces, the data they gather has been used to create a virtual tour of the castle and surrounding outbuildings so that visitors who are interested can use museum iPads to explore what would have been there. Like much of the rest of the museum, this fascinating technology—which allows you to gaze out from the window of the museum's rest area, for example, and see the castle that once stood a hundred feet away—allows visitors to explore the space between what remains hidden and what is not.

Since 2015, visitors to the site have had access to this virtual tour. This liminal space—the castle is and is not there—symbolizes the way the history of Hideyoshi can never be uncontested, never be fully explicated in

FIGURE 5.6   View of Genkai Sea from Saga Nagoya Castle ruins. Photo by author.

representations of him today. This technology, much like Pokémon GO or other popular virtual reality games, allows visitors to traverse the castle grounds and see images of the buildings and streets that are not actually there. Looking at the iPad, visitors find themselves walking the streets of Hizen in the late sixteenth century, surrounded by the massive structures Hideyoshi created. Taking one's eyes off the screen brings one back to reality, where one is surrounded by beautiful vistas, rock outcroppings, and crumbling and covered remains but sees no magnificent castle (fig. 5.6). Anecdotally, during a visit to the museum on June 20, 2016, I spent two hours exploring and appreciating the space in ways I never had before, as the iPad in my hand took me to the far corners of the castle grounds (fig. 5.7).

Is this leaving history hidden or taking a cutting-edge approach to dealing with budgetary constraints and a desire to preserve a historical site? The museum's staff members would argue it is the latter. They observe that this technology allows visitors to experience the Nagoya castle of old without requiring a costly rebuilding process that would put the

FIGURE 5.7   An image of the virtual tour of Saga Nagoya Castle, with the castle remains visible in the background. Photo by author.

remains at risk. I would argue that it is both. The use of virtual reality to show the castle is cheaper than actually reconstructing it and targets a younger demographic, but it also results in keeping the controversial history of the space out of sight. Rebuilding the castle would honor Hideyoshi in a very visible way in which he is not honored now, and there would be no minimizing of him and his aggressive intentions. Thus, the symbolism at work here is hard to overlook.

As this technology demonstrates, the museum staff has relied on a combination of erasure and selective seeing to ultimately marginalize any narrative of Japan in the late sixteenth century that includes Hideyoshi and his quest to expand its borders into the rest of East Asia. The majority of the exhibit space focuses on the positive relations that have occurred over the many years of exchange between Japan and Korea. Unable to completely divorce Hideyoshi from his castle and knowing that any overly positive depiction of him would make it impossible to achieve their goals, curators have left him just vaguely present. The introduction of virtual technology has served to highlight the liminality of Hideyoshi in this space.

Samurai Cute

A different kind of narrative shift is happening at Kyoto's Kōdaiji Temple, where Onene lived after Hideyoshi's death. Whereas Saga Nagoya Castle Museum struggles to contend with the violent history that the space represents, Kōdaiji seems to be attracting tourists by emphasizing parts of Hide-yoshi's history that are anachronistic to the temple. While Hideyoshi is missing from a place where we would expect to find him at Saga Nagoya Castle, he is increasingly (and oddly) present at Kōdaiji, and his unexpected presence highlights the way the temple has sought to attract younger visitors.

As was common at the time, Onene removed herself from secular life when she became a widow. She lived at Kōdaiji until her death in 1624. Kōdaiji was established in 1606 and named after Onene, who was then known as Kōdai-in.[20] Tokugawa Ieyasu, Hideyoshi, and Kōdai-in have all been credited with the creation and patronage of Kōdaiji, and Kōdai-in's influence in its construction demonstrates the power she had.[21] The size and splendor of the temple and its grounds have been cited as a testament to her influence. In a world where it was difficult for women to amass power, a woman who had no male heir found herself in a vulnerable position once her husband was gone. Yet Onene lived to the age of seventy-six and remained influential in politics during some of the most significant years in Japanese history. As William Samonides argues, not only is Kōdaiji a testament to her resilience and commitment to carrying on the Toyotomi name, but it is also an excellent symbol of her power and wealth at a time when most women had very little of either.[22] At a time when women in general were relegated to the inner sanctums and were seldom to be seen or heard, and when childless women in particular were especially vulnerable once they no longer had the support of a father or husband, Onene's successes are particularly striking. These successes have traditionally been the focus of the stories docents tell at Kōdaiji.

Over the past ten years, however, the narrative of the temple has shifted from this emphasis on Onene's strength and wisdom to a narrative more focused on Hideyoshi and the fate of their relationship. Despite the fact that Onene and Hideyoshi never lived together at the temple, he has become more and more present there. Furthermore, at Kōdaiji, Hideyoshi is no longer a fierce warrior but a loving and supportive husband. This shift is particularly surprising, given the ways in which Hideyoshi is believed to have often abandoned Onene or overlooked her needs. Nobunaga's famous "bald rat" missive (discussed in chapter 4) is one historical source that calls into question any narrative that paints Hideyoshi as a doting spouse.

The cute-ification and idealization of the Hideyoshi and Onene narrative illustrates another way his image has transitioned into this century. This narrative turn is marked by a growing emphasis on romance and marriage for love (as opposed to the arranged political marriages common at the time). At the temple today, Onene and Hideyoshi's relationship is described as Japan's first love marriage. Along with this shift comes a seeming flood of cute, popular Onene and Hideyoshi goods as well as an increasing emphasis on the temple's growing wedding business.

Kōdaiji Temple sits at the foot of the Higashiyama Ryozen Mountains in Kyoto, not far from Yasaka and Hokanji Temples. Though located along one of the busiest tourist routes—between Kiyomizu Shrine and Maruyama Park—the temple grounds are a peaceful oasis. Today, the temple consists of six original structures: Kaisando (Founder's Hall), Otama-ya (Sanctuary), Kasatei (Teahouse), Shiguretei (Teahouse), Omotemon (Gate to the Sanctuary), and Kangetsudai (Moon Viewing Pavilion).[23] All of them have been designated Important Cultural Properties.[24] In many ways, Kōdaiji is a quintessential Kyoto temple. There, you can meditate next to one of Kyoto's finest *karesansui* (dry landscape) rock gardens, walk through a bamboo forest, take tea in one of Hideyoshi's teahouses, view various family treasures, buy trinkets at the gift shop, and enjoy a brief rest with matcha and vanilla soft-serve ice cream at the café. The temple is also famous for its preservation of the *Kōdaiji maki-e* black-and-gold lacquer design that graces structures throughout the temple grounds.[25] The temple's rich cultural heritage provides an interesting backdrop for the narrative shifts that have happened there over the past several years.

My first visit to Kōdaiji was in 2008, when I was beginning to explore Hideyoshi-related sites in Kyoto for my research. Even though it was rainy and late in the day when I arrived, two things struck me on my first encounter with the temple: the beauty of the landscape and buildings and how quiet and secluded it felt, despite its location in one of Kyoto's busiest tourist areas. The docents' narratives on that first visit were familiar ones. They talked of Onene's strength, highlighting the grace and poise that enabled her not only to survive the death of her husband but also to transition to a life at the temple that was both contemplative and highly successful. The guides also emphasized Onene's commitment to Hideyoshi, pointing out that her resting place high on the hill overlooking the temple grounds enabled her to keep watch over him in his grave at Hokokubyo, across the city and above Kyoto Women's University. This story of Onene's commitment to the life and death of her husband and of her strength and perseverance in a time when it was hard to be a woman and even harder to be a childless one has been a staple at Kōdaiji. Indeed, the impressive beauty of the temple and its buildings conveys the story of Onene's power to visitors today. Before the move toward an *en-musubi* (marriage or, more literally, tying together of destinies) narrative at the temple, this story of her determination and strength dominated.

When I went back to Kōdaiji in the fall of 2013, I discovered some surprising additions to the temple's aesthetic that pointed to a shift in the narrative that guides would tell about Onene. In particular, what I found there were side-by-side statues of Hideyoshi and Onene. In the "chibi-manga" style, with large heads and overly cute features, the statues are about two feet high and stand on a pedestal (bringing them to about elbow height) (fig. 5.8). What struck me most about the statues, aside from the fact Hideyoshi was there at all, was how happy they both looked. Upon closer inspection, I learned why. "Touch these beloved Buddhist statues and altar objects to earn merit," a nearby sign urged in English. "Wishing for a happy marriage just like Hideyoshi and Nene, who slipped through the Warring States period. Wishing for peaceful remaining years surrounded by many people like Nene" (fig. 5.9). Somehow, in the five years since I had last visited the temple, the narrative had changed from one about Onene's constancy and strength to one about her happy marriage or, a marriage so successful that others could earn merit by simply acknowledging it. In an attempt to attract visitors, therefore, the temple has not only altered the way it tells Onene's story, but it has also reintroduced Hideyoshi's—creating a sort of time warp in which Hideyoshi has returned from the dead and joined Onene at her widow's temple.

FIGURE 5.8 "Chibi" Buddhist statues of Onene and Hideyoshi at Kōdaiji. Photo by author.

With the introduction of the new statues, the temple's gift shop started to carry a series of cute-ified Hideyoshi and Onene goods for purchase. Even before this, the shop had a number of goods with Hello Kitty versions of Onene, but now there are also socks, cloth wraps, keychains, file folders, and towels with chibi-manga-style pictures of a grinning Onene with Hideyoshi lurking in the background or of Onene standing happily next to a somewhat fierce-looking Hideyoshi. The number of goods sold has continued to increase with the introduction of *yurukyara* mascots of Hideyoshi and Onene in 2015 (fig. 5.10).

The cute-ification of places and things in Japan is not new, and the *yurukyara* boom is in many ways its logical extension. *Yurukyara* are character mascots often designed by amateur artists and used to promote local cities, events, or goods. As Debra Occhi explains, "*Yurukyara* are *yurui* ('loose,' 'wobbly,' or 'slack') in comparison to more polished and better-known characters such as Hello Kitty."[26] The popularity of character goods and *yurukyara* mascots follows from an overall move toward the promotion of "cool Japan" and cultural goods as "soft power."[27] As Michal Daliot-Bul explains, Japan has been undergoing a transition away from the promotion of hard (or industrial or corporate) power and toward

FIGURE 5.9   Sign explaining the statues of Onene and Hideyoshi. Photo by author.

promoting "playful teen-centric products and services—fashion, tele-communication, entertainment and in particular the multimedia culture of anime, manga and computer and video games, including all related merchandising, collectibles and toys."[28] Images of corporate Japan have been replaced with "Cool Japan," and Japanese popular culture and goods have become some of Japan's greatest exports. Although the popularity of *kawaii* (cute) goods took off in the 1970s with the introduction of Hello Kitty and other characters, they soon "[jumped] beyond the bounds of children's goods into gradually more and more of the general adult world."[29] More recently, characters are used to soften the image of certain entities to make them more appealing to a broader market.

FIGURE 5.10   Hideyoshi and Onene *yurukyara* goods for sale at Kōdaiji. Photo by author.

The director of the temple cites the power of popular culture to draw in younger crowds when explaining his decision to introduce the *yurukyara* mascots at Kōdaiji. This focus on appealing to a younger audience certainly seems to align with a noticeable pattern at the temple in recent years: it has become popular for its night illuminations that are set up in the everchanging rock gardens and all around the grounds and has become a trendy date spot.[30] And in the summer of 2019, Mindar, a robot priest, was introduced by the temple in the hope of keeping it relevant even as the practicing population of Buddhists in Japan ages.[31] The temple also has a Facebook page and YouTube channel. All of these efforts and the introduction of chibi-manga characters and *yurukyara* mascots are clearly meant to increase visits to the temple.

By using *yurukyara* to appeal to young people's desire for cuteness and *kawaii* goods and by simplifying the complex and often violent history of a distant past into something much more palatable, the temple is following a well-known pattern.[32] *Yurukyara* mascots are ambassadors between something potentially unpleasant or scary and the general, money-paying audience. Noriko Manabe writes: "According to a survey by toy maker Bandai's Character Research Institute in 2004, character goods (e.g. stuffed toys, pencils, or other items with an imprint of the character) were popular among not only children but also adults, with 90 percent of women and 60 percent of men in their forties owning them. . . . This affection for characters has led corporations to use them to foster intimacy between their goods and consumers. . . . Local governments and organizations also employ *yurukyara*—'loose' or 'wobbly' characters—as mascots to create a favorable image of towns, local products or events."[33] Christine Yano observes: "[The] use of cute kyarakutā [characters] by governmental institutions 'softens' their image and message for the general populace. This is the affective labor of kawaii. Kyarakutā allow more typically distant, formal institutions, such as police departments, to seem congenial and approachable."[34] The Hideyoshi and Onene *yurukyara* mascots used at the temple were chosen from thousands of entries as part of the Gotochi-chara Grand Prix contest celebrating the twenty-fifth anniversary of the temple's opening to the public. The *yurukyara* versions of Onene and Hideyoshi can be seen on posters at the gate and throughout the temple complex. The fact that both mascots were designed by amateur artists (Onene's by Matsuo Ayako, from Fukuoka, and Hideyoshi's by Ono Masatō, from Tokyo)

FIGURE 5.11   Heart-shaped Hideyoshi and Onene *ema* from Kōdaiji. Photo by author.

highlights the accessibility to visitors of these two historical figures and the history they represent. If Onene and Hideyoshi can walk cheerfully among us today, the complicated and violent relationship Japan has had with East Asia (as represented by Hideyoshi) is potentially softened, or even forgotten. Temple staff members understand the value of tempering Hideyoshi's story, and what better way to do this than to create a Hideyoshi who is willing to come back, even from the dead, to be with his beloved Onene?

Of all the depictions of these *yurukyara* mascots available at the temple, the heart-shaped *ema* in bright pink lacquer with images of "wobbly" Onene and Hideyoshi plastered across one side perhaps best exemplifies the way the culture of cute has been mobilized to redeem Hideyoshi's image at the temple (see fig. 5.11). *Ema* are small wooden plaques that visitors use to write down the wishes or prayers they want to leave at the temple or shrine to be answered by the resident deity. *Ema* tend to be the wood's natural color and far from ostentatious. Not only are the new *ema* sold by Kōdaiji nothing like those found at other temples, they also seem to demand that visitors leave prayers related to romance or marriage (even the most cursory look at the messages left on these boards reveals that this seems to be the case), crowding out any potential for more

nuanced thoughts about life in the sixteenth century and the roles that
Hideyoshi and Onene played in it.

How and why has the temple's narrative changed so much in such a
short period of time? In many ways, what is happening at Kōdaiji mirrors
what is happening at other sites of contents tourism (*kontentsu tsūrizumu*)
in Japan. The term "contents tourism" refers broadly to the tourism in-
duced by popular culture and more specifically to the growing tourism
market that seeks to use the soft power of manga, anime, and other forms
of Japanese culture to attract visitors.[35] However, what we see at Kōdaiji is
a sort of reverse contents tourism. Tourists are not coming to Kōdaiji
because of something they saw in a manga or a popular drama, but when
they arrive, they are greeted with a fun and cute narrative that appeals to
them and works to continue building an audience.

According to docents at Kōdaiji, this *en-musubi* narrative has become a focus of the temple over the past ten years and the central focus
in the past five. They explained that the *en-musubi* narrative now used at
the temple makes it much easier for them explain the temple's significance to children and people who have no knowledge about Hideyoshi.
One argued that the *en-musubi* narrative was not much of a stretch. She
gave three reasons for this argument. First, the marriage between Onene
and Hideyoshi was one of the first love marriages (if not the first) in Japan. Second, throughout their marriage Onene and Hideyoshi helped
each other succeed, regardless of the various pressures being placed upon
them. And third, even though Hideyoshi behaved as other men of his
time did and had mistresses, he always valued and supported Onene.
The docents agree that Onene's successes after his death are a sign of how
he supported her and made sure her affairs were in order before he died.
Though this description of Hideyoshi and Onene's marriage is fairly
one-sided, one docent explained, "Young people today could learn a lot
from the example set by Onene and Hideyoshi. Men should seek to rise
up in the world (*shusse*) like Hideyoshi, and women should assert their
power in the background, supporting their husband and his men like
Onene did. The modern love story should look more like the relationship
between Hideyoshi and Onene and less like what people see on TV."[36]
Hideyoshi as *sakuhingun* is alive and well at Kōdaiji.

The constant and repeated presence of historical narratives in Japanese society, as realms of memory and/or *sakuhingun*, attracts curious

tourists to history-related sites that might otherwise have been forgotten. Philip Seaton and coauthors argue that Japanese history provides one type of content being pursued by contents tourists. Although much of contents tourism is associated with fictional pop culture and anime in particular, the authors found that representations of history in popular culture such as manga, anime, and the NHK's *Taiga dorama* have led to contents tourism at various heritage sites: "If we think of history as a story with historical characters performing important deeds in various locations, we can think of history as contents. The most famous events of Japanese history are depicted repeatedly across various media formats from television dramas to manga, and visitation to heritage sites in Japan is influenced by these depictions of history in popular culture."[37] Although they are not an example of a television show, manga, or anime attracting people to a site, the changes that have happened at Kōdaiji over the past five years reflect an intentional effort to combine a well-known, if slightly altered, narrative with popular cultural trends to draw visitors. With the changes, the story of Onene and Hideyoshi continues to be told, but it has necessarily taken on this veneer of romance that did not exist before.

The move to make Onene and Hideyoshi more relatable by altering the focus of the narratives told about them and making them impossibly cute coincides with a citywide effort to increase tourism among international and young visitors. When Daisuke Kadokawa was elected as Kyoto's mayor in 2008, the city was well on its way to reaching its goal of attracting fifty million tourists annually by 2010.[38] Since then, tourism has continued to increase, hitting 56.8 million in 2015. Given the city's population of just 1.4 million, the number of tourists in Kyoto can seem staggering. Most tourists to Kyoto are older Japanese domestic tourists who tend to come for just a day and to visit multiple times over their lives. One of the city's goals is to attract new and younger tourists—chiefly younger women. Due to Japan's promotion of itself as a tourism nation, the number of tourists in Japan has increased significantly over the past ten years, and in Kyoto, it has risen fivefold. The increase in tourists has been almost entirely in Asian tourists, as China's outbound tourism industry has boomed. Both of these trends—the increased focus on young women and the increased draw of tourists from Asia, particularly from China—help explain the kind of contents tourism–based market strategy in which Kōdaiji

seems to be engaged and how and why Hideyoshi has been transformed at the temple.

Conclusion

At popular sites related to Hideyoshi, the reliance on manipulating his
visibility or invisibility demonstrates how challenging his history can
be in the twenty-first century, particularly as Japan seeks to increase
tourism among young and nondomestic populations. Thus, the fact that
he continues to appear so frequently in popular culture and at historical
sites remains problematic. As Ota of Nagahama Castle Museum so elo-
quently suggests, the image of Hideyoshi is fraught with deeper symbolism that can and should no longer be ignored, and any partial telling of his
story has become increasingly difficult in East Asia in the twenty-first
century. But as the conflicting discourses of Saga Nagoya Castle Museum
and Kōdaiji highlight, telling the stories that historical sites beg to have
told is no easy task.

Epilogue

Whither Hideyoshi?

Taikōki-based historical fiction illustrates the various ways the narrative of Hideyoshi has shifted since his death. The capacity for tales of the past to attract a broad and diverse readership makes historical fiction in general, and historical fiction about Hideyoshi in particular, a useful and effective tool for considering the impact of these changes in twentieth and twenty-first-century narratives about heroes of the past.

Tessa Morris-Suzuki writes about "the series of mediations through which narratives and images of the past reach us" and argues that "understanding the possibilities, limitations and communicative codes of various media . . . is an essential part of learning to understand the past."[1] This continues to be the case with Hideyoshi. The number of sites of reproduction and interpretation of his image seems to have increased exponentially in the late twentieth and early twenty-first centuries. Stories about Hideyoshi are no longer limited to works of literary fiction and the stage but have expanded to movies, television, manga, and museum displays. The contested nature of his legacy has become clearer as Japan has been forced to confront its own wartime past in East Asia, yet stories about him, both positive and negative, seem to be no less prevalent. Over the past fifty years, there has been no lack of representations of Hideyoshi in popular culture. He can be seen anywhere from video game ads to mobile phone commercials and car showroom displays in downtown Tokyo.

The challenge of undertaking a project such as this one is that it cannot possibly cover everything and therefore cannot hope to elucidate all the nuances inherent in Hideyoshi's image. Books could be composed, for example, on how he has appeared in Japanese visual culture and theater during the past four hundred years. Hideyoshi's afterlife in manga and film has been as rich as his afterlife in print.

The NHK's *Taiga dorama* offers a useful example. Hideyoshi has been the subject of many of these annual programs from the inauguration of the series in 1963 to the present. The series has a significant impact on viewers' ideas about Japanese history, and many of its programs have been the NHK's most viewed program in the year they appeared. They even fuel booms in tourism and consumerism.[2] Hideyoshi has appeared regularly since early in the history of the series. Yoshikawa Eiji's *Shinsho Taikōki* was the source for the program that aired in 1965, and the 1981 *Onna Taikōki* (Women's Taikōki) and the 1996 *Hideyoshi* (fig. E.1) were based on works by Nagai Michiko and Shiba Ryōtarō, respectively. Including these three *Taikōki*-based series, Hideyoshi has been portrayed or at least mentioned in more than 40 percent of all programs in the series.[3] In twenty-four of the first forty-nine years that the *Taiga dorama* series aired, it ranked either first or second for overall NHK viewership, and *Taikōki*, *Onna Taikōki*, and *Hideyoshi* all ranked number one in the year they aired. Based on viewership records, then, Hideyoshi has remained a popular character on NHK television. He has also been the subject of many made-for-television movies, including the highly entertaining 1987 *Taikōki* on Tokyo Broadcasting System, the 2003 *Taikōki: A Man Called Monkey* on Fuji Television, and the 2006 *Taikōki* on TV Asahi.

Hideyoshi was also a regular topic for the *Sono toki rekishi ga ugoita* (That's when history changed) series. Airing at 10:00 p.m. on Wednesday nights starting in March 2000 and running for 355 episodes in all, this program reintroduced its audience to various pivotal moments in Japanese history. Many of its episodes were then turned into comic books (*komikku-ban*) that sold millions of copies. The NHK's *Sono toki rekishi ga ugoita* franchise, with its weekly program and comic series, was one of the most influential reimaginations of Japanese history in the first decade of the twenty-first century, and the way Hideyoshi thrived there speaks to his malleability in the twenty-first century. Some of the most successful renditions of him in manga can be found in this comic series, which

FIGURE E.I   Takenaka Naoto as Hideyoshi in the 1996 *Taiga dorama* series *Hideyoshi*.
Photo credit NHK (Japan Broadcasting Corporation).

began in July 2003 and has the stated purpose of creating easily understood manga renditions of complete episodes. Over the six years that new issues were being published (the last was published in June 2009), more than fifty different manga artists contributed to the series by watching the NHK show and then creating a manga version based on their interpretation of it.[4] The manga versions of these episodes exponentially increased the cultural capital of the *Sono toki* enterprise. By April 2006, just over halfway through the program's run, more than 1.3 million copies of the manga had been sold.[5] Although the NHK programs were available in limited release reruns, the relatively cheap and widely available manga volumes have virtually unlimited power to reach a broad audience of manga readers, who are known to consume manga quickly before passing them on to friends or sellers of used books.

The first manga adaptation in this series is a volume called the *Sengoku-ban* (The Warring States issue), which is focused on the unification of Japan under Oda Nobunaga and Hideyoshi and on the role various women played in the events leading up to the Battle of Sekigahara, after which Tokugawa Ieyasu took control of Japan. Four of the six episodes that make up this issue are about Hideyoshi or other members of the Toyotomi clan. As a point of reference, in this NHK series, 62 of the 355 total episodes (roughly 17 percent) covered the years between 1560 and 1600, when the three unifiers were vying for power, and 9 had Hideyoshi as their primary focus.

There are other individual manga and manga series about Hideyoshi as well. Some examples are Yokoyama Mitsuteru and Yamaoka Sōhachi's *Toyotomi Hideyoshi: Ihon Taikōki* (Toyotomi Hideyoshi: A variant *Taikōki*; Kodansha, 1995), Yamada Fūtarō's 2003 *Yōkai Taikōki* (Monster's *Taikōki*; Kodansha, 2003), Izawa Motohiko and Kojima Goseki's *Ōgon Taikōki* (Golden *Taikōki*; Reedsha, 2004), Saitō Takao's *Tenkabito Hideyoshi no yume to genjitsu* (Ruler Toyotomi Hideyoshi's dream and reality; Kadokawa shoten, 2005), Yamada Yoshihiro's *Hyōge mono* (A jocular person; Kodansha, 2005), Tsuchiyama Shigeru's *Toyotomi Hideyoshi* (Reedsha; 2005), Tanaka Kanako's *Hideyoshi de gozaru!!* (I am Hideyoshi!!; Shueisha, 2007) (fig. E.2), and Tsuda Hōkō's *Tensei Taikōki—gendai chishiki de sengoku no yo o musō suru* (Reincarnated *Taikōki*—take down the Warring States period with modern knowledge; Kadokawa, 2017).

FIGURE E.2   Cover art from the manga *Hideyoshi de gozaru!!* (I am Hideyoshi!!), written and illustrated by Tanaka Kanako (Shūeisha, 2007).

Films about Hideyoshi were being produced as early as the 1920s, starting with one called *Taikōki* that was directed by Shirō Nakagawa. Others include *Shusse Taikōki* (*Taikōki* of success in life; 1938), directed by Inagiki Hiroshi; *Hanamuko Taikōki* (Groom *Taikōki*; 1945), directed by Marune Kintaro; *Taikōki* (1958), based on Yoshikawa's novel and directed by Ōsone Tatsuo; *Horafuki Taikōki* (Braggart *Taikōki*; 1964), directed by Furusawa Kengo; *Manzai Taikōki* (Comic dialogue *Taikōki*; 1981), directed by Takayashiki Hideo; and *Taikōki* (1987), directed by Okamoto Kihachi, to name a few. Like novels and manga about Hideyoshi, these films are more examples of what the historical fiction scholar Kikuchi Masanori calls "confessions of the author's view of history."[6] Teshigahara Hiroshi's 1989 *Rikyū* (fig. E.3) offers an interesting example. This film, based on Nogami Yaeko's 1964 novel *Hideyoshi to Rikyū* (Hideyoshi and Rikyū), traces the story of Hideyoshi's worsening relationship with the tea master and trusted confidant Sen no Rikyū, addressing issues of politics versus culture and arguing that the pursuit of wealth leads to corruption—a particularly pertinent message for Japan in the late 1980s. From the opening credits, Teshigahara sets up the tension in the film as a conflict between ambition and culture with the following introduction: "This is the story of the duel between art and politics, between the beliefs of one man and the ambitions of another."[7] He interprets Rikyū's death as a result of Hideyoshi's failure to understand the true nature of *wabisabi* (the Japanese art aesthetic that focuses on the acceptance of imperfection) that Rikyū represents.

Teshigahara follows Nogami's lead when he provides an explanation for Rikyū's death, though he removes much of the nuance of Nogami's novel in the process." There are a variety of theories about why Rikyū fell out of Hideyoshi's favor. The first is that Rikyū voiced criticism of Hideyoshi's actions in Korea. The second is that Hideyoshi was outraged by a statue of Rikyū that had been created and displayed at a temple in such a way that Hideyoshi had to pass under the statue's sandaled feet to enter the building. The third reason is that Rikyū refused to give his daughter to Hideyoshi as a concubine. The fourth is that Hideyoshi was displeased with the way that Rikyū used his role as confidant to Hideyoshi to help him sell more tea ware. Finally, it has been speculated that the growing discontent of other daimyo regarding Rikyū's proximity to power is what led to his downfall.[8]

FIGURE E.3 The actor Rentarō Mikuni as Hideyoshi in Teshigahara Hiyoshi's film *Rikyū* (Shochiku, 1989).

Though Teshigahara's film refers to some of these possibilities, most notably the one involving the statue, it also clearly shows that Rikyū's forced suicide was a direct result of the growing difference of opinion between the two men regarding the invasion of China. This difference is couched within the context of "the beliefs of one man" and "the ambitions of another," which is in many ways an oversimplification of Nogami's novel. But for a 1989 viewing audience, as Japan neared the end of its economic bubble, this criticism of Hideyoshi's selfishness and ambition was particularly resonant. The closing line of Teshigahara's film again focuses on this: "On February 28, 1591, Rikyū committed ritual suicide. But his way of tea influenced the nation forever. Hideyoshi died six years later during his invasion of Korea."[9] Ultimately, both men died untimely deaths, but as Teshigahara told it, only one of them died honorably and left a lasting legacy that "influenced the nation forever."

The novels, film, television shows, and manga about Hideyoshi can seem endless, and it is certainly not possible to do them all justice here. That said, Hideyoshi's example offers productive guidelines for thinking critically about the relationship between popular culture and historical narrative and how the portrayal of well-known historical figures in popular culture influences the ways people think about the past. Mass and simultaneous consumption of historical events serves to solidify notions of Japanese memory or national character. But popular representations of history almost always give readers an interpretation that says as much about the current moment as it does about the past.

Hideyoshi-*den* continue to resonate with Japanese consumers today, even as the story of Hideyoshi becomes harder and harder to sell abroad. As Barbara Ruch points out, some national tales do not translate across national boundaries, and *Taikōki* is one of them.[10] Why does *Taikōki* speak so effectively to a Japanese audience, and what does this say about the production and consumption of historical narrative in Japan? What does it say about this audience that Hideyoshi can still be a source of entertainment? Is it okay to circle back to national origin stories that feature great, yet flawed, leaders like Hideyoshi, despite what he has come to represent for many people outside Japan? Some of the authors and sites analyzed here seem to indicate that Hideyoshi's flawed nature should disqualify him from his position in the pantheon of Japan's founding fathers. But others continue to disaggregate his actions from the way he is remembered. Ultimately, the story of Hideyoshi and *Taikōki* is the story of the power of popular historical narrative.

As chapter 1 showed, Hideyoshi was a particularly malleable character from the beginning, and building on that malleability, Oze Hoan created a *Taikōki* that was an ideal model for the explosion of tales that came later. Chapter 2 demonstrated the ways this held true during World War II. During the war, Hideyoshi was primed to return from the dead and did so quite ably in the hands of Yoshikawa, becoming a symbol of the ideal and loyal soldier and representing the ultimate human and altruistic pan-Asianist. Chapter 3 showed how, following the war, Hideyoshi's narrative flexibility paved the way for him to become a model businessman and human resource manager. Good with money and people, this Hideyoshi not only served as a mythic point of origin that people could look back to as an anchor during the challenging early postwar years of the 1950s and early 1960s, but he also came to represent the possibility of social and economic ascendance.

Looking at these interpretations of Hideyoshi now, a reader is struck by how lacking in nuance many of them are. Like many other figures, Hideyoshi (as well as the historical source material about him) is both vague and complex, and thus writers of history and other authors have chosen to emplot Hideyoshi differently over the years. Writers like Nagai, and Ariyoshi Sawako (discussed in chapter 4) acknowledge this in implicit and explicit ways in their writing and highlight the problematic nature of hero-centered, patriarchal history. In the process, they greatly complicate their readers' understanding of Hideyoshi. Their novels demand that readers consider what is at stake when they embrace a certain understanding of Hideyoshi and the historical tradition that made him without questioning the ways those understandings misrepresent the past and/or marginalize certain groups.

So, whither Hideyoshi? How will his image hold up in the twenty-first century? If the ongoing outpouring of television shows, commercials, video games, manga, and advertisements with his likeness is any indication, Hideyoshi will remain a visible part of Japanese popular culture for the foreseeable future. But as Japanese leaders seek to promote tourism and internationalization in efforts to mitigate the impacts of the economic crisis caused by rapid depopulation and aging, nuanced and careful reinterpretation and positioning of Hideyoshi's legacy must embrace the fullness of his literary afterlife. Ultimately, this study of literature about Hideyoshi demonstrates how he is a figure who has been continually renewed by the stories that have been woven around his memory over the years. Hideyoshi's example illustrates just how vital it is to understand the role of popular culture in influencing people's understanding of history, identity, and the past. The figure of Hideyoshi cannot and should not be separated from the many stories told about him.

Notes

Introduction

1. Japanese *Taikōki* scholars such as Kuwata Tadachika and Abe Kazuhiko—in their works *Taikōki no kenkyū* (Taikōki studies) and *Taikōki to sono shūhen* (Taikōki and its environs), respectively—have written at length on the historical sources for and discrepancies within Oze's original *Taikōki*. This work has by no means been completed, but both authors do an excellent job of elucidating the major points of comparison and contention between historical records and Oze's adoption of these records in his biography of Hideyoshi.

2. In *Hideyoshi eiyū densetsu no nazo* (The enigma of Hideyoshi hero legends), Tsuda Saburō also discusses the various tales and events honoring Hideyoshi posthumously, but his book focuses primarily on historical events (not narratives) on the years immediately after Hideyoshi's death through the end of the Meiji era (1868–1912). Not only does this current work expand the analysis to focus on narrative tales but it also picks up chronologically from where Tsuda left off.

3. For more on Hideyoshi's invasions of the Korean peninsula, see Berry, *Hideyoshi*, 207–17.

4. In English, see, for example, Ravina, *The Last Samurai*; Wert, *Meiji Restoration Losers*; Shimoda, *Lost and Found*; Tasgold, "Popular Realms of Memory in Japan"; Prough, "Meiji Restoration Vacation."

5. Greenblatt, *Renaissance Self-Fashioning*.

6. Narita, *Shiba Ryōtarō no bakumatsu/Meiji* (Shiba Ryōtarō's bakumatsu and Meiji), 23.

7. Narita, 11.

8. Nora, "From *Lieux de mémoire* to Realms of Memory," xxiii–xxiv.

9. Bukh, "Historical Memory and Shiba Ryōtarō," 96.

10. Berry, *Hideyoshi*, 213.

11. Boscaro, *101 Letters of Hideyoshi*, 70–72.

12. Tamir, "The Enigma of Nationalism," 439.

13. Lukács, *The Historical Novel*, 25.

14. de Groot, *The Historical Novel*, 2.

15. Haruo Shirane, "Warrior Tales (Gunki–mono)," 704–6. See also Tyler, *The Tale of the Heike*.

16. For more on this phenomenon, see Sugawa-Shimada, "Rekijo, Pilgrimage and 'Pop-Spiritualism.'"

17. Jones, introduction to *An Edo Anthology*, 1.

18. Jones, 24. See also Berry, *Japan in Print*.

19. For more on historical fiction and popular literature in Japan, see Ozaki, *Taishū bungaku*, 5–18. For a further discussion of the relationship between historical fiction, popular literature, and reader reception, see Ozaki, *Taishū bungakuron*, 12; Torrance, "Literacy and Literature in Osaka"; Langton, "A Literature for the People"; Hirano, *Jun bungaku to taishū bungaku* (Pure literature and popular literature); Sakai, *Nihon no taishū bungaku*.

20. Shively, *The Love Suicides at Amijima*, 16–17. See also Satō Tadao, *Chūshingura*; Keene, *The Major Plays of Chikamatsu*.

21. See Strecher, "Purely Mass or Massively Pure?" See also Maeda, *Text and the City*, 163–222.

22. See Strecher, "Purely Mass or Massively Pure?" See also Mack, *Manufacturing Modern Japanese Literature*.

23. Mori, "History as It Is and History Ignored," 181.

24. Mori, 182.

25. Marcus, *Paragons of the Ordinary*, 30. See also Marcus, "Mori Ōgai and the Biographical Quest," 237.

26. Sakai (*Nihon no taishū bungaku*), Torrance ("Literacy and Literature in Osaka"), and Langton ("A Literature for the People") have written at length about the popularity of historical fiction in Japan. See also Shimura, *Rekishi shōsetsu to taishū bungaku*.

27. Discussions of the original incident and its consequences can be found in numerous sources. I have relied on Satō Tadao, *Chūshingura*; Ikegami, *The Taming of the Samurai*, 223–30; Hiroaki Satō, *Legends of the Samurai*, 304–21; "The Way of the Warrior II"; Keene, "Variations on a Theme," 1–13; Smith, "The Capacity of Chūshingura."

28. Takeda, Miyoshi, and Namiki, *Kanadehon Chūshingura*.

29. Interestingly, however, he expressed doubt about how *Chūshingura* would fare in the twenty-first century. Henry Smith also writes about this ("The Media and Politics of Japanese Popular History").

30. Satō, *Chūshingura*, 114.

31. Satō, 114.

32. Smith has also written about this ("The Capacity of Chūshingura").

33. Since the 1983 publication of Eric Hobsbawm and Terence Ranger's groundbreaking *The Invention of Tradition*, there has been ongoing discourse about the so-called mobilization of tradition in the modern era. In the field of Japanese studies, a series of texts has been published in the past thirty years that contributes to this discussion of how the past and tradition have been appropriated for the modern good. These works provide insights into how both positive and negative renderings of the past can be used as a means of redefining the present. Recent works such as Michael

Foster's *Pandemonium and Parade* and Gergana Ivanova's *Unbinding the Pillow Book* look at how specific stories or literary works from the past have made their way into the present. As Foster and Ivanova demonstrate, tales from the past have not only successfully navigated the centuries, but they have also served as barometers for how society has changed and how and why certain narratives continue to resonate despite these changes.

34. Ruch, "Medieval Jongleurs and the Making of a National Literature," 291–92.
35. Ruch, 291–92.
36. Ruch, 291–92.
37. Ozaki, *Taishū bungaku* (Popular literature), 5. See also Ozaki, *Taishū bungakuron* (Theory of popular literature), 12.
38. Ozaki, *Taishū bungakuron*, 7. See also Tsurumi, *Taishū bungakuron* (Theory of popular literature), 12.
39. Ozaki, *Taishū bungakuron*, 8.
40. Kuwata, *Taikōki no kenkyū*, 15.
41. Ozaki, *Taishū bungaku*, 75.
42. This form of historical storytelling most likely began during the Sengoku period (1467–1615), when daimyo employed men referred to as *otogishū* (attendant) to entertain them with stories about famous battles or moments in history. It could also be argued that the practice goes back even further, to the time of the *biwa hōshi* in the Heian period (794–1185).
43. Anderson, *Imagined Communities*, 32–36.
44. Yada Sōun's *Taikōki* stands out as the first popular fiction (*taishū bungaku*) version of Oze's story.
45. Yada, *Edo kara Tōkyō e* (From Edo to Tokyo).
46. This appears to be a mistake on Kuwata's part. The story was serialized for a little more than nine years, from October 4, 1925, to December 17, 1934.
47. Kuwata, *Taikōki no kenkyū*, 231.
48. Ruch, "Medieval Jongleurs," 292.
49. Henry, *Momotarō, or the Peach Boy*.

1. Toyotomi Hideyoshi and Taikōki

1. Yoshida, introduction to *Taikōki* by Oze Hoan, 1:27.
2. The provenance of this Edo-era poem is unclear, but it continues to be quoted today.
3. At birth, Hideyoshi was called Hiyoshimaru or Hiyoshi. After he went to work for Oda Nobunaga, he received his first surname and was called Kinoshita Tokichirō. Later his surname was changed to Hashiba, and at one point he was called Hashiba Chikuzen no Kami Hideyoshi. He became the imperial regent (*kampaku*) in 1585 and the grand minister of state (*dajō daijin*) in 1587. At this time he was given the family name Toyotomi and so became Toyotomi Hideyoshi. The name by which he is most commonly known, *Taikō*, is the honorary title given to a retired *kampaku*.
4. As Mary Berry notes, some chroniclers give Yaemon a surname, but others do not (*Hideyoshi*, 8).

5. Information about Hideyoshi's life and career in this chapter has been taken from the following sources: Berry, *Hideyoshi*; Dening, *The Life of Toyotomi Hideyoshi*; Hall, *Japan from Prehistory to Modern Times* and *The Cambridge History of Japan*, vol. 4; Kaku, *Gendaigoyaku bukōyawa* (An evening tale); Kuwata, *Toyotomi Hideyoshi kenkyū* (Toyotomi Hideyoshi studies), *Toyotomi Hideyoshi no subete* (Everything about Toyotomi Hideyoshi), *Taikō Hideyoshi no tegami* (The letters of the retired imperial regent Hideyoshi), and *Taikōki no kenkyū* (Taikōki studies); Sansom, *A History of Japan*; Totman, *Early Modern Japan*; Turnbull, *Toyotomi Hideyoshi*; and Wakita, "The Emergence of the State in Sixteenth-Century Japan."

6. White, *The Content of the Form*, 44.

7. White, 5.

8. Narita, *Shiba Ryōtarō no bakumatsu/Meiji*, 9.

9. Berry, *Hideyoshi*, 71–72.

10. Tokyo Teikoku Daigaku and Tokyo Daigaku, *Dai Nihon shiryō*, 11:1.

11. Oze, *Taikōki*, 62–65.

12. Oze, 62–65.

13. Oze, 589.

14. Yoshikawa, *Yoshikawa Eiji zenshū* (*YEZ*) (The collected works of Yoshikawa Eiji), vol. 47, *Sōshidō zuihitsu* (Jottings from Sōshidō), 141.

15. "Taikō o kataru" (Talking about the Taikō), *Yomiuri Shinbun*, March 3, 1939.

16. Shiba, "Watashi no shōsetsu sahō," 440.

17. Shimura, "Sōsaku hōhō" (Methods of literary production), 87. See also Suekuni, "Shijitsu to kyokō" (Historical fact and fabrication).

18. Quoted in Ariyoshi Nobuto, "Shiba Ryōtarō no benkyōhō" (Shiba Ryōtarō study methods), 106. The title of the special issue of the magazine is a pun on the title of Shiba's most famous novel, *Ryōma ga yuku*. The novel's title is deceptively simple and notoriously difficult to put into English. *Yuku* (meaning "to go") has been translated in a variety of ways, including *Ryōma Goes!*, *Ryōma on His Way*, *Ryōma on the Move*, *Ryōma Sets Out*, and *Ryōma!* Given the pun being used here to title this posthumous collection of essays about Shiba, I am inclined to translate it as "Shiba Ryōtarō Sets Out."

19. Matsuo, "Shiba Ryōtarō no sakuhin ni miru rekishikan," 100.

20. Quoted in Matsuo, "Rekishikan," 363.

21. Narita, *Shiba Ryōtarō no bakumatsu/Meiji*, dust jacket back cover.

22. Greenblatt, *Renaissance Self-Fashioning*.

23. Hall, "Hideyoshi's Domestic Policies," 197.

24. Hall, 197.

25. Elison, "Hideyoshi, the Bountiful Minister," 226.

26. Elison, 229–30.

27. For more on this, see Abe, *Taikōki to sono shūhen* (Taikōki and its environs); Kuwata, *Taikōki no kenkyū*.

28. Berry, *Hideyoshi*, 6.

29. The translation is from Elison, "Hideyoshi, the Bountiful Minister," 223.

30. St. Pedro Bautista Blanquez, "Audience with Hideyoshi at Nagoya, 1593," in Cooper, *They Came to Japan*, 111.

31. Elison, "Hideyoshi, the Bountiful Minister," 226.

32. Watsky, *Chikubushima*, 81.

33. The analysis here is based on the discussion of the parallels between the two Great Buddha statues found in Andrew Watsky's *Chikubushima* (76–83). Watsky also illuminates how the Toyotomi clan continued to align itself with various religious projects as a means of self-legitimation (197–230).

34. Murdoch, *History of Japan*, 2:305.

35. For a detailed description of how Toyotomi supporters deified Hideyoshi after his death in an attempt to consolidate Toyotomi power, see Watsky, *Chikubushima*, 199–208.

36. Greenblatt, *Renaissance Self-Fashioning*, 13.

37. Other early biographies include Omura Yūko, *Tenshōki* (Chronicles of the Tenshō era, 1580–1590), and Ōta Gyūichi, "Taikōsama gunki no uchi" (From the Taikō's war tales, 1610).

38. Tsuda, *Hideyoshi eiyū densetsu no nazo* (The enigma of Hideyoshi hero legends), 245.

39. Oze, *Taikōki*, 3.

40. The Toyotomi forces were first defeated at the Battle of Sekigahara in 1600 and, in 1615, they suffered their final defeat after a series of battles at Satōsaka Castle.

41. Kuwata, *Taikōki no kenkyū*, 10.

42. Yoshida, introduction to *Taikōki* by Oze Hoan, 1:15.

43. Watsky, *Chikubushima*, 199.

44. Watsky, 200.

45. Watsky, 203.

46. For a detailed discussion of the significant role the temple played in early Hideyoshi worship, see Watsky, 204–8.

47. The translation of Hideyoshi's posthumous name was taken from Berry, *Hideyoshi*, 1.

48. Watsky, *Chikubushima*, 208.

49. Watsky, 209.

50. Watsky, 220.

51. The last twenty or so years of the Azuchi-Momoyama period (1568–1600).

52. Oze, *Taikōki*, 29.

53. Kornicki, *"Nishiki no ura,"* 155.

54. Tsuda, *Hideyoshi eiyū densetsu no nazo*, 246.

55. Tsuda, 246. See also Davis, "The Trouble with Hideyoshi"; Kornicki, *The Book in Japan*.

56. Davis, "The Trouble with Hideyoshi," 285.

57. Kornicki, "The Enmeiin Affair of 1803," 509.

58. Watsky, *Chikubushima*, 213.

59. *Jōruri* is the sung narrative that accompanies Bunraku performances. *Jōruri* based on *Taikōki* include Chikamatsu Monzaemon (1653–1724), *Honchō sangokushi* (The record of the Japanese imperial three kingdoms, 1719), and Chikamatsu Yanagira, *Ehon Taikōki* (Pictured notes of great achievement, 1799). In Kabuki, Tsuruya Nanboku IV (1755–1829) created *Tokimoki kyō shusse no ukejō* (The truth about the bellflower's rise to the top, 1808). Other plays directly influenced by *Taikōki* include Namiki Gohei's *Sanmon gosan no kiri* (The paulownia crest at the Sanmon Gate, 1778) and Nakamura

Akei, Toyotake Ōritski, Kokuzōsu, Mitsu Inshi, and Asada Itchō's *Gion sairei shinkōki* (The records of faith from the Gion Festival, 1757).

60. Kornicki, *The Book in Japan*, 341. See also Davis, "The Trouble with Hideyoshi," 286–88. Davis in particular argues that the banning of *Ehon Taikōki* was due not simply to the fact that it stirred up a Hideyoshi frenzy, but also because it led others to depict Hideyoshi in the floating world, challenging Confucian notions of respect and indirectly questioning the propriety and legitimacy of Tokugawa rule.

61. Kuwata, *Taikōki no kenkyū*, 213.

62. Tsuda, *Hideyoshi eiyū densetsu no nazo*, 256.

63. "Yushutsu yunyū mo engeki kara" (Exports and imports also come from plays), in Nakayama, *Shinbun shūsei Meiji hennen-shi*, 5:279.

2. Hideyoshi's War

1. The text, which was originally published in 1950 as *Shinsho Taikōki* (The new Taikōki), was originally serialized in the newspaper as *Taikōki*. When talking about the serialized version, I will call the work *Taikōki*. Otherwise, I will refer to it as *Shinsho Taikōki*.

2. The notice was just twenty-nine characters long.

3. See Hashimoto, *The Long Defeat*, 8–9, for a discussion of the challenges inherent in naming the war that occurred in the 1930s and 1940s.

4. One incident recorded in the *Yomiuri Shinbun hyaku nijū nen shi* (The 120-year history of the *Yomiuri*) illustrates the story's popularity and the degree to which readers were invested in the story. Yomiuri reports that following Hideyoshi's acceptance into Oda Nobunaga's service, the paper was flooded by readers concerned about the fate of his mother. The outpouring of concern was so great that Yoshikawa was obliged to add a section describing his filial piety and how he ran out to buy some exotic fruit for his mother as soon as he learned of the promotion. See Yomiuri shinbuň-sha, *Yomiuri Shinbun hyaku nijū nen shi*, 160.

5. Cook, "Reporting the 'Fall of *Nankin*,'" 121.

6. See Young, *Japan's Total Empire*, 55–114; Yomiuri shinbun-sha, *Yomiuri Shinbun hyaku nijū nen shi*, 123–25.

7. Uchiyama, *Japan's Carnival War*, 23.

8. Cook, "Reporting the 'Fall of *Nankin*,'" 121.

9. Young, *Japan's Total Empire*, 55–114.

10. Uchiyama, *Japan's Carnival War*, 4.

11. Quoted in Yomiuri shinbun-sha, *Yomiuri Shinbun hyaku nijū nen shi*, 157.

12. Young, *Japan's Total Empire*, 55–114.

13. The Toranomon Incident occurred on December 27, 1923, when an attempt was made on the life of Hirohito, who was then the crown prince.

14. Gotō was a politician who, among other achievements, not only played a significant role in Japan's governance of Taiwan but also created the recovery plan that was used in Tokyo after the Great Kanto Earthquake.

15. Yomiuri shinbun-sha, *Yomiuri Shinbun hyaku nijū nen shi*, 108.

16. The Mukden Incident, also called the Manchurian Incident, occurred on September 18, 1931, when Japanese troops seized the Manchurian city of Mukden. Follow-

ing this, Japan invaded Manchuria and established the state of Manchukuo. This was the first step in Japan's entry into war with China and eventually World War II. According to Kasza, under the leadership of Shōriki, whom he refers to as "a former career officer in the so-called 'thought police,'" *Yomiuri Shinbun* had become the strongest supporter of the war out of all the major daily newspapers in Japan at the time (*The State and Mass Media in Japan*, 213–14).

17. Kasza, *The State and Mass Media in Japan*, 170–71.

18. Yomiuri shinbun-sha, *Yomiuri Shinbun hyaku nijū nen shi*, 161. The newspaper was not removed from the trials and suffering of the war, however. Besides suffering from paper shortages, it also experienced loss of life. From the start of the China war in 1937 to the end of the Pacific War in 1945, 177 Yomiuri employees were killed. Forty-five were special correspondents who died between 1937 and 1945, 111 were drafted soldiers killed between 1939 and 1945, and 21 died in fires and bombings between 1944 and 1945. Of course, the largest number of special correspondent casualties came on the front line, and not only reporters were killed there—so were people from management and the marketing, plate making, type printing, dispatch, engineering, editing, layout, planning, and general affairs departments. In short, all sections of the paper were affected by wartime deaths. On one island in Indonesia on the night of January 23, 1943, the paper lost fourteen people. And on the night of May 25, 1945, the main office in Ginza and the branch office in Yurakuchō were burned in the last major air raid of the war.

19. Yomiuri shinbun-sha, *Yomiuri Shinbun hyaku nijū nen shi*, 161. Presumably the second article led to a ban because it would have reminded readers how severe rationing had become.

20. See Selden, "A Forgotten Holocaust," for a detailed description of the Tokyo air raids.

21. Details about Yoshikawa's life have been taken from Yoshino, *Bungaku hōkokukai no jidai* (The era of the Patriotic Association for Literature), 155, and McClellan, *Fragments of a Past*, x.

22. Yomiuri shinbun-sha, *Yomiuri Shinbun hyaku nijū nen shi*, 108.

23. Yomiuri shinbun-sha, 666. In 1924, when Shōriki took over the paper, its circulation was 55,296. Just fifteen years later, when Yoshikawa began serializing his novel in 1939, circulation was up to 1,201,142. The readership reached a wartime peak of 1,919,368 in 1944—the highest it would go under Shōriki's leadership. On December 3, 1945, Shōriki was accused of war crimes, and he entered Sugamo prison on December 12, ending his run as the paper's manager (656). He was released from prison on September 1, 1947 (655). For more details on Shōriki's life, see Mitarai, *Denki Shōriki Matsutarō* (Biography of Shōriki Matsutarō).

24. Radio broadcasts started in 1925 in Japan, just a year after Shōriki took the paper's helm.

25. See Mitarai, *Denki Shōriki Matsutarō*; Fitts, *Banzai Babe Ruth*. The 1934 baseball series is perhaps Shōriki's most enduring legacy and an excellent example of how he was able to assess and maneuver within a given situation. When he realized that the fee necessary to secure a visit from the Major League Baseball players was beyond his budget, he brokered a deal with Connie Mack, their manager, convincing Mack to accept half of the usual guarantee fee in exchange for all of the profits from the exhibition games.

All Shōriki asked for in return was sole advertising rights. The players ended up earning two times their usual commission, and Shōriki became forever known as the father of baseball for his role in initiating professional baseball fever in Japan.

26. Nawata, "*Shinsho Taikōki.*"

27. Yoshikawa, *Yoshikawa Eiji zenshū*, 47:146.

28. Yoshikawa, 47:138–39.

29. A more detailed explanation of why Yoshikawa decided to write *Taikōki* appears below in this chapter.

30. Nawata, "*Shinsho Taikōki*," 130. Nawata argues that Yoshikawa was immediately persuaded when Shōriki suggested *Taikōki* as the basis for his new novel. Nawata implies that Yoshikawa felt some sort of connection to Hideyoshi. However, Yoshikawa seems to make no such statement.

31. Yoshino, *Bungaku hōkokukai no jidai*, 72. The association was the 1942 incarnation of the Novelists' Association (Shōsetsuka kyōkai), which had been formed in 1921 and renamed the Arts' Association (Bungei kyōkai) in 1926. After World War II, the group became the Japanese Arts' Association (Nihon bungei kyōkai).

32. Sakai, *Nihon no taishū bungaku*, 73.

33. Yoshino, *Bungaku hōkokukai no jidai*, 66.

34. Yoshino, 66.

35. Yoshino, 78.

36. The term "China Incident" here refers to the Manchurian Incident and its aftermath. "Greater East Asian War" became the term used to refer to post–Pearl Harbor engagements with East Asia as well as the Allies. The name was decided upon by the Japanese cabinet and released to the public soon after the December 8, 1941 (Japan time), attack. It references Japan's goal to create the Greater East Asia Co-Prosperity Sphere, which, Japanese leaders argued, would establish a new international order that ensured prosperity and peace for all of Asia, free from Western colonialism.

37. Yoshino, *Bungaku hōkokukai no jidai*, 76–77.

38. Yoshino, 78.

39. This incident was an attempted coup by young naval officers on May 15, 1932, during which Prime Minister Inukai Tsuyoshi was assassinated.

40. Yoshino, *Bungaku hōkokukai no jidai*, 154.

41. Ozaki, *Yoshikawa Eiji denki* (Biography of Yoshikawa Eiji), 318–19.

42. Yoshino, *Bungaku hōkokukai no jidai*, 79.

43. Sakai, *Nihon no taishū bungaku*, 67.

44. *Tokyo Asahi Shinbun*, September 15, 1938.

45. Yoshikawa, "Sakusha no kotoba" (A word from the author), *Yomiuri Shinbun*, November 5, 1938.

46. Yoshikawa.

47. Yoshikawa.

48. Tōkichirō is one of the early names given to Hideyoshi.

49. Yoshikawa, "Sakusha no kotoba."

50. Keene, "Japanese Writers and the Greater East Asia War," 210-11.

51. Ozaki, *Taishū bungakuron* (Theory of popular literature), 228. Cécile Sakai writes: "After the war, Yoshikawa himself made corrections to and deletions from

Miyamoto Musashi, taking care of any spots that might cause trouble [with the Occupation censors]" (*Nihon no taishū bungaku*, 65). For a thorough discussion of the debate about Yoshikawa's fascist leanings as it pertains to *Miyamoto Musashi*, see Langton, "A Literature for the People," particularly pages 333–36.

52. Sakai, *Nihon no taishū bungaku*, 67.

53. Yoshikawa, *Yoshikawa Eiji zenshū*, 47:110.

54. Yoshikawa, 47:114–15.

55. Suzuki, "Yoshikawa Eiji no rekishi kan," 43.

56. Sakai, *Nihon no taishū bungaku*, 73.

57. Sakai, 74.

58. See, for example, Sugimoto, "Songokū, budda no te o hashiru."

59. Chūken seinen shōkō dan, "Kōgun honzen no ninmu nitsute."

60. Chūken seinen shōkō dan, 819–20.

61. According to two eighth-century texts, the *Kojiki* (The record of ancient matters, 712) and the *Nihon shoki* (Chronicles of Japan, 720), Empress Jingū led an invasion of Korea and returned victorious. Emperor Meiji presided over Japan during the successful Sino-Japanese and Russo-Japanese wars (1894–95 and 1904–5, respectively), which increased the Japanese colonial empire. And the leaders of the Manchurian Incident helped secure the Japanese foothold there.

62. Cho, "Discourses of Nation," 138–54.

63. As Cho demonstrates, the connection between Hideyoshi's so-called military success in Korea and Japanese national pride dates back to the early modern era (125–54).

64. "*Taikōki* sanbu saku" (*Taikōki* in three parts), *Yomiuri Shinbun*, November 5, 1938.

65. "*Taikōki* sanbu saku." The claim that Yoshikawa would focus all of his energy into the writing of this text is ironic at best, given that he was then in the middle of his wildly popular *Miyamoto Musashi* and about to begin a second work—*Sangokushi* (Romance of the Three Kingdoms)—that started serialization in August 1939 and ran until September 1943.

66. "*Taikōki* sanbu saku."

67. Uchiyama, *Japan's Carnival War*, 5.

68. This reference is to the introduction to the work by Yoshikawa that accompanied this article. It is translated below.

69. "*Taikōki* sanbu saku."

70. Yomiuri shinbun-sha, *Yomiuri Shinbun hyaku nijū nen shi*, 160.

71. "Hō Taikō ten: Yoku mo atsumeta kono chinpin, meishi zokzoku to raikan shi zessan no arashi" (Hō Taikō exhibit: This impressive collection of rare articles opens to a surging wave of famous admirers), *Yomiuri Shinbun*, February 26, 1939. Hideyoshi never traveled from Japan to the Korean peninsula, so of course this is misleading.

72. Yomiuri shinbun-sha, *Yomiuri Shinbun hyaku nijū nen shi*, 160.

73. "Mōriagaru Taikō netsu" (Taikō fever builds), *Yomiuri Shinbun*, January 27, 1939.

74. "Mōriagaru Taikō netsu," January 27, 1939.

75. Tokutomi, "Three Qualifications of the Leader of Greater East Asia," 137–38. For more on Tokutomi in English, see Pierson, *Tokutomi Sohō*.

76. The titles and dates of publication of the roundtable articles (cited below by the series title "Taikō o kataru" [Let's Talk about Taikō] and number within the series) are

as follows: 1. "Hideyoshi, Japan's (Historical) Figure" (February 12, 1939); 2. "High Position without Lineage: Fast Action, Broad-Minded Spirit" (February 15, 1939); 3. "Hideyoshi's Era and His Relationship with Oda Nobunaga" (February 16, 1939); 4. "The Dawn of Modern Japan: Hideyoshi and Legal Tender" (February 17, 1939); 5. "For the Sake of the Nation: Why Hideyoshi Refused the Title of Shogun and Became Kampaku" (February 18, 1939); 6. "Placing Hope in the Taikō: A New Technique for Osaka" (February 19, 1939); 7. "Comparing Hideyoshi and Napoleon: Time Period and Human Fate" (February 22, 1939); 8. "Hideyoshi and Christianity: Exchanging Culture with the West" (February 23, 1939); 9. "The Battle of Hideyoshi's Life: The Battle of Yamazaki against Mitsuhide" (February 24, 1939); 10. "The Hypnotic Conditions of the Decisive Battle: The Reason for Victory at Yamazaki" (February 26, 1939); 11. "War and the Problem of [inadequate] Provisions: The Flavor of Art in History" (February 28, 1939); 12. "Hideyoshi and Absolute Japanism: General Yamamoto's View of Taikō Hideyoshi" (March 1, 1939); 13. "The Battle of Komaki: Hideyoshi and the Japanese Spirit" (March 2, 1939); 14. "The Greatness of the Human Taikō: How Does an Author Choose What to Write?" (March 3, 1939); 15. "Keen Eyesight and False Moustaches: Absolute Sentiments about Mother" (March 4, 1939); 16. "Kita-no-mandokoro and Yodo-gimi: The Customs of the Time and the Resulting Lifestyle" (March 5, 1939); 17. "Emperor-ism: An Image of Sovereign and Subject Living in Harmony" (March 8, 1939); 18. "Hideyoshi and His Policy on the Continent: Aspirations to Consume Asia" (March 9, 1939); and 19. "Momoyama Culture and Golden Yield: Toyokuni Shrine and the Spirit of Restoration" (March 10, 1939).

77. "Taikō o kataru" 1.

78. Tokutomi tries to compensate for what he must know is a weak point regarding Hideyoshi's relationship with his wife—Hideyoshi was a well-known womanizer, and she was the mother of none of his heirs—by arguing that Hideyoshi's philandering was not uncommon given his rank and the period in which he lived.

79. "Taikō o kataru" 1.

80. "Taikō o kataru" 2.

81. Yoshikawa, *YEZ*, 19:18–19.

82. Yoshikawa, 19:18–19.

83. *Nihon kokugo daijiten*, 2nd ed., s.v. "tōjin"; and *Kokushi daijiten*, 1st ed., s.vv. "tōjinza," "tōjin yashiki," "tōjin machi."

84. Yoshikawa, *YEZ*, 19:18–19.

85. Yoshikawa, 22:116.

86. Yoshikawa, 22:138.

87. *Hideyoshi jikki*, *Mōri-ke nikki*, *Ikeda kafu shūsei*, *Kuroda Kafu*, and Oze's *Taikōki* all offer slightly different versions of how Hideyoshi concluded the peace treaty with the Mōri before seeking revenge at Yamazaki.

88. "Taikō o kataru" 2.

89. Taikō-sama is a name commonly used for Hideyoshi. It refers to the title *Taikō*, which was given to the father of the imperial advisor (*kanpaku*).

90. "Taikō o kataru" 2.

91. "Taikō o kataru" 9.

92. "Taikō o kataru" 10.

93. Yoshikawa, *YEZ*, 19:188.

94. Yoshikawa, 19:188.
95. Yoshikawa, 19:237.
96. Yoshikawa, 19:242.
97. Yoshikawa, 19:244–45.
98. Yoshikawa, 47:140–41.
99. Yoshikawa, 47:141–42. This and the next quote are from an essay titled "Shōsetsu to shijitsu" (Novels and historical fact) that was published in 1938.
100. Yoshikawa, 47:142.
101. Yoshikawa, 23:408.
102. Nawata, *"Shinsho Taikōki,"* 130.
103. Quoted in Matsumoto, "Yoshikawa Eiji no miryoku," 11.

3. The Salaryman Samurai

1. Parts of a previous version of this chapter were published as Susan Westhafer Furukawa, "Deconstructing the Taikō: The Problem of Hideyoshi as Postwar Business Model," *Mechademia 10: World Renewal—Counterfactual Histories,* ed. Frenchy Lunning (Minneapolis: University of Minnesota Press, 2015), 81–96, copyright 2015 by the Regents of the University of Minnesota.

2. Throughout this chapter, I will follow the lead established by Earl Kinmonth and others in translating the term *sarariiman* as "salaryman" to indicate a white-collar worker in the Japanese context.

3. Miyazawa, *Meiji isshin no saikōzō,* 29.

4. Miyazawa, 28.

5. Sakai, *Nihon no taishū bungaku,* 73. For more on early censorship, see Etō, *Tojisareta gengo kūkan,* 6–20. See also Rubin, "From Wholesomeness to Decadence."

6. Yoshikawa Eiji's ability to publish *Taikōki* so soon after the end of the war (see chapter 2) highlights just how lax the censorship rules were.

7. Quoted in Sakata, *Keizai shōsetsu no yomikata,* 13–14.

8. Prindle, *Made in Japan and Other Japanese "Business Novels,"* xi. See also Sakata, *Keizai shōsetsu no yomikata,* 14.

9. Quoted in Dower, *Embracing Defeat,* 44.

10. John Dower puts the number of war dead at around 2.7 million (*Embracing Defeat,* 48–49), while Andrew Gordon states that it was close to 2.5 million (*A Modern History of Japan,* 225 and 229). Gordon puts the number of people needing repatriation after the war at 6.9 million, or nearly 10 percent of Japan's population at the time.

11. Tipton, *Modern Japan,* 179 and 187; Kōsai, "The Postwar Japanese Economy," 512.

12. Tipton, *Modern Japan,* 193.

13. Kōsai, "The Postwar Japanese Economy," 512–15.

14. Tipton, *Modern Japan,* 180. See also Kōsai, "The Postwar Japanese Economy," 512–15; Bullock, *The Other Women's Lib,* 16–17.

15. For a description of the origins and development of the salaryman class of workers, see Kinmonth, *The Self-Made Man in Meiji Japanese Thought,* 277–325.

16. Earl Kinmonth explains that these salaried white-collar employees were known first as *koshiben* (lunch-bucket men). They started to be referred to as salarymen in the

1910s, and use of the term "salaryman" became widespread in Japan in the 1920s (277–78 and 289–90).

17. Kasahara rose to fame as a scenario writer for movies and television. Some of his famous screenplays include *Shachō Sandaiki* (The company president's record of three generations, 1958), *Shachō Taiheiki* (The company president's *Taiheiki*), *Sarariiman Chūshingura* (The salaryman's treasury of loyal retainers), *Shachō Yōkōki* (The company president's journey to the west, 1962), and *Horafuki Taikōki* (The braggart's Taikōki, 1964). He also wrote screenplays for several movies about Sazae-san, one of Japan's most popular animated figures. She started out as a character in a manga named after her and moved on to her own television series about her life as a housewife, which has run since 1968. See Orbaugh, "Sazae-san."

18. Kōfū-sha was the first to offer novels based on the movies, with a two-volume series published in 1957 and 1958 and released again in 1962 that covered the events of the first three movies. A separate *bunkobon* (small paperback) book version published by Shun'yō Bunko covers what the Kōfū-sha version covers but also includes episodes from the final two movies. The Shun'yō Bunko books are: *Sarariiman shusse Taikōki* (A Taikōki of a salaryman rising up in the world, 1960), *Sarariiman funsensu: Sarariiman shusse Taikōki dai 2 bu* (A Taikōki of a salaryman rising up in the world, part 2, 1960), and *Zoku sarariiman shusse Taikōki: kachō ichiban kura hanamuko buchō nanbaa wan* (A Taikōki of a salaryman rising up in the world: head of the number one storehouse and the bridegroom department head, number one, 1961). The novels faithfully reproduce the content of the films word-for-word and scene-for-scene. Where there is overlap between the novels published from the two different companies, the content is identical. The texts discussed here are those published by Shun'yō Bunko.

19. As noted in chapter 1, Hideyoshi underwent several name changes throughout his life. As a boy, he was called Hiyoshimaru or Hiyoshi, and when he worked for Oda Nobunaga, he received his first surname, Kinoshita. At that time, he was known as Kinoshita Tokichirō. Later his surname became Hashiba, and eventually he was granted the name Toyotomi. The Chinese characters for Hideyoshi's name can also be read Hidekichi.

20. *Naniwabushi*, also known as *ryōkyoku*, is a type of traditional Japanese narrative singing that originated in the latter part of the Edo period. This style of music was especially popular in Japan in the first half of the twentieth century.

21. Kasahara, *Sarariiman shusse Taikōki*, 46. Because the Kōfū-sha versions of these texts are not in print, all page numbers refer to the three volumes published by Shun'yō Bunko.

22. Hokkaido was not formally incorporated into Japan until 1869, and the people of Hokkaido were not recognized officially as Japanese until 1872. In 1947, with the revision of the Local Autonomy Act—which established the current structure of local government—Hokkaido was finally classified as a prefecture and seen as being on a par with other prefectures.

23. The word *shusse* can be defined alternatively as success in life, advancement in one's career, rising to greatness, or making a name for oneself.

24. Kasahara, *Sarariiman shusse Taikōki*, 46 and 219; *Zoku Sarariiman shusse Taikōki*, 72 and 193; and *Sarariiman funsensu*, 2.

25. Kasahara, *Zoku Sarariiman shusse Taikōki*, 3.

26. Maki, *A Yankee in Hokkaido*, ix.

27. Shiba, *Shinshi Taikōki*, vol. 1, back cover.

28. Matsuo, "Rekishikan" (Views of history), 363. Narita Ryūichi also discusses Shiba's merchant perspective in *Shiba Ryōtarō no Bakumatsu/Meiji*.

29. Maari, "Shōnin bungaku," 302.

30. Narita, *Shiba Ryōtarō no Bakumatsu/Meiji*, 39–40.

31. Suekuni, "Shijitsu to kyokō," 90.

32. Shimura, "Sōsaku hōhō."

33. Narita, *Shiba Ryōtarō no Bakumatsu/Meiji*, 8.

34. Shiba, "Watashi no Hideyoshi kan," 360.

35. Suekuni, "Shijitsu to kyokō," 90.

36. Shiba, "Watashi no Hideyoshi kan," 361.

37. NHK Taiga dramas are annual year-long historical dramas that have been aired during prime time since 1963.

38. Statements about viewership information have been taken from NHK yoron chōsa jo, *Terebi-rajio bangumi shichōritsu chōsa—zenkoku kekka hyō*, volumes for 1963–2010. This information is published by Nihon hōsō kyōkai (NHK) hōsō bunka kenkyū sho.

39. Throughout the serialization of *Shinshi Taikōki*, *Shōsetsu shincho* published reader responses to Shiba's novel. Some of these comments are analyzed below in this chapter.

40. Sugaya Masayoshi, letter to editor, *Shōsetsu Shincho*, August 1966, 381.

41. Nishikawa Osamu, letter to editor, *Shōsetsu Shincho*, January 1967, 387.

42. Shiba, *SRZ*, 17:10.

43. Shiba, 17:11.

44. Shiba, 17:11.

45. Shiba, 17:102.

46. Shiba, 17:275.

47. Shiba, 17:275.

48. The word *akindo* can also be read *shōnin*.

49. Shiba, *SRZ*, 17:268.

50. Shiba, 17:268.

51. O'Bryan, *The Growth Idea*, 7.

52. Shiba, *SRZ*, 17:94–96. This refers to a supposed first marriage for Hideyoshi, an incident related in Shiba's *Shinshi Taikōki* that does not appear in any other texts (novels, movies, manga, or television shows) discussed in this book. It includes a description of Hideyoshi that is truly unflattering: young but already bald; with a pointy chin, bulging eyes, narrow forehead, flat nose, and dark skin; and wrinkled. Interspersed with this description of how ugly Hideyoshi is are the internal musings of the bride that reveal her utter shock at how unattractive and unimpressive he is.

53. Shiba, *SRZ*, 17:484.

54. "Ōgonki no Daiyamondo-sha" (The golden years of Diamond), Daiyamondo sha, accessed July 26, 2021, https://www.diamond.co.jp/ishiyama/memorial/c16_2.htm.

55. The details provided in this section are from Shashi hensan iinkai, *Daiyamondo shichijūgo nen shi* and "Ōgonki no Daiyamondo-sha."

56. Shashi hensan iinkai, *Daiyamondo shichijūgo nen shi*, 441.

57. As an example, some Hideyoshi-related titles published over the years include "Taihen na jidai wo kakenuketa otoko Toyotomi Hideyoshi: Nihon shijō saidaikyū no sakkusesu sutorii wo yomu" (Toyotomi Hideyoshi, the man who overcame a difficult time: Read of the greatest success stories in Japanese history), a special issue published by *Purejidento* in January 1996; Kokubu Yasutaka, "Hideyoshi wa ningen kankei no tatsujin de aru: Sengoku zuiichi no 'ningen tsū' ni manabu" (Hideyoshi is a master of human relations: Learn from the best 'human being' of the Warring States period), *Purejidento*, May 1996, 176–80; Shino Masafumi, "Toyotomi Hideyoshi ga Oda Nobunaga yori sugurete-ita ten to wa? Rekishi ni manabu 'tatakawazu shite katsu-hō'" (What made Toyotomi Hideyoshi superior to Oda Nobunaga? Learn the 'win-without-fighting method from history'), *Daiyamondo*, March 14, 2016, https://diamond.jp/articles/-/87776; and Suzuki Hiroki, "'Nihon ichi shusse shita otoko' Toyotomi Hideyoshi kara manabu sonota taisei kara nukedasu chōryaku-hō" (Learn how to stand out from the crowd from Toyotomi Hideyoshi, 'Japan's most successful man,'" *Daiyamondo*, August 8, 2016, https://diamond.jp/articles/-/97538. Only recently have negative stories about Hideyoshi and other figures from the Sengoku period begun to appear in these magazines. In the March 2020 issue of *Purejidento*, for example, all of the three unifiers were listed in Hongō Kazuto's article "Seikaku saiaku, jinbō zero, ningen fushin, kamidanomi . . . 'sengoku bushō' de ichiban damena ningen wa dare ka?" (Worst personality, no human desire, misanthrope, reliance on God . . . who is the worst human being of the "Sengoku warlords"?), *Purejidento*, May 17, 2020, https://president.jp/articles/-/33750.

58. Even today numerous books and magazine articles are published each year in Japan that analyze these three figures in terms of the current business climate.

59. Shimizu and Kojima, *Hideyoshi to ningen kankei*; Fuji, *Sengoku o ikiru*; Naganuma, *Hideyoshi no seikōhō* and *Hideyoshi ni manabu tōsotsuryoku*.

60. Naganuma, *Hideyoshi ni manabu tōsotsuryoku*, 1.

61. Naganuma, 2.

62. Fuji, *Sengoku o ikiru*, i–ii.

63. Fuji, iii.

64. Nora, "From *Lieux de mémoire* to Realms of Memory," xxiv.

65. Shimizu and Kojima, *Nobunaga no ningen kankei* and *Ieyasu no ningen kankei*.

66. Shimizu and Kojima, *Hideyoshi to ningen kankei*, 3.

67. Shimizu and Kojima, 4. *Kagakuteki no susumekata* is followed by *saientifikku apuroochi*, or "scientific approach" in the original.

68. Shimizu and Kojima, inside cover flap. The authors also wrote *Purejidento Nobunaga* (President Nobunaga), published by Nihon Sono Saabisu Sentaa in 1967, before Kojima set off on a solo career. He continued to write books on the Sengoku period and modern management well into the 1990s.

69. Shimizu and Kojima, *Hideyoshi to ningen kankei*, 4–5.

70. Shimizu and Kojima, 245.

71. Shimizu and Kojima, 245–46.

72. Shimizu and Kojima, 246.

73. Citations for this chapter refer to the 1994 version of Tsutsui's "Yamazaki."

74. Ozaki, "Tsutsui Yasutaka no rekishi ninshiki," 71.

75. Tsutsui, "Yamazaki," 365.

76. In 1871, domains were reorganized into prefectures and their names were changed.

77. See Tsutsui, "Yamazaki," 379, for example.

78. Tsutsui, 365. Kanbei was from a family of prominent daimyo in Harima province (modern Hyōgō prefecture) and served Hideyoshi until 1589. He became a Christian in 1585, which makes the quotation cited by Tsutsui even more unbelievable, since Nobunaga died in 1582.

79. Tsutsui, *Tsutsui Junkei*, 114.

80. Tsutsui, "Yamazaki," 378.

81. At this point, Toyotomi Hideyoshi is known as Hashiba Tokichirō.

82. Tsutsui, "Yamazaki," 378–79. Ōtsu is modern Shiga prefecture, or the opposite direction from Kyoto than where Hideyoshi really was.

83. Tsutsui, 379–80.

84. Tsutsui, 380.

85. Tsutsui, 382.

86. Tsutsui, 382.

87. Tsutsui, 383.

4. *The Women of the Realm*

1. Parts of a previous version of this chapter were published in Susan Westhafer Furukawa, "Nagai Michiko and Ariyoshi Sawako Rewrite the Taikō," *US-Japan Women's Journal* 51 (2017): 59–79. Republished here with permission from the University of Hawai'i Press.

2. Nolte and Hastings, "The Meiji State's Policy toward Women," 152.

3. Miyake, "Doubling Expectations," 267.

4. See, for example, Bardsley, "Discourse on Women in Postwar Japan"; Bullock, *The Other Women's Lib*; Gordon, "Managing the Japanese Household: The New Life Movement in Postwar Japan," 245–83; Uno, "The Death of 'Good Wife, Wise Mother'?" See also Ochiai, *The Japanese Family System in Transition*.

5. Bardsley, "Discourse on Women in Postwar Japan," 5.

6. Orbaugh, "The Body in Contemporary Japanese Women's Fiction," 121.

7. Bullock, *The Other Women's Lib*, 2.

8. Bullock, 8; Orbaugh, "The Body in Contemporary Japanese Women's Fiction," 127.

9. Bullock, *The Other Women's Lib*, 8.

10. Nagai, "Rekishi no naka no josei no hatsumei" (The invention of women in history).

11. Nagai, *Nagai Michiko rekishi shōsetsu zenshū* (*NMRSZ*), 14:621.

12. Background information on Nagai Michiko has been taken from Ichiko, Kan, and Asai, *Nihon josei bungaku daijiten*, and Muramatsu and Watanabe, *Gendai josei bungaku jiten*.

13. Nagai, *NMRSZ*, 14:334.

14. Nagai, 14:334.

15. For example, when Kuwata Tadachika discusses Onene, he emphasizes her inability to bear any children for Hideyoshi (*Taikō Hideyoshi no tegami* [The letters of the

retired imperial regent Hideyoshi], 29). See also Kitagawa, "An Independent Wife during the Warring States."

16. Nagai, *Nihon no suupaa reidii monogatari* (Stories of Japanese superwomen), 114.

17. Nagai, 118.

18. For example, see Shiba, *Shinshi Taikōki* (The new historical Taikōki), 84–87.

19. Nagai, *NMRSZ*, 14:17–27.

20. Nagai, 14:74.

21. Nagai, 14:85 and 89.

22. Nagai, 14:188–89.

23. Nagai, 14:267–68.

24. Nagai, 14:269.

25. Quoted in Berry, *Hideyoshi*, 57.

26. Berry, 56.

27. Nagai, *NMRSZ*, 14:210.

28. Nagai, 14:362.

29. Nagai, 14:458.

30. Nagai, 14:456–60.

31. Sievers, *Flowers in Salt*, 5–6.

32. Nagai, *NMRSZ*, 14:304.

33. Nagai, 14:361.

34. Nagai, 14:373.

35. Nagai, 14:534.

36. Nagai, 14:615.

37. Nagai, 14:326.

38. Nagai, 14:317.

39. Nagai, 14:317.

40. Nagai, 14:317.

41. Nagai, 14:318.

42. Nagai, 14:319–20.

43. Nagai, 14:326.

44. Nagai, 14:149–51.

45. Nagai, 14:312–13.

46. Ariyoshi Sawako, *Izumo no Okuni* (*INO*), 1:23.

47. Background information on Ariyoshi has been taken from Ichiko, Kan, and Asai, *Nihon josei bungaku daijiten*, and Muramatsu and Watanabe, *Gendai josei bungaku jiten*, as well as from Tahara, "Ariyoshi Sawako."

48. Ariyoshi, *INO*, 1:92–93.

49. Ariyoshi, 1:224.

50. Ariyoshi, 1:228.

51. Ariyoshi, 2:34–37.

52. Ohnuki-Tierney, *Kamikaze, Cherry Blossoms, and Nationalisms*, 34. See also Berry, *Hideyoshi*, 191–92.

53. Ariyoshi, *INO*, 2:99–100.

54. Ariyoshi, 1:251–52.

55. Ariyoshi, 2:172.

56. Ariyoshi, 2:174.

57. The Japanese word, *tenkaichi*, literally means "the only one in the realm" or "the only one under heaven." I concur with James Brandon's rendering of this phrase as "best in the world" (Ariyoshi Sawako, *The Kabuki Dancer*), though I would add that the use of this particular term serves to put Okuni on a par with both Nobunaga and Hideyoshi, who were seeking to become *tenka* (leaders of the realm).

58. Ariyoshi, *INO*, 3:63–65.

59. Ariyoshi, 2:120.

60. Ariyoshi, 2:252–53.

61. Ariyoshi, 3:37.

62. Ariyoshi, 1:133.

5. *Things Best Left Unseen*

1. Japan has the oldest and one of the most rapidly shrinking populations in the world. For up-to-date data on these numbers, see Statistics Bureau, Japan, *Japan Statistical Handbook 2021*.

2. Arai, "Intellectual Property Strategy in Japan," 5; McGray, "Japanese Gross National Cool."

3. Seaton and Yamamura, "Japanese Popular Culture and Contents Tourism," 6.

4. Seaton and Yamamura, 7.

5. These observations about the shrine and the mound are based on annual visits to both sites between 2008–10 and 2013–19.

6. Foer, Thuras, and Morton, *Atlas Obscura*, 159.

7. Interigen-chan, January 2017, Trip Advisor; Miruku 733851, February 2020, Trip Advisor; temperature6, July 2016, Trip Advisor.

8. Yuzuki Kaori, 2019, Google Reviews; Tamakyō, 2020, Google Reviews.

9. Tamakyō.

10. Quoted in Murai, Ota, and Morita, "Hideyoshi no henbō" (Hideyoshi's transformation), 26.

11. While this chapter looks at sites specific to Japan, it should be noted that there are museums related to Hideyoshi's invasions of Korea in both Korea and China. In Korea, the JinJu National Museum in particular has done a thorough job of depicting the conflict between Hideyoshi's troops and Korean soldiers (Imjinwaeran in Korean). Unsurprisingly, that museum's depiction of the war years is quite different from that of Nagoya Castle Museum. In particular, in contrast to how he is depicted at the Japanese museum, in the Korean one Hideyoshi is highly visible in presentations about the conflict and depicted as a large and intimidating character.

12. Saga Prefectural Nagoya Castle Museum, "Guide to Saga Prefectural Nagoya Castle Museum," 3. Throughout the chapter, I use English translations of materials provided by the museum. All the translations fairly and accurately represent the original Japanese.

13. Since 2001, the museum has held thirty-seven special exhibits, running on average four to six weeks each. Just two of the special exhibits have focused on Hideyoshi: an exhibit in 2008 about sentence style in Hideyoshi's letters and one that ended in January 2021

that explored Hideyoshi's image in paintings and print. In contrast, the museum has hosted ten special exhibits related to Korean history and culture and Japan-Korean relations.

14. Takenaka, "Reactionary Nationalism and Museum Controversies," 87.

15. Saga Prefectural Nagoya Castle Museum, English-language museum pamphlet.

16. Known as *geobukseon*, the turtle ship earned its name from shell-like armor that covers it. Turtle ships were used in Korean naval battles from the fifteenth to nineteenth centuries. The Japanese *atakebune* were used primarily in the sixteenth and seventeenth centuries.

17. Saga Prefectural Nagoya Castle Museum, English-language museum pamphlet.

18. Saga Prefectural Nagoya Castle Museum, "Guide to Saga Prefectural Nagoya Castle Museum," 21.

19. Informal conversation at the Saga Nagoya Castle site, July 19, 2006.

20. Like Hideyoshi, his wife had several names and titles over the course of her life. She was Nene, Ne, Onene, One, Toyotomi Yoshiko, Kita no Mandokoro, and Kōdai-in. For more details, see Samonides, "Patronizing Images," 106fn31. Furthermore, while temple guides and tour books have referred to her as Kōdai-in, more recently she has been called Onene, which seems quite anachronistic. The name shift alone somehow transports her back in time to her role as Hideyoshi's wife, taking from her the power and prestige she managed to gather during the two decades she lived and oversaw activities at the temple.

21. Samonides, "Patronizing Images," 100.

22. Samonides, 104 and 106.

23. The English translations of the names of these buildings have been taken from the English-language pamphlet distributed to guests at the temple.

24. Samonides, "Patronizing Images," 101.

25. Samonides, 102.

26. Occhi, "Wobbly Aesthetics, Performances, and Message," 113.

27. See Yano, *Pink Globalization*; Daliot-Bul, "Japan Brand Strategy"; Allison, *Millenial Monsters*; McGray, "Japanese Gross National Cool."

28. Daliot-Bul, "Japan Brand Strategy," 247.

29. Yano, *Pink Globalization*, 61.

30. In February 2021, for example, Kōdaiji participated in the seventh annual Valentine Photo Contest by giving young couples access to newly painted interior sliding panel doors at the temple, depicting large images of the lovers Akane and Kan'ichi from Baron Yoshimoto's well-known manga series *Gendai Jukyoden* (Modern Jukyoden). Kōdaiji encouraged couples to take their picture in front of the doors and post it to social media with the hashtag "Lovers' Kōdaiji."

31. Mindar was created by a team led by Hiroshi Ishiguro. See, for example, Peter Holley, "Meet Mindar, the Robotic Buddhist Priest," *Washington Post*, August 22, 2019, https://www.washingtonpost.com/technology/2019/08/22/introducing-mindar-robotic -priest-that-some-are-calling-frankenstein-monster/.

32. See Yano, *Pink Globalization*, 61.

33. Manabe, "Monju-kun," 268. See also Allison, *Millenial Monsters*, 89–90.

34. Yano, *Pink Globalization*, 61.

35. Seaton and Yamamura, "Japanese Popular Culture and Contents Tourism," 2.
36. Interview with a docent at Kōdaiji, June 10, 2018.
37. Seaton et al., *Contents Tourism in Japan*, 10.
38. Prough, *Revisiting Kyoto*, chapter 2.

Epilogue

1. Morris-Suzuki, *The Past within Us*, 28 and 232.
2. See, for example, Seaton, "Taiga Dramas and Tourism."
3. The data here and below in the paragraph have been taken from data found in NHK yoron chōsa jo, *Terebi·rajio bangumi shichōritsu chōsa—zenkoku kekka hyō*, vols. Shōwa 38–Heisei 21. The data here been updated with information from the NHK Taiga dorama website, "Taiga dorama zen risuto" (A complete list of Taiga drama).
4. Though fifteen manga artists wrote the bulk of these stories, new artists were being added to the list of contributors until the end of the series.
5. The publisher announced this fact in bold letters on the *obi* wrapped around the cover of the second edition of *Nobunaga, Hideyoshi, Ieyasu-ban*, published in 2005. NHK "Sono toki rekishi ga ugoita" shuzai-han, *Sono toki rekishi ga ugoita*.
6. Kikuchi, *Rekishi shosetsu to wa nani ka* (What is historical fiction?), i.
7. Teshigahara, *Rikyū*. These words appear on the screen before the opening credits.
8. See Bodart, "Tea and Counsel," for a detailed description of these theories.
9. Teshigahara, *Rikyū*.
10. Ruch, "Medieval Jongleurs and the Making of a National Literature," 291–92.

Bibliography

Abe Kazuhiko. *Taikōki to sono shūhen* (Taikōki and its environs). Osaka: Shohan, 1997.

Allison, Anne. *Millenial Monsters: Japanese Toys and the Global Imagination*. Berkeley: University of California Press, 2006.

Anderson, Benedict. *Imagined Communities: Reflections on the Origins and Spread of Nationalism*, 2nd ed. London: Verso, 1991.

Arai, Hisamitsu. "Intellectual Property Strategy in Japan." *International Journal of Intellectual Property: Law, Economy and Management* 1 (2005): 5–12.

Ariyoshi Nobuto. "Shiba Ryōtarō no benkyōhō" (Shiba Ryōtarō study methods). "Shiba Ryōtarō ga yuku" (Shiba Ryōtarō sets out), special issue, *Purejidento* (President), March 1997, 106–13.

Ariyoshi Sawako. *The Doctor's Wife*. Translated by Wakako Hironaka and Ann Siller Kostant. Tokyo: Kodansha International, 1978.

———. *Izumo no Okuni* (The Kabuki dancer). 3 vols. Tokyo: Chūō Kōron-sha, 1969–1972.

———. *The Kabuki Dancer*. Translated by James Brandon. Tokyo: Kodansha International, 1994.

———. *The River Ki*. Translated by Mildred Tahara. Tokyo: Kodansha International, 1980.

Bardsley, Jan. "Discourse on Women in Postwar Japan: The Housewife Debate of 1955." *US-Japan Women's Journal: English Supplement*, no. 16 (1999): 3–47.

Berry, Mary Elizabeth. *Hideyoshi*. Cambridge, MA: Harvard University Asia Center, 1982.

———. *Japan in Print: Information and the Nation in the Early Modern Period*. Berkeley: University of California Press, 2006.

Bodart, Beatrice M. "Tea and Counsel: The Political Role of Sen Rikyū." *Monumenta Nipponica* 32, no. 1 (1977): 49–74.

Boscaro, Adriana. *101 Letters of Hideyoshi: The Private Correspondences of Toyotomi Hideyoshi*. Tokyo: Sophia University Press, 1975.

Bukh, Alexander. "Historical Memory and Shiba Ryōtarō: Remembering Russia, Creating Japan." In *The Power of Memory in Modern Japan*, edited by Sven Saaler and Wolfgang Schwentker, 96–115. Leiden, the Netherlands: Brill, 2008.
Bullock, Julia. *The Other Women's Lib: Gender and Body in Japanese Women's Fiction.* Honolulu: University of Hawai'i Press, 2010.

Cho, Ilsoo David. "Discourses of Nation: Tensions in Early Modern Korea-Japan Relations." Ph.D. diss., Harvard University, 2017.
Chūken seinen shōkō dan. "Kōgun honzen no ninmu nitsute" (On the mission of the Imperial Army). In *Gendaishi shiryō* (Contemporary historical materials), vol. 5: *Kokka shugi undo* (Nationalist movements), pt. 2, edited by Takahashi Masae, 811–24. 2nd ed. Tokyo: Misuzu Shobō, 1964.
Cook, Haruko Taya. "Reporting the 'Fall of *Nankin*' and the Suppression of a Japanese Literary 'Memory' of the Nature of a War." In *Nanking 1937: Memory and Healing*, edited by Fei Fei Li, Robert Sabella, and David Liu, 121–53. New York: Routledge, 2002.
Cooper, Michael, ed. *They Came to Japan: An Anthology of European Reports on Japan, 1543–1640.* Berkeley: University of California Press, 1965.

Daiyamondo sha. "Ōgonki no Daiyamondo-sha" (The golden years of Diamond). Accessed July 26, 2021. https://www.diamond.co.jp/ishiyama/memorial/c16_2.htm.
Daliot-Bul, Michal. "Japan Brand Strategy: The Taming of 'Cool Japan' and the Challenges of Cultural Planning in a Postmodern Age." *Social Science Journal* 12, no. 2 (2009): 247–66.
Davis, Julie. "The Trouble with Hideyoshi: Censoring Ukiyo-s and the *Ehon Taikōki* Incident of 1804." *Japan Forum* 19, no. 3 (November 2007): 281–315.
de Groot, Jerome. *The Historical Novel.* London: Routledge, 2010.
Dening, Walter. *The Life of Toyotomi Hideyoshi*, 3rd ed. Tokyo: Hokuseido Press, 1955.
Dower, John. *Embracing Defeat: Japan in the Aftermath of World War II.* London: W. W. Norton, 1999.

Elison, George. "Hideyoshi, the Bountiful Minister." In *Warlords, Artisans, and Commoners: Japan in the Sixteenth Century*, edited by George Elison and Bardwell Smith, 223–44. Honolulu: University of Hawai'i Press, 1981.
Etō Jun. *Tojisareta gengo kūkan: Senryōgun no ken'etsu to sengo Nihon* (Sealed linguistic space: Censorship by Occupation forces and postwar Japan). Tokyo: Bungei Shunjū, 1989.

Fitts, Robert. *Banzai Babe Ruth: Baseball, Espionage, and Assassination during the 1934 Tour of Japan.* Lincoln: University of Nebraska Press, 2012.
Foer, Joshua, Dylan Thuras, and Ella Morton. *Atlas Obscura.* New York: Workman, 2016.
Foster, Michael. *Pandemonium and Parade: Japanese Monsters and the Culture of Yokai.* Berkeley: University of California Press, 2009.
Fuji Kimifusa. *Hideyoshi ni manabu ketsudan to jikkō no ningen gaku* (Learn from the humanity of Hideyoshi's resolutions and actions). Tokyo: Mikasa Shobō, 1988.
———. *Ieyasu "nin" no keiei* (Ieyasu's "endurance" management style). Tokyo: Daiyamondo-sha, 1978.

————. *Sengoku o ikiru: Hideyoshi ni manabu ningen katsuyōhō* (Living in the Sengoku period: Learning human management from Hideyoshi). Tokyo: Daiyamondo-sha, 1974.

————. *Shōgun ni manabu ningen kanri* (Learn personnel management from the shogun). Tokyo: Karuchā Shuppan-sha, 1972.

Gluck, Carol. "The Invention of Edo." In *Mirror of Modernity: Invented Traditions of Modern Japan*. Edited by Stephen Vlastos, 262–84. Berkeley: University of California Press, 1998.

————. *Japan's Modern Myths: Ideology in the Late Meiji Period*. Princeton, NJ: Princeton University Press, 1985.

Gordon, Andrew. "Managing the Japanese Household: The New Life Movement in Postwar Japan." In *Gendering Modern Japanese History*, edited by Barbara Malony and Kathleen Lee, 423–62. Cambridge, MA: Harvard University Asia Center, 2005.

————. *A Modern History of Japan: From Tokugawa Times to the Present*. Oxford: Oxford University Press, 2003.

Greenblatt, Stephen. *Renaissance Self-Fashioning: From More to Shakespeare*. Chicago: University of Chicago Press, 1980.

Hall, John W. "Hideyoshi's Domestic Policies." In *Japan before Tokugawa: Political Consolidation and Economic Growth, 1500–1650*, edited by John W. Hall, Nagahara Kenji, and Yamamura Kozo, 194–223. Princeton, NJ: Princeton University Press, 1981.

————. *Japan from Prehistory to Modern Times*. New York: Dell, 1970.

Hashimoto, Akiko. *The Long Defeat: Cultural Trauma, Memory, and Identity in Japan*. Oxford: Oxford University Press, 2015.

Henry, David. "*Momotarō, or the Peach Boy*: Japan's Best-Loved Folktale as National Allegory." Ph.D. diss., University of Michigan, 2009.

Hirano Ken. "Jun bungaku to taishū bungaku" (Pure literature and popular literature). *Gunzō* 40 (December 1961): 152–74.

Hobsbawm, Eric, and Terence Ranger, eds. *The Invention of Tradition*. Cambridge: Cambridge University Press, 1983.

Ichiko Natsuo, Kan Satōko, and Asai Kiyoshi, eds. *Nihon josei bungaku daijiten* (Dictionary of women's literature). Tokyo: Nihon Tosho Sentaa, 2006.

Ikegami, Eiko. *The Taming of the Samurai: Honorific Individualism and the Making of Modern Japan*. Cambridge, MA: Harvard University Press, 1995.

Ivanova, Gergana. *Unbinding the Pillow Book: The Many Lives of a Japanese Classic*. New York: Columbia University Press, 2018.

Jones, Sumie. Introduction to *An Edo Anthology: Literature from Japan's Mega-City, 1750–1850*, edited by Sumie Jones and Kenji Watanabe, 1–41. Honolulu: University of Hawai'i Press, 2013.

Kaku Kōzō, ed. *Gendaigoyaku bukōyawa: Hideyoshi Hen* (An evening tale: Brilliant military exploits related to Toyotomi Hideyoshi, a modern translation). Tokyo: Shin Jinbutsu Ōraisha, 1992.

Kasahara Ryōzō. *Sarariiman funsensu: Sarariiman shusse Taikōki dai 2 bu* (A Taikōki of a salaryman rising up in the world, part 2). Tokyo: Shun'yō Bunko, 1960.

————. *Sarariiman shusse Taikōki* (A Taikōki of a salaryman rising up in the world). Tokyo: Shun'yō Bunko, 1960.

————. *Zoku sarariiman shusse Taikōki* (A Taikōki of a salaryman rising up in the world continued). Tokyo: Shun'yō Bunko, 1961.

Kasza, Gregory. *The State and Mass Media in Japan, 1918–1945.* Berkeley: University of California Press, 1993.

Keene, Donald. "Japanese Writers and the Greater East Asia War." *Journal of Asian Studies* 23, no. 2 (February 1964): 209–25.

————. *The Major Plays of Chikamatsu.* New York: Columbia University Press, 1990.

————. "Variations on a Theme: Chūshingura." In *Chūshingura: Studies in Kabuki and Puppet Theater*, edited by James Brandon, 1–22. Honolulu: University of Hawai'i Press, 1982.

Kikuchi Masanori. *Rekishi shosetsu to wa nani ka* (What is historical fiction?). Tokyo: Chikuma shobo, 1979.

Kinmonth, Earl. *The Self-Made Man in Meiji Japanese Thought: From Samurai to Salary Man.* Berkeley: University of California Press, 1981.

Kitagawa, Tomoko. "An Independent Wife during the Warring States: The Life of Kitamandokoro Nei (1548–1624) in Letters." Ph.D. diss., Princeton University, 2009.

Kornicki, Peter. *The Book in Japan: A Cultural History from the Beginnings to the Nineteenth Century.* Leiden, the Netherlands: Koninklijike, 1998.

————. "The Enmeiin Affair of 1803: The Spread of Information in the Tokugawa Period." *Harvard Journal of Asiatic Studies* 42, no. 2 (1982): 503–33.

————. "*Nishiki no ura*: An Instance of Censorship and the Structure of a *Sharebon*." *Monumenta Nipponica* 32, no. 2 (1977): 153–88.

Kōsai, Yutaka. "The Postwar Japanese Economy, 1945–1973." In *The Cambridge History of Japan*, vol. 6: *The Twentieth Century*, edited by Peter Duus, 494–537. Cambridge: Cambridge University Press, 1988.

Kuwata Tadachika. *Taikō Hideyoshi no tegami* (The letters of Taiko Hideyoshi). Tokyo: Bungei Shunjū, 1965.

————. *Taikōki no kenkyū* (Taikōki studies). Tokyo: Tokuma Shoten, 1965.

————. *Toyotomi Hideyoshi kenkyū* (Toyotomi Hideyoshi studies). Tokyo: Kadokawa Shoten, 1975.

————. *Toyotomi Hideyoshi no subete* (Everything about Toyotomi Hideyoshi). Tokyo: Shinjinbutsuōrai-sha, 1981.

Langton, Scott. "A Literature for the People: A Study of jidai shōsetsu in Taishō and Early Shōwa Japan." Ph.D. diss., Ohio State University, 2000.

Lukács, Georg. *The Historical Novel.* Translated by Hannah Mitchell and Stanley Mitchell. London: Merlin Press, 1962.

Maari Sumika. "Shōnin bungaku" (Merchant literature). In *Shiba Ryōtarō jiten* (Shiba Ryōtarō encyclopedia), edited by Shimura Kunihiro, 301–2. Tokyo: Bensei Shuppan, 2002.

Mack, Edward. *Manufacturing Modern Japanese Literature: Publishing, Prizes, and the Ascription of Literary Value.* Durham, NC: Duke University Press, 2010.

Maeda Ai. *Text and the City: Essays on Japanese Modernity.* Edited and translated by James Fujii. Durham, NC: Duke University Press, 2004.

Maki, John. *A Yankee in Hokkaido: The Life of William S. Clark.* New York: Lexington Books, 2002.

Manabe, Noriko. "Monju-kun: Children's Culture as Protest." In *Child's Play: Multi-Sensory Histories of Children and Childhood in Japan.* Berkeley: University of California Press (2017): 264–85.

Marcus, Marvin. "Mori Ōgai and the Biographical Quest." *Harvard Journal of Asiatic Studies* 51, no. 1 (June 1991): 233–62.

———. *Paragons of the Ordinary: The Biographical Literature of Mori Ōgai.* Honolulu: University of Hawai'i Press, 1993.

Matsumoto Akira. "Yoshikawa Eiji no miryoku" (The charm of Yoshikawa Eiji). Special issue, *Kokubungaku* 10 (October 2000): 10–13.

Matsuo Masashi. "Rekishikan" (Views of history). In *Shiba Ryōtarō jiten*, edited by Shimura Kunihiro, 362–63. Tokyo: Bensei Shuppan, 2002.

———. "Shiba Ryōtarō no sakuhin ni miru rekishikan" (The perspective on history seen in Shiba Ryōtarō's works). In *Kokubungaku kaishaku to kanshō bessatsu: Shiba Ryōtarō no sekai*, edited by Shimura Kunihiro, 100–104. Tokyo: Shibundō, 2002.

McClellan, Edwin. *Fragments of a Past: A Memoir.* Tokyo: Kodansha, 1992.

McGray, Douglas. "Japanese Gross National Cool." *Foreign Policy* 130 (2002).

Mitarai Tatsuo. *Denki Shōriki Matsutarō* (Biography of Shōriki Matsutarō). Tokyo: Kodansha, 1944.

Miura Satōshi, ed. *Ehon Taikōki* (The illustrated chronicles of Toyotomi Hideyoshi). Tokyo: Yūhōdō Bunko, 1917.

Miyake, Yoshiko. "Doubling Expectations: Motherhood and Woman's Factory Work under State Management in Japan in the 1930s and 1940s." In *Recreating Japanese Women, 1600–1945*, edited by Gail Lee Bernstein, 267–95. Berkeley: University of California Press, 1991.

Miyazawa Seiichi. *Meiji isshin no saikōzō: Kindai nihon no "kigen shinwa"* (The second Meiji Restoration: Modern Japan's origin myth). Tokyo: Aoki Shoten, 2005.

Mori Ōgai. "History as It Is and History Ignored." In *The Historical Fiction of Mori Ōgai*, edited by David Dilworth and J. Thomas Rimer, 179–84. Honolulu: University of Hawai'i Press, 1991.

Morris-Suzuki, Tessa. *The Past within Us: Media, Modernity, History.* London: Verso, 2005.

Murai Shigetoshi, Ota Satōru, and Morita Naoki. "Hideyoshi no henbō: *Shinshi Taikōki* no seikai" (Hideyoshi's transformation: The world of *Shinshi Taikōki*). In *Shiba Ryōtarō III*, edited by Yamaguchi Kazuomi, 19–82. Tokyo: Asahi Shinbunsha, 2008.

Muramatsu Sadataka and Watanabe Sumiko, eds. *Gendai josei bungaku jiten.* Tokyo: Tōkyō-do Shuppan, 1990.

Murdoch, James. *A History of Japan.* Vol. 2. New York: Frederick Ungar, 1964.

Nagai Michiko. *Nagai Michiko rekishi shōsetsu zenshū* (The collected historical fiction of Nagai Michiko). Vol. 8: *Enkan/Emaki* (Ring of fire/The picture scroll). Tokyo: Chūō Kōron-sha, 1995.

———. *Nagai Michiko rekishi shōsetsu zenshū* (The collected historical fiction of Nagai Michiko). Vol. 9: *Hōjō Masako* (Hōjō Masako). Tokyo: Chūō Kōron-sha, 1995.

———. *Nagai Michiko rekishi shōsetsu zenshū* (The collected historical fiction of Nagai Michiko). Vol. 14: *Ōja no tsuma: Hideyoshi no tsuma Onene* (The monarch's wife: Hideyoshi's wife Onene). Tokyo: Chūō Kōron-sha, 1995.

———. *Nihon no suupaa reidii monogatari* (Stories of Japanese super ladies). Tokyo: Nihon keizai shinbun-sha, 1969.

———. "Rekishi no naka no josei no hatsumei (The invention of women in history)." Lecture at the NHK Broadcast Museum, Tokyo, March 22, 2008.

———. *Rekishi o sawagaseta onnatachi* (Women who disturbed history). Tokyo: Bungei Shunjū, 1979.

Naganuma Hiroaki. *Hideyoshi ni manabu tōsotsuryoku* (Learning leadership strength from Hideyoshi). Tokyo: Karuchā Shuppan-sha, 1974.

———. *Hideyoshi no seikōhō* (Hideyoshi's path to success). Tokyo: Karuchā Shuppan-sha, 1973.

Nakayama Yasumasa, ed. *Shinbun shūsei Meiji hennen-shi* (Compilation of Meiji era newspapers). Vol. 5. Tokyo: Zaisei Kezai Gakkai, 1934.

Narita Ryūichi. *Shiba Ryōtarō no bakumatsu/Meiji: Ryōma ga yuku to Saka no ue no kumo o yomu* (Shiba Ryōtarō's bakumatsu and Meiji: Reading *Ryōma Moves On* and *The Clouds over the Hills*). Tokyo: Asahi Shinbun-sha, 2003.

Nawata Kazuo. "Shinsho Taikōki" (The new Taikōki). Special issue, *Kokubungaku* 10 (October 2000): 130–37.

NHK yoron chōsa jo, ed. *Terebi rajio bangumi shichōritsu chōsa—zenkoku kekka hyō* (Television and radio audience rating survey—nationwide results). Vols. Shōwa 38–Heisei 21. Nihon hōsō kyōkai hōsō bunka kenkyū sho, 1963–2010.

NHK "Sono toki rekishi ga ugoita" shuzai-han. *Sono toki rekishi ga ugoita: Nobunaga, Hideyoshi, Ieyasu ban* (That's when history changed: The Nobunaga, Hideyoshi, and Ieyasu issue). Tokyo: Hōmu-sha, 2005.

Nolte, Sharon, and Sally Hastings. "The Meiji State's Policy toward Women, 1890–1910." In *Recreating Japanese Women, 1600–1945*, edited by Gail Lee Bernstein, 151–74. Berkeley: University of California Press, 1991.

Nora, Pierre. "From *Lieux de mémoire* to Realms of Memory." In *Realms of Memory: The Construction of the French Past*, vol. 1: *Conflicts and Divisions*, edited by Pierre Nora and Lawrence D. Kritzman, translated by Arthur Goldhammer, xv–xxiv. New York: Columbia University Press, 1996.

O'Bryan, Scott. *The Growth Idea: Purpose and Prosperity in Postwar Japan*. Honolulu: University of Hawai'i Press, 2009.

Occhi, Debra J. "Wobbly Aesthetics, Performances, and Message: Comparing Japanese Kyara with Their Anthropomorphic Forebears." *Asian Ethnology* 71, no. 1 (2012): 109–32.

Ochiai, Emiko. *The Japanese Family System in Transition: A Sociological Analysis of Family Change in Postwar Japan*. Tokyo: LTCB International Library Foundation, 1997.

Ohnuki-Tierney, Emiko. *Kamikaze, Cherry Blossoms, and Nationalisms: The Militarization of Aesthetics in Japanese History*. Chicago: University of Chicago Press, 2002.

Orbaugh, Sharalyn. "The Body in Contemporary Japanese Women's Fiction." In *The Woman's Hand: Gender and Theory in Japanese Women's Writing*, edited by Paul Gordon Schalow and Janet Walker, 119–64. Stanford, CA: Stanford University Press, 1996.

———. "Sazae-san." In *Encyclopedia of Contemporary Japanese Culture*, edited by Sandra Buckley, 439. New York: Routledge, 2002.

Ozaki Hotsuki. *Rekishi shōsetsu, jidai shōsetsu sōkaisetsu* (Historical fiction, period fiction: A critical introduction). Tokyo: Jiyū Kokumin-sha, 1984.

———. *Taishū bungaku* (Popular literature). Tokyo: Kinokuniya Shoten, 1980.

———. *Taishū bungakuron* (Theory of popular literature). Tokyo: Kodansha, 2001.

———. "Tsutsui Yasutaka no rekishi ninshiki" (Tsutsui Yasutaka's understanding of history). *Kokubungaku* 26, no. 11 (August 1981): 67–71.

———. *Yoshikawa Eiji denki* (Biography of Yoshikawa Eiji). Tokyo: Kodansha, 1970.

Oze Hoan. *Eiri Taikōki* (The illustrated chronicles of Toyotomi Hideyoshi). Kyoto: Izumoji Izumi Jo, 1710.

———. *Taikōki* (The chronicles of Toyotomi Hideyoshi). Vol. 60 of *Shin Nihon koten bungaku taikei*. Tokyo: Iwanami Shoten, 1996.

Pierson, John D. *Tokutomi Sohō, 1863–1957: A Journalist for Modern Japan*. Princeton, NJ: Princeton University Press, 1980.

Prindle, Tamae. *Made in Japan and Other Japanese "Business Novels."* London: M. E. Sharpe, 1989.

Prough, Jennifer. "Meiji Restoration Vacation: Heritage Tourism in Contemporary Kyoto." *Japan Forum* 30, no. 4 (2018): 564–88.

———. *Revisiting Kyoto: Heritage Tourism in Contemporary Kyoto*. Honolulu: University of Hawai'i Press, 2022.

Ravina, Mark. *The Last Samurai: The Life and Battles of Saigō Takamori*. Hoboken, NJ: John Wiley and Sons, 2004.

Rubin, Jay. "From Wholesomeness to Decadence: The Censorship of Literature under the Allied Occupation." *Journal of Japanese Studies* 11, no. 1 (1985): 71–103.

Ruch, Barbara. "Medieval Jongleurs and the Making of a National Literature." In *Japan in Muromachi Age*, edited by John Whitney Hall and Toyoda Takeshii, 279–310. Berkeley: University of California Press, 1977.

Saga Prefectural Nagoya Castle Museum. "Guide to Saga Prefectural Nagoya Castle Museum." Saga Prefectural Nagoya Castle Museum, 2000.

Sakai, Cécile. *Nihon no taishū bungaku (1900–1980)* (Japanese popular fiction [1900–1980]). Translated from the French by Asahina Kōji. Tokyo: Heibon-sha, 1997.

Sakata Makoto. *Keizai shōsetsu no yomikata* (How to read business novels). Tokyo: Kōbun-sha, 2004.

Samonides, William. "Patronizing Images: Kōdai-in and Toyotomi Hideyoshi at Kōdaiji." In *Nichibunken Japan Review* 7 (1996): 99–126.

Sansom, George. *A History of Japan: 1334–1615*. Stanford, CA: Stanford University Press, 1961.

Satō, Hiroaki. *Legends of the Samurai*. New York: Overlook Press, 1995.

Satō Tadao. *Chūshingura: Iji no keifu*. Tokyo: Asahi Shinbun-sha, 1976.

Seaton, Philip. "Taiga Dramas and Tourism: Historical Contents as Sustainable Tourist Resources." *Japan Forum* 27, no. 1 (2015): 82–103.

Seaton, Philip, and Takayoshi Yamamura. "Japanese Popular Culture and Contents Tourism: Introduction." *Japan Forum* 27, no. 1 (2015): 1–11.

Seaton, Philip, Takayoshi Yamamura, Akiko Sugawa-Shimada, and Kyungjae Jung. *Contents Tourism in Japan: Pilgrimages to "Sacred Sites" of Popular Culture*. Amherst, NY: Cambia Press, 2017.

Selden, Mark. "A Forgotten Holocaust: US Bombing Strategy, the Destruction of Japanese Cities and the American Way of War from World War II to Iraq." *Asia-Pacific Journal* 5, no. 5 (May 2, 2007). http://japanfocus.org/-Mark-Selden/2414.

Shashi hensan iinkai. *Daiyamondo shichijūgo nen shi* (The Diamond seventy-five-year history). Tokyo: Daiyamondo-sha, 1988.

Shiba Ryōtarō. *Shiba Ryōtarō zenshū*. Vol. 17: *Shinshi Taikōki* (The new historical Taikōki). Tokyo: Bungei Shunjū, 1972.

———. *Shinshi Taikōki* (The new historical Taikōki). Vol. 1. Tokyo: Shinchōsha, 1968.

———. "Watashi no Hideyoshi kan" (My view of Hideyoshi). In *Shiba Ryōtarō ga kangaeta koto 2* (Shiba Ryōtarō's thoughts, 2), 360–63. Tokyo: Shincho-sha, 2001.

———. "Watashi no shōsetsu sahō" (My approach to fiction). In *Shiba Ryōtarō zenshū*. Vol. 32: *Hyōron zuihitsu shū* (Collection of critical writings), 440–42. Tokyo: Bungei Shunjū, 1974.

Shimizu Sadakichi and Kojima Kōhei. *Hideyoshi to ningen kankei: Hyūman rirēshonzu* (Hideyoshi and interpersonal relationships: Human relations). Tokyo: Chūbu Zaikaisha, 1965.

———. *Ieyasu to ningen kankei* (Ieyasu and interpersonal relationships). Tokyo: Chūbu Zaikaisha, 1965.

———. *Nobunaga to ningen kankei* (Nobunaga and interpersonal relationships). Tokyo: Chūbu Zaikaisha, 1965.

———. *Purejidento Nobunaga* (President Nobunaga). Tokyo: Nihon Sono Saabisu Sentaa, 1967.

Shimoda, Hiraku. *Lost and Found: Recovering Regional Identity in Imperial Japan*. Cambridge, MA: Harvard University Asia Center, 2014.

Shimura Kunihiro. *Rekishi shōsetsu to taishū bungaku* (Historical fiction and popular literature). Tokyo: Miyamoto Kikaku, 1990.

———. "Sōsaku hōhō" (Methods of literary production). In *Kokubungaku kaishaku to kanshō bessatsu: Shiba Ryōtarō no sekai* (Shiba Ryōtarō's world), edited by Shimura Kunihiro, 84–87. Tokyo: Shibundō, 2002.

Shirane Haruo. "Warrior Tales (Gunki mono)." In *Traditional Japanese Literature: An Anthology, Beginnings to 1600*, edited by Shirane Haruo, 704–6. New York: Columbia University, 2012.

Shively, Donald. *The Love Suicides at Amijima: A Study of a Japanese Domestic Tragedy by Chikamatsu Monzaemon*. 2nd ed. Ann Arbor: University of Michigan Press, 1991.

Sievers, Sharon. *Flowers in Salt: The Beginnings of Feminist Consciousness in Modern Japan*. Stanford, CA: Stanford University Press, 1983.

Smiles, Samuel. *Self Help*. London: J. Murray, 1905.

Smith, Henry. "The Capacity of Chūshingura: Three Hundred Years of Chūshingura." *Monumenta Nipponica* 58, no. 1 (Spring 2003): 1–42.

———. "The Media and Politics of Japanese Popular History: The Case of the Ako Gishi." In *Historical Consciousness, Historiography, and Modern Japanese Values*, edited by James Baxter, 75–97. Kyoto: International Research Center for Japanese Studies, 2006.

Statistics Bureau, Japan. *Japan Statistical Handbook 2021*. Tokyo: Ministry of Internal Affairs and Communication, Statistics Bureau, Japan, 2021.

Strecher, Matthew. "Purely Mass or Massively Pure? The Division between 'Pure' and 'Mass' Literature." *Monumenta Nipponica* 51, no. 3 (Autumn 1996): 357–74.

Suekuni Yoshimi. "Shijitsu to kyokō" (Historical fact and fabrication). In *Kokubungaku kaishaku to kanshō bessatsu: Shiba Ryōtarō no sekai* (Shiba Ryōtarō's world), edited by Shimura Kunihiro, 88–91. Tokyo: Shibundō, 2002.

Sugawa-Shimada, Akiko. "Rekijo Pilgrimage, and 'Pop-Spiritualism': Pop-Culture-Induced Heritage Tourism of/for Young Women." *Japan Forum* 27, no. 1 (2015): 37–58.

Sugimoto Sonoko. "Songokū, budda no te o hashiru: Shi, Yoshikawa Eiji sensei" (The Monkey King runs on Buddha's hand: My teacher Yoshikawa Eiji). Special issue, *Kokubungaku* (October 2000): 33–35.

Suzuki Sadami. "Yoshikawa Eiji no rekishi kan" (Yoshikawa Eiji's view of history). Special issue, *Kokubungaku* (October 2000): 42–51.

Tahara, Mildred. "Ariyoshi Sawako: The Novelist." In *Heroic with Grace: Legendary Women of Japan*, edited by Chieko Irie Mulhern, 297–322. New York: M. E. Sharpe, 1991.

Taiga dorama zen risuto (A complete list of Taiga drama). Accessed July 28, 2021. https://www2.nhk.or.jp/archives/search/special/detail/?d=taiga000.

Takeda Izumo, Miyoshi Shōraku, and Namiki Senryū. *Kanadehon Chūshingura*. Translated by Donald Keene. New York: Columbia University Press, 1971.

Takenaka, Akiko. "Reactionary Nationalism and Museum Controversies: The Case of 'Peace Osaka.'" *Public Historian* 36, no. 3 (May 2014): 75–98.

Takeuchi Kakusai. *Ehon Taikōki* (Illustrated Taikōki). Tokyo: Yūhodo Shoten, 1914.

Tamir, Yael. "The Enigma of Nationalism." *World Politics* 47, no. 3 (1995): 418–40.

Tasgold, Christian. "Popular Realms of Memory in Japan: The Case of Sakamoto Ryōma." *Contemporary Japan* 25, no. 1 (2013): 41–59.

Teshigahara Hiroshi, dir. *Rikyū*. Tokyo: Shochiku, 1989.

Tipton, Elise. *Modern Japan: A Social and Political History*. New York: Routledge, 2002.

Tokutomi Sohō. "Three Qualifications of the Leader of Greater East Asia." In *Sources of Japanese Tradition*, vol. 2, pt. 2: *1868–2000*, edited by William Theodore de Bary, Carol Gluck, and Arthur Tiedemann, 137–38. New York: Columbia University Press, 2006.

Tokyo Teikoku Daigaku and Tokyo Daigaku, eds. *Dai Nihon shiryō*. Vol. 11, *Tenshō 10 to Keichō 9 (1582–1585)*. Tokyo: Tokyo Teikoku Daigaku, 1927.

Torrance, Richard. "Literacy and Literature in Osaka, 1890–1940." *Journal of Japanese Studies* 31, no. 1 (Winter 2005): 27–60.

Totman, Conrad. *Early Modern Japan*. Berkeley: University of California Press, 1993.

Tsuda Saburō. *Hideyoshi eiyū densetsu no nazo* (The enigma of Hideyoshi hero legends). Tokyo: Chūō Kōron-sha, 1997.

Tsurumi Shunsuke. *Taishū bungakuron* (Theory of popular literature). Tokyo: Rokko Shuppan, 1985.

Tsutsui Yasutaka. *Tsutsui Junkei* (Tsutsui Junkei). Tokyo: Shinkō-sha, 1969.

———. "Yamazaki" (Yamazaki). In *Jidai shōsetsu: Jisen tanpenshū* (Period fiction: a self-selected collection of stories), 363–386. Tokyo: Chūō Kōron-sha, 1994.

Turnbull, Stephen. *Toyotomi Hideyoshi: Leadership, Strategy, Conflict*. Oxford: Osprey, 2010.

Tyler, Royall, trans. *The Tale of the Heike*. New York: Penguin Books, 2014.

Uchiyama, Benjamin. *Japan's Carnival War: Mass Culture on the Homefront, 1937–1945*. Cambridge: University of Cambridge Press, 2019.

Uno, Kathleen S. "The Death of 'Good Wife, Wise Mother'?" In *Postwar Japan as History*, edited by Andrew Gordon, 293–322. Berkley: University of California Press, 1993.

Vlastos, Stephen, ed. *Mirror of Modernity: Invented Traditions of Modern Japan*. Berkeley: University of California Press, 1998.

Wakita, Osamu. "The Emergence of the State in Sixteenth-Century Japan: From Oda to Tokugawa." *Journal of Japanese Studies* 8, no. 2 (1982): 343–67.

Watanabe Takeru, Uchida Kusuo, and Nakamura Hiroshi. *Shashin Taikōki* (Taikōki in photographs). Osaka: Hōiku-sha, 1983.

Watsky, Andrew. *Chikubushima: Developing the Sacred Arts in Momoyama Japan*. Seattle: University of Washington Press, 2004.

"The Way of the Warrior II." In *Sources of Japanese Tradition*, vol. 2, pt. 1: *1600 to 2000*, edited by William Theodore de Bary, Carol Gluck, and Arthur Tiedemann, 353–93. New York: Columbia University Press, 2006.

Wert, Michael. *Meiji Restoration Losers: Memory and Tokugawa Supporters in Modern Japan*. Cambridge, MA: Harvard University Asia Center, 2013.

White, Hayden. *The Content of the Form*. Baltimore, MD: Johns Hopkins University Press, 1987.

Yada Sōun. *Edo kara Tōkyō e* (From Edo to Tokyo). Tokyo: Tōkōkaku Shoten, 1924.

———. *Taikōki*. Tokyo: Chūō Kōron-sha, 1935.

———. *Toyotomi Hideyoshi: Hashiba Chikuzen no maki* (Toyotomi Hideyoshi: The Hashiba Chikuzen volume). Tokyo: Kodansha, 1938.

———. *Toyotomi Hideyoshi: Taikō no maki* (Toyotomi Hideyoshi: The Taikō volume). Tokyo: Kodansha, 1938.

Yano, Christine. *Pink Globalization: Hello Kitty's Trek across the Pacific.* Honolulu: University of Hawai'i Press, 2013.

Yomiuri shinbun-sha. *Yomiuri Shinbun hyaku nijū nen shi* (The 120-year history of the *Yomiuri*). Tokyo: Yomiuri Shinbun-sha, 1994.

Yoshida Yutaka. Introduction to *Taikōki* by Oze Hoan. Translated by Yoshida Yutaka. Tokyo: Kyōikusha, 1979.

Yoshikawa Eiji. *Yoshikawa Eiji zenshū* (The collected works of Yoshikawa Eiji). Vols. 19–23: *Shinsho Taikoki* (The new Taikōki). Tokyo: Kodansha, 1980.

———. *Yoshikawa Eiji zenshū* (The collected works of Yoshikawa Eiji). Vol. 47: *Sōshidō zuihitsu* (Jottings from Sōshidō). Tokyo: Kodansha, 1980.

Yoshino Takao. *Bungaku hōkokukai no jidai* (The era of the Patriotic Association for Literature). Tokyo: Kawade Shoho Shin-sha, 2008.

Young, Louise. *Japan's Total Empire: Manchuria and the Culture of Wartime Imperialism.* Berkeley: University of California Press, 1998.

Index

Page numbers for maps and figures are in italics.

Harvard East Asian Monographs
(most recent titles)